Intellectual Property Rights (IPRs) and Economic Development

Edited by

Md. Zafar Mahfooz Nomani
Professor, Department of Law,
Aligarh Muslim University (AMU), Aligarh

and

Faizanur Rahman
Assistant Professor, Faculty of Law,
Jamia Millia Islamia (JMI), New Delhi

New Century Publications
New Delhi, India

NEW CENTURY PUBLICATIONS
4800 / 24, Bharat Ram Road,
Ansari Road, Daryaganj,
New Delhi - 110 002 (India)

Tel.: 011-2324 7798, 4358 7398, 4101 7798
E-mail: indiatax@vsnl.com • info@newcenturypublications.com
www.newcenturypublications.com

Editorial office:
LG – 7, Aakarshan Bhawan,
4754-57/23, Ansari Road, Daryaganj,
New Delhi – 110 002

Tel.: 011-4356 0919

First Published: **2018**

ISBN: **978-81-7708-467-2**

Published by New Century Publications and printed at Milan Enterprises, New Delhi.

Designs: Patch Creative Unit, New Delhi.

PRINTED IN INDIA

Dedicated

to

Ghayas Ahmad Gaddi and Ilyas Ahmad Gaddi

The Cherished Loadstar

of

Urdu Fiction

Justice R. K. Agrawal
Judge
Supreme Court of India

8, Moti Lal Nehru Marg
New Delhi-110011
Ph.: 23012825

February 27, 2018

FOREWORD

I feel immensely privileged to put pen to this foreword for the book on "Intellectual Property Rights and Economic Development" edited by Md. Zafar Mahfooz Nomani and Faizanur Rehman which is going to be published soon by the New Century Publications, New Delhi.

With the emerging fields of law, the Intellectual Property Rights have become precious commodities and are being fiercely protected. I believe that this book would be the gift of wisdom to those who are keen to understand the Intellectual Property Rights and with rich knowledge it plays a positive role in encouraging new business development, rationalization of inefficient industry including technology acquisition and creation.

The scope of Intellectual Property Rights granted, and the degree to which those are enforced, reflect what a Nation considers to be its best interest. The challenges relating to IPR are particularly seen in developing nations where IP system is undergoing substantial expansion, modernization and a global push to have open trade practices. The present work provides for easily comprehensible solution to various issues relating to the subject.

The beauty of the book is that it does not confuse, rather it clarifies the material presented in a simple language by the authors with years of their academic knowledge and experience.

I convey my best wishes to the learned authors who with their zeal and hardwork have provided with an outstanding service in the field of Intellectual Property Rights.

RKAgrawal
(R.K. AGRAWAL)

About the Book

Intellectual property rights (IPRs) refer to the legal ownership by a person or business of an invention/discovery attached to a particular product or process which protects the owner against unauthorized copying or imitation. With the emergence of the knowledge society and virtual products, the issue of safeguarding the investment in the information-based products has certainly gained high importance.

Globalization and the rapid proliferation of technology have elevated the significance of intellectual property protection. The importance of IPRs has increased in recent years in the wake of rapid advancements and proliferation of technology. Intellectual property protection is a key factor for economic growth and advancement in the high technology sector. IPRs are good for business, benefit the public at large and act as catalysts for technical progress. The intangible nature of intellectual property and the worldwide inconsistency of standard practices create challenges for those wishing to protect their inventions, brands, and business methods in foreign markets. The three most common vehicles for protecting intellectual property are patents, trademarks, and copyrights.

The Agreement establishing the World Trade Organization (WTO) contains, *inter alia*, an Agreement on Trade-related Aspects of Intellectual Property Rights (TRIPS). TRIPS Agreement, which came into effect on January 1, 1995, is presently the most comprehensive multilateral agreement on intellectual property. It provides for norms and standards in respect of various areas of intellectual property.

This book contains 13 research papers, authored by experts in the field, which explain and examine various aspects of the TRIPS Agreement and the corresponding Indian laws for its implementation.

Editors' Profile

Professor Md. Zafar Mahfooz Nomani is presently with the Department of Law, Aligarh Muslim University (AMU), Aligarh, Uttar Pradesh. He specializes in ecology law and intellectual property rights and is engaged in teaching and research for the last 20 years. He successfully collaborated with World Bank and Ministry of Environment and Forests on Capacity Building Project on Environmental Law in India (Law Component) during 1998-2003. He successfully completed University Grants Commission's major research project on Wetland Law during 2009-2011. Currently, he is engaged in a major research project on Socio-Economic Impact of Special Economic Zones (SEZs) on the Land Owners and Local Inhabitants of Uttar Pradesh and Uttarakhand States of India sponsored by the Indian Council for Social Science Research (ICSSR). Professor Nomani has authored 5 books and published more than 100 research papers in prestigious refereed and peer reviewed journals covering diverse areas of environmental, intellectual property and corporate laws. His insight into the subject is laced with erudite explanation and cited across the discipline of visceral affinity.

Dr. Faizanur Rahman is an Assistant Professor in the Faculty of Law, Jamia Millia Islamia (JMI), New Delhi and specializes in intellectual property rights. After obtaining law degree from Aligarh Muslim University (AMU) in 2007, he continued with his studies in the same University, earning LL.M. degree in 2009 and Ph.D. degree in 2014. Dr. Rahman has to his credit several research papers on trade secrets law, competition law and IPRs. His extensive research is widely recognized in academic circles around the world. His research work is cited in national and international refereed journals of repute. His work has achieved remarkable acceptance by practitioners across multiple fields.

Contents

Contributors

Ashish Kumar Srivastava	Assistant Professor, National Law University, Jodhpur, Rajasthan.
Chandan	Lecturer, Faculty of Juridical Sciences, MITS University, Lakshmangarh, Rajasthan.
Anis Ahmad	Assistant Professor, Department of Law, SLS B.B. Ambedkar University, Lucknow, Uttar Pradesh.
Anushka M. Nayak	Lecturer and Research Scholar, Barkatullah University, Bhopal, Madhya Pradesh.
Md. Zafar Mahfooz Nomani	Professor, Department of Law, Aligarh Muslim University (AMU), Aligarh, Uttar Pradesh.
Faisal Sherwani	Senior Associate, Parekh and Co., Advocates and Attorneys, New Delhi.
Faizanur Rahman	Assistant Professor, Faculty of Law, Jamia Millia Islamia (JMI), New Delhi.
Farooq Ahmad Mir	Former Head of Department of Law, University of Kashmir, Srinagar, Jammu and Kashmir.
Mir Farhatul Aen	Research Scholar and Project Fellow, Department of Law, University of Kashmir, Srinagar, Jammu and Kashmir.
Mir Junaid Alam	Assistant Professor, Department of Law, University of Kashmir, Srinagar, Jammu and Kashmir.
Mohammed Saheb Hussain	UDSM School of Law, (Formerly Faculty of Law), Department of Private Law, University of Dar-Es-Salaam, Tanzania.
Mutakyahwa Charles	Advocate, High Court of Tanzania.
N.R. Madhava Menon	Honorary Professor and IBA Chair on Continuing Legal Education, NLSIU, Bangalore; Chairman, Menon Institute of Legal Advocacy Training,

Trivandrum; formerly Vice Chancellor, National Law School, Bangalore and National University of Juridical Sciences, Kolkata.

Syeda Nishat Shadmani Senior Legal Officer, Oil India Limited, Duliajan, Assam.

B.K. Prasad Associate Professor, Department of Genetics and Plant Breeding, Amar Singh Post-graduate College, Lakhaoti, Bulandshahar, Uttar Pradesh.

Rashid. A. Faridi, Associate Professor, Department of Geography, Amar Singh Post-graduate College, Lakhaoti, Bulandshahar, Uttar Pradesh.

S.Z. Amani Associate Professor, Jamia Millia Islamia (JMI), New Delhi.

S.K. Verma Former professor, Faculty of Law, University of Delhi; former Director, Indian Law Institute, New Delhi.

Shiva Kanaujia Sukula Assistant Librarian, Central Library, Jawaharlal Lal Nehru University (JNU), New Delhi.

Preface

Intellectual property rights (IPRs) refer to the legal ownership by a person or business of an invention/discovery attached to particular product or process which protects the owner against unauthorized copying or imitation. With the emergence of the knowledge society and virtual products, the issue of safeguarding the investment in the information-based products has certainly gained high importance.

Globalization and the rapid proliferation of technology have elevated the significance of intellectual property protection. The importance of IPRs has increased in recent years in the wake of rapid advancements and proliferation of technology. Intellectual property protection is a key factor for economic growth and advancement in the high technology sector. They are good for business, benefit the public at large and act as catalysts for technical progress. The intangible nature of intellectual property and the worldwide inconsistency of standard practices create challenges for those wishing to protect their inventions, brands, and business methods in foreign markets. The three most common vehicles for protecting intellectual property are patents, trademarks, and copyrights.

World Trade Organization (WTO) deals with the global rules of trade between nations. Its main function is to ensure that trade flows as smoothly, predictably and freely as possible.

The Agreement establishing the World Trade Organization (WTO) contains, *inter alia*, an Agreement on Trade-related Aspects of Intellectual Property Rights (TRIPS). TRIPS Agreement is Annex 1C of the Marrakesh Agreement establishing the World Trade Organization (WTO), signed in Marrakesh, Morocco on April 15, 1994.

The TRIPS Agreement, which came into effect on January 1, 1995, is to date the most comprehensive multilateral agreement on intellectual property.

TRIPS provides for norms and standards in respect of following areas of intellectual property:

1. Copyright and related rights (i.e. the rights of performers, producers of sound recordings and broadcasting organizations).
2. Trademarks including service marks.
3. Geographical indications including appellations of origin.
4. Industrial designs.
5. Patents including the protection of new varieties of plants.
6. Layout-designs of integrated circuits.
7. Undisclosed information including trade secrets and test data.
8. Control of anti-competitive practices in contractual licences.

Following are the three main features of the TRIPS Agreement:

Standards: In respect of each of the main areas of intellectual property covered by the TRIPS Agreement, the Agreement sets out the minimum standards of protection to be provided by each Member. Each of the main elements of protection is defined, namely the subject-matter to be protected, the rights to be conferred and permissible exceptions to those rights, and the minimum duration of protection.

The Agreement sets these standards by requiring, first, that the substantive obligations of the main conventions of the WIPO, the Paris Convention for the Protection of Industrial Property (Paris Convention) and the Berne Convention for the Protection of Literary and Artistic Works (Berne Convention) in their most recent versions, must be complied with. With the exception of the provisions of the Berne Convention on moral rights, all the main substantive provisions of these conventions are incorporated by reference and thus become obligations under the TRIPS Agreement between TRIPS Member countries. The relevant provisions are to be found in Articles 2.1 and 9.1 of the TRIPS Agreement, which relate, respectively, to the Paris Convention and to the Berne Convention. Secondly, the TRIPS Agreement adds a substantial number of additional obligations on matters where the pre-existing conventions are silent or were seen as being inadequate. The TRIPS Agreement is thus sometimes referred to as a Berne and Paris-plus agreement.

Enforcement: The second main set of provisions deals with domestic procedures and remedies for the enforcement of intellectual property rights. The Agreement lays down certain general principles applicable to all IPR enforcement procedures. In addition, it contains provisions on civil and administrative procedures and remedies, provisional measures, special requirements related to border measures and criminal procedures, which specify, in a certain amount of detail, the procedures and remedies that must be available so that right holders can effectively enforce their rights.

Dispute Settlement: The Agreement makes disputes between WTO Members about the respect of the TRIPS obligations subject to the WTO's dispute settlement procedures.

In addition, the Agreement provides for certain basic principles, such as national and most-favoured-nation treatment, and some general rules to ensure that procedural difficulties in acquiring or maintaining IPRs do not nullify the substantive benefits that should flow from the Agreement. The obligations under the Agreement will apply equally to all Member countries, but developing countries will have a longer period to phase them in. Special transition arrangements operate in the situation where a developing country does not presently provide product patent protection in the area of pharmaceuticals.

The TRIPS Agreement is a minimum standards agreement, which allows Members to provide more extensive protection of intellectual property if they so wish. Members are left free to determine the appropriate method of implementing the provisions of the Agreement within their own legal system and practice.

Another main set of provisions deals with domestic procedures and remedies for the enforcement of intellectual property rights. The Agreement lays down certain general principles applicable to all IPR enforcement procedures. In addition, it contains provisions on civil and administrative procedures and remedies, provisional measures, special requirements related to border measures and criminal procedures, which specify, in a certain amount of detail, the procedures and remedies that must be available so that right holders can effectively enforce their rights.

The Agreement makes disputes between WTO Members in respect of the TRIPS obligations subject to the WTO's dispute settlement procedures.

The Doha Round of negotiations at the World Trade Organization (WTO), which began in 2001, is still under way. The scope of the negotiations includes agriculture, market access for non-agricultural products, services trade, trade-related aspects of intellectual property rights (TRIPS), rules (covering anti-dumping and subsidies), trade facilitation and so on.

Md. Zafar Mahfooz Nomani
Faizanur Rahman

Part I
Intellectual Property, Agricultural Biotechnology and Political Economy

1

Suicide Seeds and Right to Food

Ashish Kumar Srivastava and Chandan

Introduction

Belly rules the mind. Food is the basis of life. Being the quintessential component of human life process, one has to honour the food and give it due importance which it deserves. Due to its importance, UDHR recognizes the right to food by affirming that "everyone has the right to a standard of living adequate for the health and well-being of himself and of his family, including food, clothing, housing and medical care and necessary social services, and the right to security in the event of unemployment, sickness, disability, widowhood, old age or other lack of livelihood in circumstances beyond his control". [1] International Covenant on Economic, Social and Cultural Rights, 1966 laid down that State Parties to the Covenant recognise "the right of everyone to an adequate standard of living for himself and for his family including food, clothing, housing and to the continuous improvement of living conditions". [2]

Food is a matter of one's existence and therefore the same cannot be negated. The issues relating to food are crucial for a country like India as agriculture continues to be the mainstay of the majority of Indian population. Agriculture and allied sectors contribute nearly 14 percent of gross domestic product (GDP) of India, while about 65-70 percent of the population is dependent on agriculture for their livelihood. The agricultural output, however, depends on monsoon as nearly 60 percent of area sown is dependent on rainfall'. [3]

Agriculture is one of the main constituent of our economy and seeds are its essential ingredients. The role of good seeds is very important as we need very large stocks of grain to feed one of the biggest populations of the world which is growing round the clock at a lightning speed. The Indian agrarian fraternity basically relies upon the traditional way of agriculture in which the farmers sow the crop and harvest the same saving a definite amount of their produce as seeds to be sown in the next season. But once suicide seeds/terminator seeds (better known as genetic restrictive use technology) get introduced in the Indian agriculture, things may not remain the same. In fact, they may emerge as one of the most potential threats to the traditional lifestyles of the agrarian community of India. The paper aims to examine the pros and cons of terminator seeds, its justification in the light of right to food and food crisis and price escalation of essential commodities and plant variety protection.

Terminator Seeds or Suicide Seeds

Terminator seeds are the brain child of big seed companies like Monsanto, Dupont etc. The terminator seeds essentially have a very limited life and normally they cannot be used as seeds for the next season. This technique is known as genetic use restriction technology under which the scientists, with the help of bio-technology, modify the crop element in the seeds. This has an antigen which tends to kill the crop when the seeds are sown next time. The justification for such type of seed usage is intellectual property right and enhancement of production of food grains. The companies claim that a particular type of crop is an outcome of labour of years of research and the companies have to bear enormous costs in the invention and evolution of these seeds. Therefore, there is no reason why the concerned companies should not reap the benefits of such research, labour and financial inputs in a fiercely competitive commercial world.

Seeds and Indian Agriculture

Seed is a critical and basic input for enhancing agricultural production and productivity in different agro-climatic regions. Indian seed programme largely adheres to the limited generation system for seed multiplication. The system recognises three generations, namely, breeder, foundation and certified seeds and provides adequate safeguards for quality assurance in the seed multiplication chain to maintain the purity of variety as it flows from the breeders to the farmers.

Green Revolution development was started in Mexico by Norman Borlaug in 1943 and was judged as a success. The program in India, was started with the help of the US-based Rockefeller Foundation and was based on high-yielding varieties of wheat, rice, and other grains that had been developed in Mexico and Philippines. Of the high-yielding seeds, wheat produced the best results. Production of coarse grains—the staple diet of the poor—and pulses—the main source of protein—lagged behind, resulting in reduced per capita availability.

Indian seed programme includes the participation of Central and State governments, Indian Council of Agricultural Research (ICAR), State Agricultural Universities (SAUs), public sector, co-operative sector and the private sector institutions. Seed sector in India consists of two national level corporations i.e. National Seeds Corporation (NSC) and State Farms Corporation of India (SFCI), 13 State Seed Corporations (SSCs) and about 100 major seed companies. For quality control and certification, there are 22 State Seed Certification Agencies (SSCAs) and 101 State Seed Testing Laboratories (SSTLs). The private sector has started to play a significant role in the production and distribution of seeds. However, the organized seed sector particularly for food crops cereals continues to be dominated by the public sector. [4]

The Seeds Act, 1966 provides for the legislative framework for regulation of quality of seeds sold in the country. The Central Seed Committee (CSC) and the Central Seed Certification Board (CSCB) are apex agencies set up under the Act to deal with all matters relating to administration of the Act and quality control of seeds. The proposed Seeds Bill, 2004 has been approved by the cabinet for moving official amendment which is still pending.

Seeds and Right to Food

The Constitution of India is not a silent spectator to this serious issue and hence it provides that, "The state shall endeavour to organize agriculture and animal husbandry on modern and scientific lines and shall, in particular, take steps for preserving and improving the breeds, and prohibiting the slaughter of cows and calves and other milch and drought cattle". [5]

Organizing agriculture includes seeds development and its proper management. The Green Revolution became a reality only because of the sumptuous seeds. The apex court in post Maneka [6] regime opened a flood gate and recognized so many rights as fundamental rights. The right to food is obviously new in the chain which was recognized by the judiciary in many cases.

The right to live guarantee in any civilized society implies the right to food, water, decent environment, education, medical care and shelter. These are basic human rights known to any civilized society. All civil, political, social and cultural rights enshrined in the Universal Declaration of Human Rights and Convention or under the Constitution of India cannot be exercised without these basic human rights. [7]

In any organized society, right to live as a human being is not ensured by meeting only the animal needs of man. It is secured only when he is assured of all facilities to develop himself and is freed from restrictions which inhibit his growth. All human rights are designed to achieve this objective. The right to live guarantee in any civilized society implies the right to food, water, decent environment, education, medical care and shelter. All civil, political, social and cultural rights enshrined in the Universal Declaration of Human Rights and Convention or under the Constitution of India cannot be exercised without these basic human rights. [8] The Supreme Court reiterated the same opinion in variety of judgments. [9]

After recognition of right to food as a fundamental right, the relationship of seeds to agriculture has become more important and delicate. But terminator seeds are causing a serious threat to it.

Intellectual Property and Terminator Seeds

Seeds and plant variety due to its potential in changing the economy are subject matter of intellectual property protection. TRIPS recognizes its value and provides that "Members may also exclude from patentability: (a) diagnostic, therapeutic and surgical methods for the treatment of humans or animals; and (b) plants and animals other than micro-organisms, and essentially biological processes for the production of plants or animals other than non-biological and microbiological processes. However, Members shall provide for the protection of plant varieties either by patents or by an effective *sui generis* system or by any combination thereof. The provisions of this sub-paragraph shall be reviewed four years after the date of entry into force of the WTO Agreement". [10]

TRIPS recognize that plant varieties or seeds are to be protected through patent or any *sui generis* system. India having ratified TRIPS, enacted a legislation entitled "The Protection of Plant Varieties and Farmers' Right Act, 2001". The regime and protection provided by the Act are very simple. The Act establishes a Plant Variety Authority and provides the same criterion of registration like inventive step, industrial use, novelty and distinctiveness. The Act for the first time places the farmers' intellectual property over traditional seeds equivalent to scientists' intellectual property over Genetically Modified Varieties. The Act affirms the breeders' right over conventional crops and gives it intellectual property protection. Being an agrarian society, we have taken due consideration of this terminator technology so provided in our municipal legislation that "every application for registration *inter alia* shall be accompanied by an affidavit sworn by the applicant that such variety does not contain any gene or gene sequence involving terminator technology". [11]

Such initiative on the part of legislator was most sought after because even after the Green Revolution, our 65 percent of population relies upon agriculture as an occupation and their cultivation is still very conventional in which the farmers use the same crop as seeds year after year which maintains the bio-diversity as well. The prominence of biological diversity cannot be ignored by any civil society having scientific temper.

Terminator Seeds and Commerce

Seeing the potential market for seeds, three major giants including Dupont, Monsanto and Delta and Pine Land Seed Co. invented terminator technology and Monsanto acquired Delta and Pine Land (DPL), the world's largest cotton seed company, which jointly holds three US patents on terminator technology with the US Department of Agriculture. In October 2005, DPL won new terminator patents in both Europe and Canada. Also, the multinational seed and agrochemical company Syngenta is requesting a Canadian patent on its terminator potatoes.

Having a self-killing technique deeply infused in itself, the world reacted against this technology in one voice because of which these companies in 1999 publicly vowed not to commercialize such crops. But despite mounting opposition from national governments and United Nations agencies, work on terminator and traitor (genetic trait control) moves full speed ahead. After Monsanto and AstraZeneca publicly vowed not to commercialize suicide seeds in 1999, governments and civil society organizations were lulled into thinking that the crisis had passed. Nothing could be further from the truth. A few years back, AstraZeneca conducted its first field trial on genetic trait control technology in the UK. According to industry sources, it is not the first company to conduct field tests. Can commercialization be far behind?

"We've continued right on with the work on Technology Protection System [Terminator]. We never really slowed down. We're on target, moving ahead to commercialize it. We never really backed off"—Harry Collins, Delta and Pine Land Seed Co., (January 2000).

Companies have a proper justification to say as it took four years and an investment of US$ 720,000 to develop the technique, according to RAFI. The USDA (United States Department of Agriculture) spent US$ 190,000 and Delta and Pine Land Co. US$ 275,000 on in-house research expenses and the two jointly spent US$ 2,55,000. The patent covers seeds of all crop varieties, including genetically modified and conventionally developed seeds. [12] The companies also justify the patenting of technology saying that it is an anti-theft technique and they want to contain unauthorised cultivation of proprietary seeds.

It is important to take note that these big giant companies are market leaders and they have the potential of deep penetration and catchment areas of these companies are quiet large. 'Delta and Pine Land Co. is the largest cottonseed company in the world, and had a turnover of US$ 183 million in 1997. Monsanto, its parent company, operates in India in the seeds and agro-chemicals market. Monsanto, which bought Delta and Pine Land for US$ 1.76 billion after the latter got the patent for terminator technology, is now the largest pesticide firm, the second largest seed company and one of the 10 largest producers of pharmaceutical and veterinary medicines in the world'. [13]

Terminator Seeds in Global Perspective

Initially, the technique was invented as measure of anti-theft technique and the companies patented the inventions in its name and the world seeing their catchment capacity alarmed the public against it and hence Monsanto took a public vow not to commercialize the crops in 1999. But the big question is how long they are going to honour their own promise.

On February 18, 2009, the Ecuadorian Congress approved a new Law on Food Sovereignty, which, among other important points, declared the country "free of transgenic crops and seeds". However, in spite of vocal popular opposition, the legislation left the door open to approvals of genetically modified organisms (GMOs) in "exceptional" cases. [14]

On the same lines, in February 2005, Canadian government officials (delegates) to a UN meeting tried to introduce new language to "allow for the evaluation" of terminator for field testing and commercial use. But its initiative was vehemently rejected by the world community. One point is clear that mounting pressure of these seeds producing giants can break the nerve of any nation at any time and we know that seeds protection are intellectual property therefore if they are allowed patents or *sui generis* protection they will not take a second to dump their suicide seeds across the globe. This will kill the conventional cultivation and enhance our dependability on these giants and which shall resultantly weaken our haggling capacity with these giants.

In India, realising the seriousness of the problem, the ICAR and the DBT set up a monitoring committee, which came out with a plan of action to ensure that this lethal technology did not enter India. The Government of India refused license to the patent holders to sell the terminator seeds in the country. It also banned the import of such seeds and directed the quarantine office of the Customs Department, which had 18 stations spread over the country, to ensure that no transgenic seed material is permitted entry and that imported seeds get the approval of the Plant Protection Authority in the Ministry of Agriculture before they are released. [15]

India's M.S. Swaminathan, former independent chairman of the FAO Council and recipient of World Food Prize, explains, "for example, in India, where there are nearly 100 million operational holdings, denial of plant-back rights or the use of the terminator mechanism will be disastrous from the socio-economic and biodiversity point of view, since over 80 percent of farmers plant their own farm-saved seeds". [16]

Conclusion

Seeing the direct connection in right to food and seeds and municipal legislation on plant variety protection, we cannot ignore this serious issue. The question is how long we can stop these corporate giants on the basis of international moratorium on the use of one of the world's most controversial GM food technologies agreed in 1999.

According to Dr. Swaminathan, there is a need for a universal declaration on Plant Genome and Farmers' Rights similar to the Universal Declaration on Human Genome and Human Rights adopted by the United Nations Educational, Scientific and Cultural Organisation (UNESCO) in Paris on November 11, 1997. The UNESCO declaration stipulates in Article 10 that "no research or research applications concerning the human genome, in particular in the fields of biology, genetics and medicine, should prevail over respect for the human rights, fundamental freedom and human dignity of individuals".

Our conventional method of cultivation and their potential and capacity in dumping the market with terminator seeds have serious implications not only for the Indian agriculture but for the very mode and methods of indigenous communities and agrarian culture of India. If these technologies are allowed in the name of better yielding crops or second green revolution as we have to feed one of the largest populations in the world it may lead to dependability on foreign players like these corporate giants which may be misused by them and we may face the food scarcity and price escalation in essential commodities. This thing, if happens, may amount to a compromise in securing social, economic and political justice for the people of India.

Endnotes

1. Universal Declaration of Human Right, Article 25(1).
2. Article 11.

3. "India 2009", Publications Division, Ministry of Information and Broadcasting, Government of India.
4. "India 2009", Publications Division, Ministry of Information and Broadcasting, Government of India.
5. Article 48, The Constitution of India.
6. AIR 1978 SC 597.
7. Chameli Singh and Ors. vs. State of U.P. and Ors., AIR 1996 SC 1051.
8. Ibid.
9. (2009) 5SCC511, Kapila Hingorani vs. State of Bihar, 20034 SCALE 712.
10. Article 27 of the TRIPS Agreement.
11. Section 18, The Protection of Plant Varieties and Farmers' Right Act, 2001.
12. Asha Krishna Kumar (1998), "Terminator of Food Security", *Frontline*, Vol. 15, No. 21, October 10-23.
13. Asha Krishna Kumar (1998), "Terminator of Food Security", *Frontline*, Vol. 15, No. 21, October 10-23.
14. www.banterminator.org.
15. Asha Krishna Kumar (1998), "Terminator of Food Security", *Frontline*, Vol. 15, No. 21, October 10-23.
16. M.S. Swaminathan (1998), "Farmers' Rights and Plant Genetic Resources", *Biotechnology and Development Monitor*, No. 36, pp. 6-9.

2

Intellectual Property Rights (IPRs) and Indian Agriculture

Anis Ahmad

Introduction

The agriculture sector performs different functions in developed and developing countries. In fact, the international, national and local efforts to increase food security and agricultural management were traditionally based on the principle of free flow sharing of knowledge and resources with global community for obtaining in return, the improved varieties developed at international agricultural research centres. But in the past two decades, there have been substantial changes in intellectual property protection law framework which has broadened its nature and scope. [1] The protection and enforcement of intellectual property rights promote market competition and convey monopoly power per se. [2]

The introduction of intellectual property rights in agriculture by the developed countries to commercialise this sector with the involvement of private actors has been linked to the decreasing importance of agriculture as an economic activity and as a provider of employment. Contrarily, in developing countries, the introduction of intellectual property rights in agriculture had taken place with the adoption of the TRIPS Agreement and the introduction of life form patents in all WTO member states. In a country like India, where a large population depends on the agricultural sector, the importance of agriculture to overall production has diminished in terms of livelihood and employment but still remains significant. Further, the problems of malnutrition and food insecurity are big challenge. [3]

The development of biotechnological advances in agriculture to improve the productivity has tremendous implications on legal policy frameworks. [4] At present, all elements of India's agriculture and food security policies are being dismantled under the pressure from the World Bank and the World Trade Organization (WTO). [5] In such a situation, the issues of food security and introduction of intellectual property rights in agriculture are important because it directly touches the questions of economic development, agricultural management, environmental management and the fulfilment of basic food needs. [6]

There is scant realization of the fact that if our agriculture goes in wrong way nothing else in our economy will have a change to go in the right direction. In such a desperate atmosphere, it is high time to look into the existing intellectual property rights framework in the broader context of sustainable development in order to achieve inclusive growth for the benefit of present and future generations. In this backdrop, the present paper analyses the impacts of international legal regime of IPRs in agriculture to arrive at a resilient indigenous model of biodiversity management—in particular the agro-biodiversity for the sustainability of agricultural sector.

Indian Agriculture and Economic Development

India is an agricultural economy and has a distinct position in agricultural production in the world. Agriculture plays an important role in the Indian economy. Though the share of this sector in the overall gross domestic product of the country has fallen from 55 percent in 1960 to about 30 percent in 1990-91 to only 18 percent in 2010 and less than 15 percent in 2015-16—a trend that is expected in the development process of any economy—yet agriculture forms the backbone of development. [7] Around 72 percent of India's population still depends on agriculture. A majority of rural people are farmers and engage in agricultural production, thus they are largely dependent on agriculture which provides livelihood, subsistence needs and employment generation at the local level. India is one of the largest agrarian economies of the world; the agriculture sector still contributes approximately 14.6 percent of India's GDP and employs a majority of the population. [8]

Further, agriculture provides raw material for agro-based industries such as cotton and jute industries which are dependent on agricultural commodities. [9] At the international level, for around 75 percent of the world's population, the mainstay of livelihood is agriculture particularly in developing countries. In India, the annual income of a farmer is around US$ 175 as against the average of US$ 480. [10]

Indian agricultural policy has been continuously evolving since Independence. The main focus across decades pursued a centrally directed, inward-oriented development strategy. This strategy emphasised on self-sufficiency and self-reliance in food grains production. Considerable progress has been made on this front in the country during last the seven decades or so. The food grains production rose from 50 million tonnes in 1950 to 275 million tonnes in 2016-17. The share of agriculture in real GDP has fallen given its lower growth rate comparison to industry and the service sectors.

Unfortunately, the budget allocations and actual expenditure for agricultural sector has been continuously declining in successive Five Years Plans from 15 percent of the total outlay in the First Five Year Plan to 3.7 percent in Eleventh Five Year Plan. The result is that the average agricultural GDP growth has shrunk as against the industrial GDP growth rate and the services GDP growth. In fact, the Ninth and Tenth Five Year Plans witnessed agricultural sector growth rate of 2.44 percent and 2.30 percent respectively compared to 4.72 percent during the Eighth Five Year Plan.

The approach paper to the Twelfth Five Year Plan emphasized the need to "redouble our efforts to ensure that 4.0 percent average growth" is achieved during the Plan if not more. Without incremental productivity gains and technology diffusion across regions, achieving this higher growth may not be feasible and has implications for the macroeconomic stability given the rising demand of the 1.2 billion people for food. [11] Achieving minimum agricultural growth is a pre-requisite for inclusive growth reduction of poverty levels, development of the rural economy and enhancing of farm incomes. Achieving an 8-9 percent rate of growth in overall GDP may not deliver much in terms of poverty reduction unless agricultural growth accelerates.

At the same time, growth with inclusiveness can be achieved only when agriculture growth accelerates and is also widely shared amongst people and regions of the country. All these factors point to just one thing that agriculture has to be kept at the centre of any reform agenda or planning process, in order to make a significant dent on poverty and malnutrition, and to ensure long-term food security for the people. India is still home to the largest number of poor and malnourished people in the world, hence a high priority to agriculture will achieve the goals of reducing poverty and malnutrition as well as of inclusive growth. Further, it may be noted that in the last two Five Year Plans, it is clearly mentioned that for the economy to grow at 9 percent, it is important that agriculture should grow by at least 4 percent per annum. [12]

Further, in the context of intellectual property rights regime, the management of agro-biodiversity or plant varieties is an important activity. In plant variety management, various actors are involved in the development of plant varieties. Smallholder or subsistence farmers have been to a large extent confined to most developing countries. The main actors involved in saving seeds, selecting specific traits to produce varieties suiting their requirements and generally managing agro-biodiversity and plant varieties belong to the developed world. This can be linked to the fact that people involved in agriculture account for 59 percent of the total population in developing countries and 73 percent in least developed countries, as well as well as 72 percent in India. Most rural people are either farmers or working in agricultural production. They are thus closely dependent upon natural resources in their vicinity for their livelihood and subsistence needs.

Overall, the population active in the agricultural sector amounts to 69 percent in least developed countries and 54 percent in developing countries. In India, 59 percent of economically active population works in the agricultural sector. This implies that an overwhelming majority of rural people have strong incentives to sustainably manage their resource base. In fact, local communities have often maintained harmonious relationship with their environment over time and have sustainably managed their resource base even when utilization has been intensive. In the recent past, plant variety conservation and enhancement has been undertaken by some other actors from government to private companies and research centres. [13]

Agriculture sector is vital for the food and nutritional security of the nation. Compared to other countries, India faces a greater challenge, since with only 2.3 percent share in world's total land area; it has to ensure food security of its population which is about 17.5 percent of the world population. This leads to excessive pressure on land and consequent fragmentation of land holdings.

Against the backdrop of the burgeoning population demands for food grains, degrading natural resource base, emerging concerns of climate change and other challenges, the Department of Agriculture and Cooperation has focused on mobilizing higher investments in agriculture, bridging yield gaps that exist across states/regions in terms of timely and adequate supply of quality inputs and providing adequate support services to the farmers to make agriculture a remunerative vocation on a sustainable basis. Increasing agriculture production with limited natural resources in a sustainable manner for ensuring food and nutritional security and providing income security to farmers are the major challenges before the government. [14]

Moreover, the challenges of food security are immense particularly in a developing country like India. The introduction of genetic engineering is a possible contribution for enhancing food security. But at the same time, these commercialized genetically modified seeds have not taken into consideration the needs of a developing country's agriculture. In a developing country, food security for most people is ensured through livelihood security in agriculture.

In fact, agricultural livelihood leads to entitlements that ensure access to food. Destruction of agricultural livelihood leads to insecure entitlement and hence creates food insecurity. At the national level, there is a need for more agricultural research in developing countries focused on subsistence crops as well as crops for low-quality lands. This is a question which needs to be addressed in view of the overall limited availability of land and the need to balance food sovereignty with the need to earn hard currency from the export of agricultural commodities. In addition to the above dimensions, the issue of food security can be judged from a human rights perspective. [15]

Agro-biotechnology and Genetically Modified Organisms

Biotechnology is a revolutionary technology. [16] It covers all technological applications using biological system, living organisms or their derivatives to make or modify products or processes. The use of biotechnology in the more specific context of agriculture, which is known as agro-biotechnology and the most relevant part, is genetic engineering. [17] Genetic engineering generally refers to the modification of an organism's genetic make-up in which DNA from one organism or cell is transferred to another without sexual reproduction. The development of genetic engineering has tremendous implications for agriculture-related policies and legal frameworks.

In developed countries, genetic engineering has been

directly associated with the move towards the patenting of life forms up till the 1980s. The development of genetic engineering in the private sector is closely linked to the introduction of patents of life forms because they are one essential legal tool to protect the products of genetic engineering. The rapid development of the biotech industry over the past couple of decades can therefore be directly linked to the expanding scope of patents on life forms in the United States in particular and also at the international level. This has no direct impact on the developing countries but the adoption of the TRIPS Agreement and the introduction of life patents in all WTO member states compel to change policy related to agriculture. [18]

It is clear that intellectual property protection is not the only relevant factor in the development of genetic engineering but it is one of the prominent ones. From an agricultural policy perspective, genetic engineering has been promoted partly as a solution to the shortcomings of chemical agriculture since some of the products are, for instance, meant to be more environmentally friendly because they are designed to require fewer chemical inputs. The development and use of genetic engineering is of tremendous significance for agricultural and environmental management. In fact, the introduction of genetically modified plant varieties and food has been extremely controversial in Europe and some of the implications of genetic engineering have already been the subject of significant debate in India and other developing countries. This includes concerns with the environmental impact of the introduction of these varieties, on human health and the legal policy. [19]

Another grave concern for Indian agriculture in recent times has been the evolution and emergence of genetically modified organisms (GMOs) such as transgenic seeds modified by the application of transgenesis or recombination DNA technology involving the insertion or deletion of genes. The revolution in plant biotechnology and genomics has opened new perspectives and opportunities for plant breeders to introduce new varieties in the agricultural crops and food crops by a handful of biotech giants such as Monsanto, Ciba-Geigy, Du pont, Mycogen, Amoco, Agracetus and Lubrizol for global trade which has changed the face of global agriculture. A number of justifications have been given for the introduction of intellectual property rights in plant varieties with a view to foster food security for long-term in developing countries. [20]

In India, according to the Department of Science and Technology, plant biotechnology has made significant strides in the past twenty years, encompassing developments in plant molecular biology and genetic engineering. The first commercial GM food crop variety 'FlavrSavr' tomato, released in 1994 was genetically engineered. About the prospects and effects of transgenic food crops, the Department of Science and Technology were of the view that the conventional technologies of agriculture are inadequate to meet formidable challenges of feeding large population with limited land and water resources. In addition, adverse effects of global climate change impose new limitations on crop production.

From an economic perspective, genetic engineering seems to be a useful proposition in the context where the commercialization of agriculture is a norm but it has not provided the equal or positive results—for example, the commercialization of Bt cotton in India has not yet yielded any results. [21]

The Parliamentary Standing Committee on Agriculture (2011-2012) constituted by the Ministry of Agriculture, Government of India submitted its Thirty Seventh Report titled "Cultivation of Genetically Modified Food Crops: Prospects and Effects" on August 9, 2012. After an exhaustive interaction with the stakeholders and considering the impact of genetically modified food crops on biodiversity, human health, the environment and the future of farming, it recommended: "for the time being, all research and development activities on transgenic crops should be carried out only in containment and the ongoing field trials in all States should be discontinued forthwith". [22]

The Committee further presented a holistic and comprehensive view on the pros and cons of the application of biotechnology in agricultural sector. The Committee was furnished with several studies and reports such as the International Assessment of Agricultural Knowledge, Science and Technology for Development (IAASTD) Report on the above subject by various stakeholders' having a contextual bearing on the Indian agriculture sector. The Committee rightly substantiated the various findings of the Report including the regulatory framework of testing GMOs, existing IPR and liability framework, ability of modern biotechnology to make significant contributions to the resilience of small and subsistence agricultural system, costs and benefits created by the modern technology, and the manner in which it has been incorporated into the society and the eco-system. As far as the cost and benefits component is concerned, in this regard, the Committee during their above mentioned study visited the Vidharba region of Maharashtra state and established that the observation of 400 experts in IAASTD Report had a sound basis on the cost and benefits front.

The Committee further lamented that "because of very high input costs and the yield loss due to development of resistance in the targeted pests, the local agrarian economy has been totally shattered with huge losses for small and marginal farmers. There have been 7,992 farmers suicides in the region during the period 2006 to 2011—the indebtedness and multitude of other problems caused by sowing of Bt. cotton being a contributory factor. [23] During the year 2012, according to the documentation done by the Vidarbha Jan Andolan Samiti, a social group working among the farmers, an estimated total of 535 farmer suicides happened in Vidarbha between January 1 and October 1 of 2012.

Apart from that, the traditional local cotton varieties have been almost wiped out while the seed companies have benefited from the transgenic Bt. Cotton. The poor and helpless farmers have suffered more of the costs than the benefits". The IAASTD Report has also drawn attention towards the threat of intellectual property and globalization as regards the public plant breeding institutions in developing countries and the transfer of knowledge away from common man. The privatization will lead to women losing economic resources and social standings as plant breeding knowledge appropriated the entire communities' knowledge and control over food security. [24]

Further, the Supreme Court appointed Technical Expert Committee (TEC) also recommended the serious concerns and apprehensions that society at large has towards all field trials of GM food crops. It opined, "knowing the casual manner in which large-scale field trials are held across the country, the absence of a regulatory mechanism, and the failure to document the damage transgenic crops have inflicted on humans and the environment during, before and after such trials, the committee has called for invoking the 'precautionary principle". [25]

In fact, the introduction of genetically modified plant varieties and foods has been extremely controversial in developing countries because it not only touches the potential impacts on environment, human health and the legal policy but it also brings socio-economic impacts for the society where a large proportion of the population is engaged in agricultural sector. It compels the farmers to buy new seeds every year which is also a matter of grave concern for the poor countries, where more than 60 percent of the population earns livelihood from agriculture. Consequently, the continuation of traditional farming practices including the right to save and exchange seeds and sell their harvest is a matter of great importance for the developing countries as this is an important process to maintain biodiversity.

Use of genetically modified plant varieties may result in displacement and promotion of monocultures of single agrochemical-dependent varieties, which may in turn result in the loss of biodiversity and reduction of crop's resilience to pests and diseases. It may decline the availability of nutritious food in the market with a high probability of weakening research on crop varieties that are less economical such as traditional crops in favour of high value crops. So it can be presumed that the extension of intellectual property rights in the seeds sector may carry a risk of restricting farmer's rights to reuse and sell seeds, which was traditionally available to them. If all fears are genuine it may destabilize the food security. [26]

International Intellectual Property Rights Instruments

TRIPS Agreement: The TRIPS Agreement came as a result of seven years of negotiations from September 1986 to December 1993 as a part of the Uruguay Round of multilateral trade negotiations of the GATT. [27] These negotiations were launched at Punta del Este, Uruguay and formally concluded in April 1994 at Marrakesh, Morocco along with the other negotiations of the Uruguay Round. TRIPS came into force on the first day of 1995, with the establishment of WTO and it is the most important intellectual property treaty for all WTO member states. The TRIPS Agreement covers different kinds of IPRs, such as patents, copyright and geographical indications. [28] The preambular language prescribes the introduction of minimum standards of protection that all countries must follow in regulated areas and have tacitly agreed to all the provisions of the new world order subject to their national legislations. [29]

From the standpoint of TRIPS, the question of food security is one that can be tackled through some of the exceptions provided in TRIPS Agreement through the two general interpretative clauses of Articles 7 and 8 to take into account the socio-economic goals. Article 7 is the only provision which evokes the balance between the rights granted to individual intellectual property right holders and the broader interests of the society at large. Further, Article 8 applies more specifically to measures adopted by the states to implement their TRIPS obligation. It provides that "States can adopt measures to protect public health and nutrition, as well as to promote the public interest in sectors of vital importance for socio-economic and technological development. [30]

As far as the introduction of intellectual property protection in agriculture is concerned, it is directly linked to food security and towards the realization of the human right to food in developing countries like India. Further, with the large-scale development of agro-biotechnology and genetic engineering, particularly in the agricultural sector, it has tremendous impacts on related policies and legal frameworks in developing countries with the adoption of the same. The patents in agro-biotechnology are important to address in two ways. Firstly, the TRIPS Agreement prescribes the patentability of micro-organisms. Secondly, it requires that all member states must introduce intellectual property protection for plant varieties. [31]

As regards the issue of plant variety protection, the provision under Article 27(3)(b) is an exception to the general rule of Article 27(1), which talks that all member states "shall provide for the protection of plant varieties either by patents or by an effective *sui generis* system or by any combination thereof. This provision will have significant impact on developing countries because they have to redesign their law and policies in this field to comply with the TRIPS Agreement. In the TRIPS context, Article 27(3)(b) is an interesting provision in the sense that it does not only impose the patentability of plant varieties but it provides significant liberty to member states to introduce an alternative system of protection regime. [32] Moreover, Article 27(3)(b) is also significant in the context of the broader and comprehensive legal regime for food security, IPRs, environmental management and human rights. It provides member states an opportunity to introduce a kind of plant variety protection which focuses on the human right to food and their obligations under FAO and its PGRFA treaty and obligation under the Biodiversity Convention for Environmental Management rather than focus on TRIPS obligations. [33]

International Convention for the Protection of New Varieties of Plants (UPOV): Apart from the patenting regime sponsored by the TRIPS Agreement, a number of European countries have also introduced a hybrid form of protection for plant breeders rights in the International Convention for the Protection of New Varieties of Plants—the (UPOV) Convention. [34] It has evolved over time in line with the increasing importance of the private sector in agricultural sector in developed countries. Though it is not a part of United Nations, the UPOV scheme of plant variety protection provides recognition to the rights of plant breeders on an international basis. It was signed in 1961 in Paris. It came into force in 1968 and was revised in 1972, 1978 and 1991. Each member state needs to ratify the specific version of the Convention by which it wants to be governed.

The UPOV Convention was first negotiated and developed mostly among western European countries and OECD countries. Its membership remained relatively small until the early 1990s and its importance was limited. The objective of the Convention is to provide and promote an effective system of plant variety protection or plant breeders' rights specifically with the aim of encouraging the development of new varieties of plants in the interests of both agricultural development and commercial plant breeders. [35]

Plant varieties can be protected under UPOV regime if they fulfil the four criteria of novelty, distinctness, stability and uniformity. The concept of novelty under UPOV is significantly different from its equivalent under the patent law. Under UPOV a variety is novel if it has not been sold or otherwise disposed of to others, by or with the consent of the breeder, for the purpose of exploitation of the variety. The criterion of distinctness requires that the protected variety should be clearly distinguishable from any other variety whose existence is a matter of common knowledge at the time of filing of the application. Stability is obtained if the variety remains true to its description after repeated reproduction or propagation. And, uniformity implies that the variety remains true to the original in its relevant characteristics when propagated. [36] The UPOV Convention provides the following privileges:

- Breeder's exemptions which allowed the breeders to use their protected varieties for research purposes and breeding new varieties;
- Farmer's privilege, which allowed the farmers to use their own harvested seeds of the protected variety for sowing the next crop in their own farm. [37]

The UPOV Convention provides a *sui-generis* form of intellectual property protection specifically adapted for the process of plant breeding and has been developed to encourage breeders to develop new varieties of plants for the benefit of public at large. A protected variety under UPOV confers a certain number of rights to the breeders. There is, however, no monopoly right of the breeder similar to near monopoly of the patent holder given the exceptions provided to the breeders' right. In general, breeders have exclusive rights to produce or reproduce protected varieties, to condition them for the purpose of propagation, to offer them for selling, to commercialize them, including exporting and importing them. The 1978 version of UPOV Convention was in force till April 1998, when the 1991 version entered into force. The 1991 version substantially enlarges the scope of breeders' rights and restricts farmers and researchers exemptions and provides for a longer term protection of plants. [38]

In the TRIPS era, the situation has significantly changed since by introducing plant breeders, it is recognized as one of the ways to satisfy the requirement of the TRIPS Agreement. Further, to build an understanding for joining UPOV or adopting a plant breeders rights system was one possibility for member states to fulfil their commitments under Article

27(3)(b) of the TRIPS Agreement. A number of developing countries that had had no form of plant variety protection before 1994 suddenly turned to UPOV either to join it or in most cases adapt the basic framework it proposes in terms of plant breeders rights protection. India has taken a consistent stand that the UPOV Convention is unsuitable for the country's needs because it is more concerned about the protection of the interests of the plant breeders rather than the farmers. The 1991 version has ignored the rights of village communities, rights of re-use and exchange of seeds. In order to comply with the mandate of the TRIPS Agreement, countries like India would have to blend elements of the 1978 and 1991 Acts in their domestic legislation. [39]

Overall, this special regime for plant varieties under the UPOV Convention and the existence of a special provision concerning plant variety provision in the TRIPS Agreement has led in the era of life patents in genetic engineering towards a search for the exact definition of a plant variety. This is important in all countries where the patentability of plant varieties is excluded.

Convention on Biological Diversity: To counter the TRIPS Agreement, the Convention on Biodiversity came into being. It was adopted in 1992 in the form of a binding framework treaty but came into force in 1993. It has been signed by 191 parties present and has thus become one of the most widely ratified of all the environmental conventions. The Convention reflects the worldwide concern to prevent unfair exploitation of the rich genetic wealth and traditional knowledge of the developing states by the developed states. [40] The Convention recognized for the first time in international law that the conservation of biological diversity is "a common concern of humankind" and is an integral part of the development process. The Agreement covers all ecosystems, species, and genetic resources. It provides an opportunity to governments to protect their agricultural biodiversity, farmers' livelihoods, and sovereign rights to biodiversity.

The Convention on biological diversity goes beyond the FAO Undertaking on Plant Genetic Resources and accords primacy to 'national sovereignty' rather than the common heritage. The Convention lays down certain general principles that will guide a state's action in biodiversity management. The preamble as well as Article 3 states that national government has the right to decide the utilization of genetic resources including collection of payment of such utilization. [41] Such access is being subjected to a new law of prior informed consent of the country where collection takes places *in situ* and must be on mutually agreed terms. [42] It also affirms of the fundamental principle that a state can exercise sovereignty over genetic resources by legislation [43] by stating that state shall endeavour to facilitate access not to impose restrictions contrary to the Convention. [44]

To promote information sharing, it ordains participation in scientific research and development through consensual approach on mutually agreed terms. Encompassing the ethical dichotomies in recognition reward system, a conflicting set of legal moralities was detected when India became a signatory to the WTO Agreement in 1995. [45] Since TRIPS mandates that IPR could be universally applied to all technologies, biodiversity, genetic resources and plant variety automatically become subjects of patent either under global patent regime or *sui generis* national system. [46] Unfortunately, arguments have not been fruitfully deployed by the Indian Governments in international negotiations to counter patentability and as a result, the individualization of plant varieties went unabated.

Impact of Intellectual Property Rights Regime

With the continuing inclemency of the new global economic order and the end of the protectionist measures, Indian agriculture sector has been directly encountering all the damaging consequences of the WTO regime. The introduction of intellectual property rights in the field of agriculture has the following adverse impacts:

1. The introduction of new seeds protected by the patent having higher yields is likely to induce the displacement of the local varieties. The loss of local varieties is in itself a loss of agro-biodiversity. It is threatening biodiversity conservation as well as farmers survival. Biodiversity erosion will in turn lead to the erosions of the rich cultural diversity of our country. [47]
2. The use of commercial varieties developed by the private sector by the farmers implies a much higher investment in input cost and leads to a circle of economic dependence. As long as crops succeed, farmers can benefit from the new system but in an under-average performance, the farmers suffer multiple losses and in worst cases, farmers cannot recover which leads to debt spiral and farmers committing suicides in various part of the country including Maharashtra, Andhra Pradesh, Karnataka, Madhya Pradesh and Chhattisgarh. [48]
3. Intellectual property protection in the area of agriculture and new plant varieties will undermine food security since the protected and patented verities are not linked to food needs but to the processing and marketing requirements of agri-business. The undermining of food security will increase food imports and thus inviting deeper conditionalities from institutions like the IMF and the World Bank.
4. The introduction of transgenic food crops came to be associated with significant environmental costs and impacts on other natural resources like declining soil fertility with excessive chemical fertiliser use, reduced ground water recharge, salt infestation, lower yields, flooding of low lands, regimentation of small tanks and reservoirs etc. [49]
5. The threat of bio-piracy is lurking deep in the Indian farming sector. For example, the patenting of *basmati, neem, haldi, karela, kalsjira and bhindi* by MNCs and

private sector genetic engineering industry. [50]

6. The patent and plant breeders' rights increase the seed prices and inhibit the development of the domestic private seed companies.
7. It also affects the subsistence of small-scale agriculture. [51]

National Intellectual Property Protection Laws

The ratification of CBD, TRIPS and membership of WTO has significant impact for India. It enjoined to undertake massive legal rehabilitation and wide-ranging legislative changes particularly in the field of patents for biotechnological inventions, plant breeders' rights and geographical indications. Patenting of innovations in the agriculture segment has been practiced all through the history of the patent system. [52] Historically, the Indian Patents Act, 1970 did not provide for the protection of agricultural products as well as limitations on the scope of the rights granted to patent holders. It is only after the ratification of the TRIPS Agreement, that a number of changes have been introduced as a part of the three amendments to the Patent Act such as the Patents (Amendment) Act, 1999 and the Patents (Amendment) Act, 2002 adopted in past decades that will have direct impacts for the Indian agriculture.

The single substantive change to the above Act has been made by the Patents (Amendment) Act, 2005. [53] The amendment includes inventions in all areas of technology including agriculture which are to be protected as long as they satisfy the basic requirements for patenting. Patents are now being filed for agro products, food processing and agrochemicals including fertilizer and biocides. Such efforts will continue and could have an impact on research in agriculture and food technology areas.

Further, in furtherance of the fulfilment of CBD and TRIPS requirements, three important legislations have been passed by the Indian government. In respect of agricultural, natural, traditional and industrial goods, there was no specific law governing geographical indications which could adequately protect the interests of producers and consumers from abuse. TRIPS does not accord legal protection to such goods unless geographical indication is protected in the country of origin. Therefore, the Parliament passed the Geographical Indication of Goods (Registration and Protection) Act, in 1999. [54] The salient features of the Act incorporate establishment of geographical indication registry, maintenance of register of geographical indications containing registered geographical indications and authorized users, compulsory advertisement for inviting objection and registration of authorized users and criterion for infringement action. The overall object is to combat the menace of bio-piracy.

Further, the exclusion of plant varieties from the scope of patentability under the Patents Act, 1970 is related to the introduction of a separate plant variety protection regime as part of the commitments taken under Article 27(3)(b) of the TRIPS Agreement. A decision was taken to adopt separate legislation, a solution adopted by a majority of WTO member states. Thereafter, India passed the Protection of Plant Varieties and Farmers Rights Act, 2001. [55]

In the wake of an inbuilt threat of bio-piracy in the second part of the 1990s and in other contexts such as the adoption of TRIPS Agreement, a national biodiversity law becomes *sine qua non*. Of late, the Government of India to implement the principles of CBD in domestic law enacted the Biological Diversity Act, 2002. The Act was developed through an extensive and intensive consultation process initiated in 1994. India is one of the few countries to have enacted such legislation. The main object of the Act is to provide for conservation of biological diversity, sustainable use of its components and fair and equitable sharing of the benefits arising out of the use of biological resources, knowledge and for matters connected therewith or incidental thereto, mentioned in the Biodiversity Convention, 1992. [56]

Thereafter, in particular, the Indian Parliament is thinking of a new seed law which may bring substantial changes to the existing intellectual property protection regime in agriculture. For that, the Seed Bill, 2004 [57] and 2010, is yet to see the light of the day. [58]

Conclusion

Thus, it is apparent from the analysis that the internationalization of TRIPS Agreement under the WTO has the potential to bite deep into the material well-being of Indian agricultural sector and encountering all the damaging consequences of intellectual property rights regime sponsored by the developed countries. This new system of hegemony which promotes individual appropriation has led to the formulation of a new set of rules concerning control over knowledge and resources. If agriculture is considered exclusively a commercial and economic activity then there is no problem, but if it is taken in a broader perspective, the impacts of intellectual property rights in agriculture and biodiversity management need to be taken into account. Biodiversity and agro-biodiversity in particular, is of primary importance for the sustainability of agricultural systems in the long-term. Agro-biodiversity is of special importance because it directly contributes to feeding millions of poor people living in developing countries like India.

In fact, the socio-economic conditions differ in developed and developing countries. In developing countries like India, the primary sector still constitutes 15 percent to the gross domestic product (GDP) and employs about two-thirds of the working population. The exclusion of patent in natural and agricultural recourses has been traditionally premised on the elements of public morality. There is a need to foster innovation at all levels, from the smallest farmer to corporate giants.

An alternative regime should be formulated by the fusion of legal and communal systems of intellectual property rights.

This regime should provide for the establishment of property rights for all actors engaged in agriculture management and seed improvement. The proposed regime should provide for non-monopoly rights implying that no single entity derives all the benefits associated with a given invention and that different inventors may have concurrent rights. To develop such a model law, following areas should be taken into consideration which includes, the interests and rights of farmers, the conservation and sustainable use of biological and genetic resources, the prevention of biopiracy, the protection of traditional knowledge, the fair and equitable sharing of benefits arising from the exploitation of resources and the realisation of human rights to food.

To conclude, it can be said that under the present socio-economic conditions, it is high time to devise novel legal and extra legal models of sustainable management of ecological, biological and agricultural resources to achieve the goals of reducing poverty and malnutrition as well as of sustainable inclusive growth in the present economic perspective.

Endnotes

1. Philippe Cullet (2005), "Intellectual Property Protection and Sustainable Development".
2. Nunopirs de Carvalho (2011), "The TRIPS Regime of Trademarks and Designs".
3. Supra note 1 at 187.
4. Jayashree Watal (1998), "Intellectual Property Rights in Indian Agriculture", ICRIER, 5.
5. Md. Zafar Mahfooz Nomani (2000), "Environment, Agriculture and Challenges of Bio-Piracy: A Blue Print of Indian Sui Generis Legal Order", *Indian Journal of Environmental Law,* 9.
6. Philippe Cullet (2003), "Food Security and Intellectual Property Rights in Developing Countries", IELRC Working Paper, available at:
   http://www.ielrc.og/content/w0303.pdf.
7. Jayati Ghosh (2012), "Structural Imbalances", *The Frontline,* September 22-October 5.
8. "Annual Report, 2010-11" Ministry of Agriculture, Government

of India.
9. Supra note 1 at 188.
10. M.D. Nair (2011), "GATT, TRIPS, WTO and CBD: Relevance to Agriculture", 3, J.I.P.R. 176.
11. "Economic Survey, 2011-2012", Ministry of Finance, Government of India.
12. "State of Indian Agriculture, 2011-12", Government of India.
13. Supra note 1 at 189.
14. Supra note 5.
15. Supra note 1 at 204.
16. Joel J. D'Silva (2005), "GM Seeds, Intellectual Property and the Corporatization of Food", 34, Ban. L.J. 7.
17. Ghayur Alam (1996), "Biotechnology, Agriculture and the Developing Countries", *Economic and Political Weekly*, March 23, 703.
18. Supra note 1 at 193.
19. Terri Raney and Prabhu Pingali (2004), "Private Research and Public Goods: Implications of Biotechnology for Biodiversity", FAO Working Paper.
20. Vandana Shiva (1996), "Agricultural Biodiversity, Intellectual Property Rights and Farmers Rights", *Economic and Political Weekly*, June 22, 1623.
21. Committee on Agriculture (2011-2012), "Thirty Seventh Report", Ministry of Agriculture, Government of India, August 19.
22. Devinder Sharma (2012), "GM Crops Should Go Back to the Lab", *The Hindu*, November 8.
23. Supra note 20 at 151.
24. *The Hindu Daily,* Allahabad Edition, October 10, 2012.
25. Supra note 21 at 07.
26. Supra note 1 at 193.
27. V.R. Krishna Iyer (2000), "GATT, TRIPS and Patent Law-I", *The Hindu Daily*, New Delhi, September 11.
28. Jayashree Watal (2000), "Intellectual Property Rights in the WTO and Developing Countries", 2.
29. Carlos M. Carrea (2007), "TRIPS: A Commentary on the Agreement".
30. M.D. Nair (2002), "Issues in TRIPS of Concern to India", *The Hindu*, New Delhi, September 23.
31. Supra note 1 at 200.
32. Vandana Shiva (2001), "Intellectual Property Protection in the

North/South Divide", in Christopher Heath and Anselm Kamperman Sanders (eds.), 'Intellectual Property in Digital Age: Challenges for Asia'.
33. Md. Zafar Mahfooz Nomani (2001), "WTO, TRIPS Agreement and Protection of Plant Variety: Imperative and Implication for Indian Intellectual Property Rights Regime", in A.K. Kaul and V.K. Ahuja (eds.), 'The Law of Intellectual Property Rights: In Prospect and Retrospect'.
34. Philippe Cullet (2000), "Farmers Rights in Peril", *Frontline*, 17(7).
35. Supra note 1 at 227.
36. Rolf Jordens and Peter Button (2011), "Effective System of Plant Variety Protection in Responding to Challenges of a Changing World: UPOV Perspective", March 16, 75.
37. Christopher Arup (2000), "The New World Trade Organisation Agreements: Globalising Law through Services and Intellectual Property", 234.
38. Supra note 2 at 10.
39. Anshu Pratap Singh, Padmavati Manchikanti and H.S Chawla (2011), "Sui Generis IPR Laws vis-à-vis Farmers Rights in Some Asian Countries: Implications under the WTO", 16 J.I.P.R. 108.
40. Patricia Birnie Alan Boyle and Catherine Redgwell (2009), "International Law and the Environment".
41. Supra note 2 at 11.
42. Article 8, Convention on Biological Diversity, 1992.
43. *Id* Article 15(1).
44. *Id* Article 15(2).
45. Md. Zafar Mahfooz Nomani (2000), "Laws and Flaws Relating to Conservation of Biological Diversity: A Kaleidoscopic View", *The Company Law Journal*, 120.
46. Philippe Cullet (2000), "Bio-Diversity Legislation Reflects India's Obligations", *The Hindu Daily,* New Delhi, February 22.
47. Supra note 20 at 1628.
48. P. Sainath (2012), "The Seeds of Suicide", *The Hindu*, July 12, and *The Hindu*, July 9.
49. Supra note 20 at 1628.
50. Suman Sahai (1998), "Protecting Basmati", *Economic and Political Weekly*, 33(9), 442.
51. Vandana Shiva (2002), "Restore Exemption to Patents in

Agriculture", *The Hindu*, New Delhi, February 17.
52. Supra note 05 at 11.
53. Feroz Ali Khader (2009), "The Law of Patents With a Special Focus on Pharmaceuticals in India", 13-16.
54. Bare Act, Intellectual Property Laws, 257 (2011).
55. Ibid. at 299.
56. Ibid. at 385.
57. S. Bala Ravi (2005), "Seeds of Trouble", *The Hindu,* New Delhi, March 8.
58. S. Bala Ravi (2010), "Fault Lines in the 2010 Seeds Bill", *Economic and Political Weekly*, 45 and 32, 13.

3

Patents in the Area of Biotechnology in India

Anushka M. Nayak

Patents add the fuel of interest to the fire of genius.
—*Abraham Lincoln*

The system of patent is subject to continuous changes in the philosophy and in its purview. The invention of new technologies has always been a subject for the system of patent with the emergence of the two pioneer technologies of modern world namely information technology and biotechnology. The system of patent is undergoing significant changes from time to time. The fact that philosophy of patent law is dynamic and prone to continuous changes has had its impact on patenting the invention of new technologies. The modern world is very much influenced by these technologies.

For the improvement of research and development, many inventions with great ability and function have been claimed in the patent. In today's world, biotechnology has become a whole new industry and patent protection for this is of immense commercial importance. This paper is focused on the role of patents in the area of biotechnology—an important tool to protect biotechnological inventions. Biotechnology and genetics research have been matter of extensive investment both by the public and private sectors, with the products and processes promising from these efforts making a significant and increasing contribution to human health and health care. Intellectual property rights (IPRs), protection of new life forms, especially related to human biological materials, raises a number of difficult technical and ethico-legal issues because of which the patentability of new biological forms and processes is still not accepted in many countries.

Introduction

India is a stockroom of biological resources and one of the world's richest biodiversity countries. In the past five years, there has been a rise in the investment in the biotech-oriented industries. In today's world, biotechnology has become a whole new industry and patent protection for this is of immense importance. The system of patent is undergoing significant changes from time to time. Patents are exclusive rights granted to inventions that satisfy the criteria of patentability in the form of novelty, non-obviousness and potential for industrial application. [1] The fundamental principle or "the object of patent law is to encourage scientific research, new technology and industrial progress. Grant of the exclusive privilege to own, use or sell the method or product patented for a limited period, stimulates new inventions of commercial utility. The price of the grant of monopoly is the disclosure of the invention at the Patent Office, which after expiry of the fixed period of monopoly, passes onto the public domain". [2]

In 1998, the U.S. Patent and Trademark Office (PTO) issued a broad patent claiming primate (including human) embryonic stem cells, entitled "Primate Embryonic Stem Cells" (Patent 5,843,780) whereas on March 13, 2001, a second patent (6,200,806) was issued with the same title but focused on human embryonic stem cells. Thus, worldwide there have been over 2,000 patent applications involving human and non-human stem cells, of which one quarter refers to embryonic stem cells. Moreover in India, it is estimated that over the next five years, biotechnology can offer opportunities for fresh investment of ` 7-8 billion.

Biotechnology is poised to take India to a different playing field where it can dominate the world market. However, to achieve its full potential, the biotech sector requires a facilitative environment. The government needs to make a concerted effort to amend its patent laws and strengthen its intellectual property regime, so as to protect the economic interests of those who innovate. Additionally, India needs to sign the Budapest Treaty on the International Recognition of the Deposit of Micro organisms for the Purposes of Patent Procedure to assist in the standardization process of biotechnology patenting.

What is Biotechnology?

Broadly speaking, biotechnology can be defined as "the application of all natural sciences and engineering in the direct or indirect use of living organisms or parts of organisms, in their natural or modified forms, in an innovative manner in the production of goods and services and/or to improve existing industrial process. The market application of outputs is typically in the general areas of human health, food production, industrial bio-processing and other public goods and environmental settings". [3]

The United Nations Convention on Biological Diversity defines 'biotechnology' as: "any technological application that uses biological systems, living organisms, or derivatives thereof, to make or modify products or processes for specific use". [4]

Nevertheless, the most frequent use of this term or its abbreviation "biotech" refers to what can be called 'modern biotechnology' unlike classical or conventional biotechnology. Classical biotechnology may be defined as the production of useful products by living micro-organisms and as such it has been with us for a long time. The production of ethanol from yeast cells is as old as history, and over 50 years ago the production of various industrial chemicals such as acetic acid and acetone by fermentation processes was well-known indeed. Even the word 'biotechnology' is not recently coined. In 1920, a Bureau of Biotechnology was established in Leeds and published a journal dealing with fermentation technology and related topics. Back in 1873, Louis Pasteur obtained a US patent claiming 'yeast free from organic germs of disease as an article of manufacture', an early case of a patent for living organisms. [5]

Modification and application of living beings for the different practical purpose is possible through biotechnology. The progress of modern world is dependent on the development of biotechnology due to its diverse and significant application. Research in this field has given rise to many inventions with enormous utility and commercial value.

More recently, the antibiotics industry was based upon the isolation of products from selected strains of micro organisms and although the majority of antibiotics is now produced synthetically, many are still made from micro organisms either found in nature or artificially mutated. Not only antibiotics but also other drugs, for example, the immune suppressant cyclosporine are produced by fermentation of a micro-organism.

On the other hand, modern biotechnology is technology that involves understanding, mapping, manipulation or change of the genetic patrimony of a living organism. It began in the 1970s with two basic techniques of recombinant DNA technology and hybridoma technology. It is important to be aware that biotechnologies are both new and very old. So, we can divide biotechnologies into three generations for the sake of better understanding. The first generation includes traditional technologies like beer brewing and bread making which is really old and second generation begins with the microbiological applications developed by Louis Pasteur culminating in the production by fermentation. Modern plant animal breeding also falls within these generations. The third generation biotechnology includes various genetic engineering techniques for transferring DNA from one life to another including cloning.

In simple terms, biotechnology brings together technology with the science of the living cells. It is the scientific manipulation of living organisms for human benefit and its best known form is genetic engineering, [6] industrial agriculture, plant and animal breeding. Applications in this area are leading to revolutionary new drugs that include Genetech t-PA to dissolve blood clots, which cause heart attack; Merck's meracore which lowers cholesterol levels in people; Amgen's new medicine to cure anaemia; and Viagra to improve sexual potentiality in men.

Patents and Biotechnology

TRIPS Agreement [7] provides the minimum standard of patent protection that require mandatory compliance by all member countries. Article 27(1) of TRIPS mandates that: "patents shall be available for any inventions, whether products or processes, in all fields of technology...and patents shall be available and patent rights enjoyable without discrimination as to...the field of technology".

However, Article 27(3)(b) specifically allows member countries to exclude from patentable subject matter, "plants and animals other than micro-organisms, and essentially biological processes for the production of plants or animals other than non-biological and microbiological processes. However, Members shall provide for the protection of plant varieties either by patents or by an effective *sui generis* system or by any combination thereof".

This forms the basis for the provisions on the exclusions from patentability under the Indian Law. The list of exclusions includes inventions which are frivolous and are contrary to the well established physical laws of nature such as a perpetual motion machine. The Patents Act also excludes all forms of discoveries, scientific theories, mathematical methods and abstractions.

Subject Matter of Biotechnological Patents

The patent protection is obtainable for most of the biotechnological innovations. The protection thus provided serves as an incentive for further development and technical innovations. Biological inventions in the patent system are similar to chemical inventions as biological, microbiological, biotechnological, genetic engineering and medical inventions.

What is Patentable in Biotechnology?

As per the Indian Patent Act, the following are patentable:

1. Micro organisms: Under the Indian Patent Act, microbiological processes can be patented. Also, patentable are processes for producing new micro organisms through genetic engineering and the products that result out of this process, such as micro organisms including plasmids and viruses if they are non-living.
2. Cell lines: A cell line is patentable if artificially produced.
3. R-DNA, RNA, Amino Acid: If the end result is non-living, it is patentable.
4. Hybridoma [8] technology: Patents are also allowed on hybridoma technology, but not on protoplast fusion.
5. Expressed sequence tag's, or ESTs, are small fragments of genetic material obtained by reverse transcriptions of messenger RNA (mRNA) from expressed genes. The gene sequence, or expressed sequence tags (ESTs), can be patented if it has a use, such as if it works as a probe.

What is not Patentable in Biotechnology?

Additionally, the Indian Patent Act defines what is not a patentable biotechnology: inventiveness does not apply to plant or animals. Accordingly, a method of producing a new form of a known plant or tissue culture method for production of plant variety is not patentable, nor is a method of treatment of a human body by surgery or operation for diagnosis. Nor is a method of improving or changing the appearance of the human body or parts of it patentable. Still, these categories are not as clear-cut as they appear. Skilful wording may decide whether a finding is an "invention" or a "discovery". Thus, it is best to consult a patent attorney prior to filing a patent.

To compete worldwide, India must decide whether to remain with the more conservative European approach, or if the

Australia/US or some other approach better suits the needs of its emerging economy. In either case, Indian companies, inventors, and investors venturing into the biotech sector must be well-informed and well aware of Indian laws, as well as the laws of other countries as they seek to join the biotechnology headliners. More importantly and immediately, these companies and investors venturing into the biotech sector need to fully realize the significant role intellectual property plays in the commercialization process for biotechnological innovation.

The biological matter includes both living as well as non-living matters (amino acids, peptides, proteins, fats and fatty acids). These kinds of compounds are best recognized when referred to by their commonly known names of anti-bodies, hormones, enzymes, antibiotics, cholesterol etc. regarding the status of patenting of these non-living genetic materials, all of these are being patented as just chemical compounds. It needs to be reiterated that their special nature is being completely ignored by the policy makers. In the normal course, none of these products are considered to be living biological matter.

However, in my view, these cannot be treated merely as chemical compounds rather are part of the living matter. Beyond the structural non-living components of living organism are the smallest, wholly viable units of life called cells. Cells are also the smallest reproducible units of life, and it is this aspect of reproducibility which is a complete invention in biotechnology. Cells come in all different shapes, sizes and have different capacities for independent survival. Microbes, for example, are unicellular organisms capable of living in the environment.

The methods or processes of manufacture in biotechnology are the next most important subject matter of biotechnology. The most commonly known type of processes which are included under the rubric of biotechnology include the fermentation process, chemical process, diagnostic process and also methods of treating human and animal bodies. It also includes methods of treating products of cells such as hormones, enzymes and the like. The area of methods and processes has raised a number of issues because the techniques that are available provide the potential for the creation of genetically altered biological matter itself.

Accepting the traditional approach, the new premise of patent law states that natural life is the creation of God, but non-natural life is the creation of human beings. So, the new idea of patent law is that the creation of God or the creation of the nature could not be patented whereas creations of human beings involves the application of human intelligence to natural things and thus could be patentable.

Patenting of Micro-organisms

Microbiological inventions generally involve the use of a new strain of micro-organism to produce a new compound or to produce a known compound [9] more efficiently. The new organism may have been found in nature or produced in the laboratory by artificially induced random mutation or by more specific techniques such as genetic engineering. Article 27(3)(b) of the TRIPS Agreement forms basis for the provisions relating to patentability of micro-organisms. Nevertheless, micro-organisms also have to satisfy the novelty, utility and non-obviousness criteria to be patented. However, TRIPS Agreement does not provide a precise definition of micro-organism.

The term 'micro-organism' is generally understood to include virus, bacteria, protozoa, unicellular algae and non-differentiated animal or plant cells. Even though micro-organism can be patented as per the Agreement, one is often faced with a dilemma whether all micro-organisms constitute a patentable subject matter since they are real 'life forms'. The law which opened the gates for inventions in the field of biotechnology, particularly micro-organism was a landmark judgement of the US Supreme Court in 1980 in the case of *Diamond vs. Chakraborthy.* [10]

A modified micro-organism was developed by Dr. Chakraborty which had the ability of breaking down the crude oil. This property was introduced into naturally occurring bacterium to produce a genetically modified organism. The dispute was with regard to a modified micro-organism developed by Ananda Chakraborty which had the ability of breaking down crude oil. The US Commissioner of Patent refused the granting of patent stating that the subject matter of the invention was a living organism and was hence not patentable. The US Supreme Court decided in favour of the patentee and stated that everything under the sun is patentable.

The landmark judgement paved the way for granting a number of such biotechnology related patents. The court's decision that 'everything under the sun is patentable', apart from a human being, should be regarded as patentable was a sweeping judgement. It sent a crucial signal to the world that patenting must be made available in any country which sought to join the race for commercial returns on biotechnological research. The decision aroused great public interest at the time but in all the fuss, it went unremarked that the British Patent Office had already granted the corresponding patent in 1976. In 1988, eight years after the court's ruling in *Chakrabarty* case, the U.S. Patent Office issued its first patent for an animal.

The Chakrabarty decision and the subsequent actions enacted by the US Congress provided great economic stimulus to the patenting of micro-organisms and cells, and in turn provided stimulus to the growth of the biotechnological industry in the 1980s. The Supreme Court of Canada in *Monsanto Canada Inc. vs. Schmeiser* [11] laid down that higher life forms were not patentable because they were not a manufacture or composition of matter within the meaning of invention of the Patent Act. However, increased patenting of biotechnological inventions has led to litigation related to patent infringement issues. The patent litigation is only likely to increase in the future considering overlapping of patent claims, the high value of products, problem of prior publication and the fact that many companies are pursuing the same product. The increase in the patent claims leads to the inability of the patent offices to process the biotechnological inventions in a timely manner.

The European Patent Office (EPO) following closely the US Patent Office practices has granted numerous patents on all sorts of biological materials. Though not explicitly mentioned, it is generally accepted that European Patent Convention (EPC) allows patent protection for micro-organisms. There are three exclusions from patentable subject matter which in the Patents Act, 1977 derive directly from EPC where in Articles 3, 4 and 5 prohibit patent in: (a) methods of treating the human and animal body, (b) plant and animal varieties and essentially biological methods for their creation and (c) inventions contrary to public order or morality.

In India, the position of patentability of the micro-organisms is parallel to that of the US and Europe. Prior to TRIPS, India's patent system had been regulated by the Patents Act, 1970. To begin making India's law consistent with TRIPS, the Patents Act was amended in 1999 and 2002 and with further modifications in 2005 in order to become fully TRIPS compliant.

Section 3 of the Patent Act, 1999 provides the patent of micro-organism as required by Article 27(1) of the TRIPS agreement. The term 'micro-organism' has not been clearly defined. The Calcutta High Court gave a path-breaking judgement in the case of *Dimminaco A.G. vs. Controller of Patents and Design* [12] which has been hailed in the Indian scenario as counter to *Diamond vs. Chakraborty* case of the US. The case related to the patentability of a process for preparation of Bursitis vaccine useful for protecting poultry against the infectious bursitis. The ground for rejection of the patent by the controller was that the examiner found that the claim did not fall within Section 2(1)(j) of the Patents Act, 1976 and therefore is not an invention. The Court held that "merely because the end product of a process containing a living organism does not preclude the process from being an invention and consequently patentable". Further, the Court found that the patent claimed was useful as it protected poultry against contagious disease and the end product resulted in a new article.

After this decision, the Indian Patents Office did not grant patents for micro-organisms but with the law permitting patenting of micro-organisms, several private sector companies, including Dr. Reddy's Research Foundation, Novo Nordisk, Procter and Gamble, Biocon India, Reliance Life Sciences, Cadila Pharmaceuticals and others have filed applications for fungi, bacteria and viruses.

Patenting of Plants and Animals

The TRIPS Agreement provides that the member states may exclude plants and animals from patentability. The option has been adopted by a number of countries such as the United Kingdom, Europe and India. One of the most controversial provisions of the Agreement surrounds protection of plant varieties. Article 27(3)(b) of the Agreement allows countries to exclude plants and essentially biological processes for their production from their patent system of protection. The same provision however, states that countries must "*provide for the protection of plant varieties either by patents or by an effective sui generis system or by any combination thereof*". Under the Agreement, a country can implement more than one form of plant protection.

The meaning of "*sui generis*" is one of the contentious issues surrounding the Agreement. It is generally believed that the term enables member countries to design their own system of protection for plant varieties if they have elected not to use their patent system for plant protection. What is a sufficient system to qualify as "sui generis" remains to be seen. The issue of the patentability of animals arises mainly because the patentability of animals is considered to be a moral issue rather than a legal one. In India, the plant varieties may be protected under the Protection of Plant Varieties and Farmer's Rights

Act, 2001 under which Plant's Breeder's right or Plant's Variety right is granted to a person coming up with the invention of such plants by asexual methods.

As we have already discussed, different types of plant varieties can be produced by using asexual methods [13] and sexual methods [14] and patent protection of 20 years can be granted to a plant which is new, distinct, uniform and stable. *Lubrizol Transgene Expression* case [15] is the first leading case in which patentability of plant was questioned containing a claim to hybrids produced in accordance with a staged sequence of selection of parent plants and then by cross-testing, evaluation and further multiplication. The Court held that a patent should be granted as it will help in the future in the creation of more food.

The first transgenic animals to be produced was the *oncomouse.* The "*Oncomouse*" [16] was genetically modified by the Harvard Medical School to develop cancer for the purposes of medical research which raised complex ethical issues for patent authorities. This case highlights issues that have arisen in some significant patent law cases concerning biotechnology and bioethics. Animals are called "transgenic" when DNA from other species has been artificially introduced into their genome. These transgenic animals have been developed for potentially beneficial applications, such as medical research, enhanced food production, and the production of proteins or organs but the genetic manipulation of animals, particularly mammals also raises a host of ethical issues that can be highly controversial. Such issues are much wider than the questions relating to patentability. The first transgenic animals to be produced was the *oncomouse* and was conceived as a valuable means of furthering cancer research which gave rise to two key issues in the patent system:

1. Should patents be granted at all for animals or animal varieties, particularly for higher-order animals such as mammals, even if they do otherwise meet the patentability criteria (novelty, industrial applicability/usefulness, inventive

step etc.)?

2. How should moral implications be addressed in relation to specific cases, e.g., the question of suffering caused to the transgenic animal?

The claims were referred to animals in general, but in the course of proceedings, the patent was amended and finally maintained with claims limited to mice. However, these issues have been resolved differently by the patent authorities of different countries. Inventions which concern plants and animals may be patentable if the technical feasibility of the invention is not confined to a particular plant or animal variety. The oncomouse case showed that the exclusion is confined to varieties of animals alone. It was acknowledged by the Board that the experimental animals must not suffer; on the other hand, there was little danger in this case of incalculable environmental damage since the animals could not reproduce their artificial genetic make-up. The history of the Harvard Oncomouse application in the EPO is a depressing saga which has been going on since the filing date in 1985 and was concluded only in July 2004 where the examining division initially refused the application on the basis that it claimed an animal variety, contrary to Article 53(b). [17]

The EPO applied the taxonomy of animals which subdivides a species into sub-species and varieties. Subsequent to Chakraborty and Oncomouse cases, it has been made clear that any life form is patentable provided that human technical intervention is required in its production. The one exception is that human beings cannot be patented because this would be a violation of the Thirteenth Amendment to the Constitution, which prohibits slavery and hence any property rights in individual human beings. Furthermore, the United States has extended patent protection to plants produced by either sexual or asexual reproduction and to plant parts including seeds and tissue cultures. [18]

The exclusion of plant varieties from plant protection was construed in a limited way in a case decided in 1984. In this case, a footnote which related to chemically treated seeds, not transgenic plants, it was held that if the claim covered plant genera without claiming individual specific varieties it did not contravene Article 53(b). However, in a later case in which transgenic plants were claimed, the decision was essentially that a transformed plant having a characteristic phonotype stably transmitted was by definition a plant variety and the prohibition of Article 53(b) was not avoided merely by using broader claim language. Claims to plant cells were granted but not claims to plants or seeds. It was also held that although the first step in the process, the transformation of the plant cell was 'microbiological', this did not make the final plant the product of a microbiological process.

Advantages

Due to improved and improving technology of genetic engineering, many diseases can be cured and new varieties of plants are breeded to produce more food. For example, the diseases of a child in the fetus can be detected and removed and with it several contagious diseases can be prevented by applying genetic engineering. Gene cloning techniques have unlimited scope for application which includes technology that can cater to humans to have prosperity.

Agriculture, animal husbandry, micro-based industry and clinical intervention in human beings in terms of genes and replacement therapy are loosely included under the global term biotechnology. In a more circumscribed sense, biotechnology also includes those enterprises that depend on the fermentation process. At present, it is vogue to restrict the definition further to fermentation based technology in which the recombinant plays an important role. Whatever be the terms of reference in using the level of biotechnology, applications of genetic engineering in plants, animals, microbes and single eukaryotic cells utilize characteristically unique ancillary techniques and of course cater to different objectives.

Pertaining to application of genes, cloning techniques are

being discovered in less traditional fields as well as in certain novel areas. These areas include the management of the environment, supplementing of mining capabilities and engineering of designer proteins. The unambiguous goal of plant, animal and microbes breeders has been to improve the quality and yield of products. This has been achieved by the traditional methods of breeding and selection and practiced since the dawn of human civilization. The discovery of artificial mutagenesis augmented these methods by providing sources of newer alleles in a shortest time period.

The other alternative is to screen naturally occurring population for desired genes. Both the strategies depend on random discoveries of wanting genes.

In agriculture, genetic manipulation of bacteria has been an incentive for similar interventions in plants and animals. The greater complexities of this higher eukaryotes have however, been the major deterrent in the development of successful genetic engineering protocols for their improvement. Based upon genetic engineering, Green Revolution took place in India. Once, India was importing food grains from foreign countries and now it is in a position to export rice to foreign countries. It is in a position to feed its growing population.

The theory and practice of gene therapy showed that gene can be transferred from one organism to another. A disease affecting the gene can be removed from plants and animals so that high quality of plants can be produced. It was detected by a German scientist that thirteen genes in a chromosome of a human being cause 'diabetes' when the level of cholesterol increases in the blood and in the same way, diseases can be cured with the help of same genetic engineering.

Patents have been a fundamental element of the biotechnology industry, driving the march of commercial investment as well as practices of public research institutions. Patents are thus sought for a number of reasons including obtaining income from licensing, increase in share prices and keep other companies out of potentially and commercially rewarding fields. The rising intellectual property protection of biotechnological products and processes can be considered successful in this regard, as private sector investment in plant breeding has increased substantially since the 1950s.

In particular, patent protection has been criticized as a means by which large biotech companies can protect and strengthen their position in the industry. There can be no doubt that patents are of greater importance in the field of biotechnology than in other fields such as engineering or electronics. If it is felt that it is immoral to make transgenic animals or human embryonic stem cell lines then surely it would be more logical to concentrate on campaigning for legislation to stop or restrict such experiments, rather than trying to lock the door after the horse has bolted by stopping patents for work which has already been done. [19] Perhaps there are three reasons.

Firstly, it is easier and cheaper to oppose a patent than to mount a lobbying campaign for a piece of legislation especially when any number of opponents are allowed to oppose for the cost of one opposition fee. [20]

Secondly, patents appear to be a potent symbol of commercial exploitation and they take on a symbolic importance which bears no relationship to the limited rights actually granted by a patent. It is either not known or ignored that patents can only be used to stop others and do not give positive rights of exploitation. In 2002, the University of Missouri obtained a US patent [21] that was condemned by various NGOs because it covered *inter alia* human cloning. The response of the University was- "*Yes, we know it does and if anyone tries to do human cloning, we will use our patent to stop it*". This seems a perfectly logical answer, to invalidate the patent and anybody can do it. And finally, a patent is seen to be a seal of official approval and by attacking the patent, one indirectly attacks the government policy. This shows a complete misunderstanding of the nature of patent rights.

A further point that needs to be made is that there is a disturbing trend to consider patents as invalid under Article 53(a) of the EPC, not for anything to do with the use of the invention, but because of what the inventor did before filing the application. As an example, if tissue samples are taken from a human patent, prior informed consent must be obtained. Some people argue that if this is not done, any patent on an invention made using such samples violates the said provision. For many NGOs, the logic is clear: all pharmaceutical companies make money out of human suffering therefore they are immoral and so all patents they obtain are contrary to morality and are invalid. [22]

A new biotechnology product may be imitated more easily and with least investment. Products in the market require a vast amount of investment, a major part of which is spent in the safety and efficacy instead of developing the synthesis of the product. It may be possible to produce cheaply, but it will still be necessary to charge a high price in order to recover the amount spent not only on the compound which is finally marketed but also on the others which do not reach this stage. In the absence of patent protection, imitator only bears the cost of research and development which again can offer the compound at a much lower price and still make a handsome profit.

Thus, biotechnology industry more than others is interested in using patents for their classical purpose, that of excluding the competition. Other than the classical purpose, most universities in the UK and US now assert ownership of inventions made by their academic scientists and use it as a source of royalty income. The universities are not themselves in a position to exploit this invention commercially. The strategy is therefore to license out the inventions to industrial companies in exchange for royalties and possibilities of payments.

Disadvantages of Granting Patents in Biotechnology

Biological Warfare: During the First World War, Germany

used gases and bacteria weapons against the enemies and these biological and chemical weapons have proven highly alluring. In American-Vietnam war, Americans used a chemical weapon named 'agent orange' which caused death and physically handicapped several thousand Vietnamese.

Ethical Consideration: Human and animal cloning raises several ethical issues and problems in the society. On the representation of several governmental as well as non-governmental organizations, press and judiciary, the American government banned the experiments on humans for the purpose of cloning. For better understanding, in 1970, when the test-tube baby took birth, the same kind of criticism was flooded but soon such criticisms calmed down. Likewise, in the near future, human cloning may be helpful to human beings for the enhancement of health and prosperity.

Human Rights Issue: IP and bioethics have a bearing on international human rights principles. The Universal Declaration of Human Rights and the International Covenant on Economic, Social and Cultural Rights provide for:

1. Recognition of the dignity of a human being.
2. Right to the enjoyment of health.
3. Right to food.
4. Right to enjoy the benefits of scientific progress.
5. Right to benefit from the protection of the moral and material interests resulting from one's scientific productions.

Similarly, such kind of patenting of life forms may cause great harm to human rights also in the following manner:

1. It fosters bio-piracy of indigenous resources.
2. Turns life forms into commodities to be used for profit.
3. Hinders the free-flow of scientific research.
4. Destroys economic sustainability of developing nations.
5. Genetic research may pose a serious threat to the human race.
6. The dangers are too substantial to permit such research to proceed.

7. May spread pollution and disease.
8. May result in a loss of genetic diversity and depreciate the value of human life.

Arguments against biotechnology per se suggests that it is the creation of such invention which is problematic. The core objective is that biotechnology and more specifically genetic engineering is wrong in itself, even if the net benefits outweigh the harm caused. Genetic engineering is considered to be intrinsically wrong for the following reasons:

1. It is an attempt at playing with the nature or God.
2. Genes represent the common heritage of mankind and should be passed from generation to generation without any technical intervention by man.
3. Genes occur naturally in organisms and should not suffer any sort of intervention .
4. It encourages inequitable sharing of profits.
5. It acts as a threat to public health, safety and human dignity.
6. It encourages commercialization of life.
7. It includes issues relating to violation of human rights.

Why Morality is an Issue in Patent in Biotechnology?

The debate concerning the legal, social and moral problems concerned with the modern biotechnology give rise to a very different attitude not only among the internal participants of the patent system namely scientists and lawyers but also the general public. Moral arguments enter the patent area directly through the gateway of Article 53 of the European Patent Convention, 1973. Article 53 provides, *inter alia,* that a patent shall not be granted for inventions, publications or exploitations of which would be contrary to public order and morality. Through this gateway have come arguments, which previously were not considered real issues in patent law. Biotechnology has changed it all. The patent law is now one of the central areas in which moral issues are raised.

Another moral argument against biotechnology is that

animal testing for the genetic engineering purpose is wrong because pain and sufferings is inflicted upon animals for ends that appears frivolous in contrast. On a purely moral basis, science should be research driven. The most complex issues arise when considering the genetic modification of human beings. Viewed from the public perspective, the threat posed by contemporary biotechnology is the possibility that will alter human nature in an irrevocable manner. Some questions arising are: do we, as humans win our genetic material or does it belong to the society as a whole?

The common heritage argument here is that is the material possessed in abundance by a vast number of people cannot be the subject of a private monopoly. The next question that arises includes, is intervention into the human genome an attack on the human dignity? Proponents of genetic engineering argue that intervention into the human genome is necessary, ultimately leading to an increase in human biodiversity, while opponents on the other hand, claim that such a step is making the sacred into the profane. Only the society can ultimately decide the degree of importance to be attached to the benefits, hazards and their impact.

Conclusion

Any science, including genetic engineering will morally amount to a mixed blessing having both advantages and disadvantages. However, on balance, patent law is primarily an instrument of economic policy. It provides an incentive to invest and to innovate. Also, the development of the society depends on the development of science and technology. The development in all spheres depends upon the encouragement and support provided through rewards for the efforts and labour in the production of new inventions.

As far as regulating biotechnological inventions are concerned, denying patentability on the basis of morality is misguided; as such a solution does not match the nature of the problem. On the other hand, for the improvement of law, science, and economics, a strong patent system is a core aspect of commercial development. Economic and moral policies are not of equal validity. If a technology is excluded from patentability, there is no incentive to invest in research. In such a situation, the public may be deprived of knowledge and also of any advantage that technology might have to offer. Patent law is a crucial component in regulating the creation of biotechnology and to deal with it, certain points must be taken into consideration such as:

1. The Patent Act be equipped to deal appropriately with higher life forms as patentable subject matter.
2. The human body or parts of the human body *per se* must be excluded from patentability.
3. Owning and selling of human tissue and body parts be prohibited.
4. Allowing patents for certain life forms and genetic material may lead to unauthorized exploitation of a country's natural resources, thus such exploitation should be stopped and be made a crime.

The use of genetic sequences or biological materials (that are identical to naturally occurring sequences and materials) for whatever purpose should not be controlled from coming under the ownership and control of any one organization or person.

By signing "Budapest Treaty on the International Recognition of the Deposit of Micro Organisms for the Purposes of Patent Procedure", India can assist in the standardization process of biotechnological patents in the country. Since the patent system cannot survive in a moral vacuum, so we must not let any conflict continue between biotechnology and patents regarding it.

Endnotes

1. The term 'Patent' has been defined under Section 2(m) of the Patents Act, 1970 as "patent" means a patent for any invention granted under this Act.
2. Bishwanath Prasad Radhey Shyam vs. Hindustan Metal

Industries, (1979) 2 SCC 511.

3. Ernst & Young as referred in A. Maria, J. Reut and M.H. Zerah, "Biotechnology in India: Final Report", www.cerna.ensmp.fr.
4. Article 2 of the Convention on Biological Diversity, United Nations, 1992.
5. Grubb Philips W. (n.d.), "Patents for Chemicals, Pharmaceuticals and Biotechnology: Fundamentals of Global Law, Practice and Strategy", 4th edition, p. 246, Oxford University Press, New York.
6. Genetic engineering is the technique of removing, modifying or adding genes to a DNA molecule in order to change the information it contains. By changing this information, genetic engineering changes the type or amount of proteins an organism is capable of producing.
7. Agreement on Trade-Related Aspects of Intellectual Property Rights (TRIPS) that came into force on January 1, 1996 sets out minimum protection that must be given for each category of intellectual property rights in the national law of each WTO member country.
8. A type of hybrid cell produced by fusing a normal cell with a tumour cell. When lymphocytes (antibody producing cells) are fused to the tumour cells, the resulting hybridomas produce antibodies and maintain rapid, sustained growth, producing large amounts of an antibody.
9. For example, by screening of soil samples.
10. Diamond vs. Chakraborty, 447 U.S. 303 (1980).
11. 2004 SCC 34.
12. (2001) AID No. 1, IPLR 2002, July 255.
13. Asexual methods includes cutting, grafting, budding, layering or through pollen grains where pollen grain of one plant is transferred to another to produce a new seed.
14. Sexual process takes place in plants having same genes.
15. (1990) O.J. EPO 476.
16. The term 'oncomouse' was derived from the Greek word for tumour.
17. Supra note 5 at 276.
18. Ex-parte Hibberd (1985) 227 USPQ 433.
19. G. Laurie (2004), "Patenting Stem Cells of Human Origin", EIPR, 59.
20. G3/99 (O.J. 2002, 347) Howard Florey/Grace period.

21. USP 6, 211, 429.
22. Supra note 5, at 286.

References

Cases Referred

1. Diamond vs. Chakraborty, 447 U.S. 303 (1980).
2. Dimminaco A.G. vs. Controller of Patents and Design (2001) AID No. 1, IPLR 2002, July 255.
3. Ex-parte Hibberd (1985) 227 USPQ 433.
4. Lubrizol Transgene Expression Case (1990) O.J. EPO 476.
5. Monsanto Canada Inc. vs. Schmeiser, 2004 SCC 34.

Books Referred

1. B.L. Wadhera (2006), "Law Relating to Patents, Trademarks, Copyright, Designs and Geographical Indications", 3rd revised edition, Universal Law Publishing Co. Pvt. Ltd., New Delhi.
2. Bonwoo Koo, G. Pandey and S. Visalakshi (2003), "Development of Agricultural Biotechnology and Patenting Pattern in India", mimeo.
3. Correa Carlos and Yususf Abdulqawi A., "Intellectual Property and International Trade: The TRIPS Agreement".
4. David Vaver and Bently Lionel (2004), "Intellectual Property in the New Millennium", Cambridge Publications.
5. Grubb Philips W. (n.d.), "Patents for Chemicals, Pharmaceuticals and Biotechnology: Fundamentals of Global Law, Practice and Strategy", 4th edition, p. 246, Oxford University Press, New York.
6. Manish Arora (2007), "Universal's Guide to Patents Law", 4th edition, Universal Law Publishing Co. Pvt. Ltd., New Delhi.
7. Mills Oliver (2004), "Biotechnological Inventions: Moral Restraints and Patent Law", Ashgate Publications.
8. N.S. Sreenivasulu (2007), "Intellectual Property Rights", Regal Publications, New Delhi.
9. Narayan, P. (1997), "Intellectual Property Law", 2nd edition, Eastern Law House, New Delhi.
10. Peter Drahos and Mayne Ruth M. (2002), "Global Intellectual Property Knowledge, Access and Development", Oxfam Publications.
11. Ramesh Chandra (2004), "Issues of Intellectual Property Rights", ISHA Publications.

12. S.K. Verma and Raman Mittal (2004), "Intellectual Property Rights: A Global Vision", Indian Law Institute, New Delhi.

Articles Referred

1. Abhinav Kumar (2008), "Towards Patentability of Essentially Biological Process", *JIPR*, Vol. 13, pp. 129-138, March.
2. Maria, J. Reut and M.H. Zerah, "Biotechnology in India: Final Report", available at:
www.cerna.ensmp.fr.
3. Correa Carlos, "Access to Plant Genetic Resources and Intellectual Property Rights", Background Study Paper No. 8, available at:
ftp://ftp.fao.org/docrep/fao/meeting/014/aj584e.pdf.
4. N.S. Sreenivasulu and C.B. Raju (2008), "Biotechnology and Patent Law: Patenting Living Beings".
5. "Intellectual Property and Bioethics: An Overview", Consultation Draft, WIPO.
6. Karnika Seth, "History and Evolution of Patent Law: National and International Perspectives".
7. Mitchell B. Waller Stein, Mary Ellen Mogee and Roberta A. Schoen (1993), "Global Dimensions of Intellectual Property Rights in Science and Technology", Part 3, National Research Council.
8. Mueller, Janice M. (2008), "Biotechnological Patenting in India: Will Bio-genetics Leads a "Sunrise Industry" to Bio-innovation?", January.
9. Resham Abraham (2008), "Issues and Controversies in Patenting Recent Biotechnological Inventions: Is the Patenting of Life Equivalent to Owning It?", August, available at:
www.legalservicesindia.com.
10. Sanjay P. Shrivastava (2010), "Patenting of Micro-organisms in India: An Overview", June 26, available at:
www.legalservicesindia.com.
11. WIPO Patent Report, 2007.

4

Copyright, Technological Revolution and Legal Implications

Md. Zafar Mahfooz Nomani and Faisal Sherwani

Introduction

The technological onslaught has seen online contracts in the form of shrink-wrap agreements and the like being upheld as legally binding by courts both in the Unites States and India. It has only been in exceptional circumstances that they have been invalidated and that too not because of their form but rather because of their content. Just like standard contracts, shrink-wrap licenses may be invalidated by courts where their form is unconscionable and not legally enforceable. Yet, firms may ultimately seek to avoid even this remote possibility by using technological protection measures (TPMs) to control access to content, with no recourse to law possible at all. Such TPMs are essentially programs that limit distribution and use of a particular item of digital content (text, video, music, software, etc.).

A TPM "could prevent content from being copied once and sent to one recipient, but deleted from the original recipient's hard drive. It could delete content automatically after a set time period. It could link a copy to a particular computer, so that it would not be playable anywhere else". [1] And there are potentially no limitations on the types of limitations encoded. These TPMs will attempt to accomplish through technology what was previously accomplished through contract. For example, a shrink-wrap license that prohibits copying can be replaced by a software code that simply prevents such copying. Likewise, a TPM can be configured to make a video unplayable after a certain period of time or on someone else's machine, and so on.

Thus, TPMs potentially bypass the state's structuring of contract law. Some have seen the internet as a giant copy machine and have argued for increased legal protection lest copyright law be rendered irrelevant by changes in technology. TPMs (backed by legal restrictions against circumvention) offer a possible response to these developments by providing owners of content with a set of tools to protect their assets. In that sense, proponents of TPMs argue they are not unlike the way in which owners of more tangible property deploy fences or locks. Yet, this is only half the story. TPMs give content providers the means to more perfectly restrict access to material. Thus, a copy-protected compact disc prevents a teacher from making a copy even if the copyright law might have deemed copying a fair use in the United States and a permitted use (if not for economic gains) in India.

Similarly, but hypothetically speaking, if such a compact disc retains any economic value (in all likelihood it would be obsolete) after the expiry of the statutory period of copyright i.e. life of the author plus 70 years, a content provider may still be able to restrict the material from falling into the public domain by continuing to use such TPMs. The paper attempts to analyze the upside and downside of the use of such TPMs. It seeks to take into account, without handing out specific answers, to what extent such TPMs may be used as a supplement or alternative to the law. More critically, the paper questions whether the very use of TPMs defeats the ends and goals of copyright law itself. The questions that are addressed in some detail are: should we be concerned about the deployment of TPMs?

On the one hand, we might view TPMs as an appropriate *self-help* mechanism to ensure that content providers can control access to their work in the digital age. On the other, TPMs threaten to supplant important balances struck by the current law. In order to explore this debate, the authors seek to direct their focus on TPMs and copyright law. Do there need to be new *limits* on the increased ability of content providers to block public access to information? The paper shall make an attempt to lay out the basic arguments on both sides concerning the use of TPMs, focusing in particular on the interaction between TPMs and the copyright law. We finally reach our own conclusion, advocating a result that would reach a balance between copyright law and free access. We attempt to support a stance, that excessive legal sanction to technological protection would lead to defeating the underlying purposes of the copyright legislation and the constitution which bestows the power to frame these legislations.

A Technological Solution to Copyright Protection

Just as discussed earlier, TPMs will attempt to accomplish through technology what was previously accomplished through contract. Thus, in a sense, TPMs potentially bypass the state's structuring of contract law. As Radin argues, TPMs function as [2]..an infallible "injunction" controlled completely by one party. The recipient has no option to breach and pay damages; efficient breach is therefore "repealed". The recipient has no option to infringe and then argue fair use to a court; the safety valve of fair use is "repealed"...No entity of the state will balance the hardships and look for irreparable harm before issuing the injunction...The recipient cannot ask the court to consider reliance, reasonable expectation, economic duress, and so forth. In other words, [TPMs] will make even non-waivable rights irrelevant, unless legal limitations on the operation of machine "injunctions" come into existence.

The question boils down to the extent of concern that ought to be expressed about the deployment of TPMs. On the one hand, one may argue that TPMs serve as an appropriate self-help mechanism to ensure that content providers can control access to their work in the digital age. On the other,

TPMs threaten to unseat and altogether remove important balances struck by the current law of intellectual property and copyright specifically. In order to explore this debate, the authors focus on TPMs, as an issue of law in cyberspace [3] and copyright law.

The Constitution of the United States authorizes Congress "[t]o promote the progress of science and useful arts, by securing for limited times to authors and inventors the exclusive right to their respective writings and discoveries". [4] Congress has used this power to grant copyright protection to "original works of authorship fixed in a tangible medium of expression." [5] Copyright protection extends to, among other things, literary works, musical works, dramatic works, sound recordings, and audiovisual works. To qualify for this protection, a work must be "original" in the sense that it represents its author's intellectual creation, but it need not be particularly inventive. Copyright protection does not extend to an idea, concept, or principle; rather, it extends to the expression of that idea in a tangible medium. [6]

In essence, copyright law grants an author a limited monopoly over the fruits of his or her creative efforts. [7] The public, in return, gains limited rights to use it once its term of protection expires. Among the exclusive rights the law secures to a copyright holder are the rights to reproduce, distribute, display, and perform the work, and to prepare derivative works based upon the copyrighted work. [8] The copyright statute, however, limits the author's exclusive rights by reserving to the public the right to make a "fair use" of a copyrighted work—as for purposes such as criticism, comment, or education. Similar defences exist under Indian copyright law with regard to permissible use. This limitation developed at common law and codified in the 1976 U.S. Copyright Act, creates an affirmative defence to a claim of infringement. [9] In addition, under the copyright law's "first sale doctrine", a person who lawfully acquires a copyrighted work generally can give it to someone else, resell it, or destroy it. [10]

Finally, protection of a copyrighted work does not extend indefinitely. For works created on or after the effective date of the current statute, January 1, 1978, the term of protection is the life of the author plus 70 years. Works of institutional authors are protected for a period of 95 years from the date of publication or 120 years from the date of creation, whichever is shorter. When the term of protection ends, a work passes into the public domain.

It may be conceded that with the development of technology and the widespread use of digital technology, an author could be reasonably assured that others seeking to exploit his or her work could not cheaply produce and distribute successive high-quality copies of the work. For instance, an analog recording of music can be recorded but subject to degradation in the quality of sound. The quality of successive generation copies would likewise degrade, and mass distribution would be quite costly.

The development of digital technology debatably removed this layer of protection and as the federal government recognized in its 1995 document *Intellectual Property and the National Information Infrastructure,* [11] widely known as the "White paper", technology posed two challenges for copyright holders. First, digital copies of intellectual property can be perfect copies—intellectual property in digital form is made up of strings of zeros and ones, and those strings can be precisely duplicated. Second, the development of the internet makes distribution of intellectual property in digital form much less costly. Thus, some have seen the internet as a giant copy machine and have argued for increased legal protection lest copyright law be rendered irrelevant for changes in technology.

TPMs (backed by legal restrictions against circumvention) offer a possible response to these developments by providing owners of content with a set of tools to protect their assets. In that sense, proponents of TPMs argue, they are not unlike the way in which owners of more tangible property deploy fences or locks. The only difference is that here the "fences" and "locks" are built into computer hardware and software and implemented via firewalls, encryption, and passwords. TPM enables a "pay-per-use" world, where the content providers can offer encrypted files for sale one at a time. At its most powerful, a TPM enables the "super distribution" of propriety information. In other words, it allows information providers to market documents that disallow certain types of uses (e.g., copying) and provide continuing revenue (e.g., charging 2 cents per access) regardless of who holds the document (e.g., including someone who obtained it post-first sale)". [12] Thus, we might view TPMs as a useful and necessary way to make digital content more accessible, by ensuring that content providers will be able to enforce copyright or trade secret claims and define contractual rights without resorting to costly and unpredictable litigation.

Yet, this is only half of the story. TPMs give content providers the means to more perfectly restrict access to materials. Thus, a copy-protected compact disc prevents a teacher from making a copy even if the copyright law might have deemed the copying a fair use. Likewise, although the first sale doctrine permits users to transfer or resell their copies, TPMs can be used to foreclose activities that the background public legal regime had made the right of the user. [13]

Accordingly, while technology changes many of the assumptions underlying copyright law, it is far from clear whether such changes result in an expansion or contraction of control over content. As a result, it is difficult to determine how copyright law should adapt. Do content providers need new legal tools to combat the increased ease of digital copying? Or do there need to be new *limits* on the increased ability of content providers to block access to information? Or are the policies underlying copyright sufficiently served by a purely market-based approach, that is, by allowing an arms race of sorts between infringement-facilitating and infringement-blocking technologies?

The authors attempt to consider the basic arguments on both sides concerning the use of TPMs, focusing in particular on the interaction between TPMs and copyright law. We feel that in each case it becomes a consideration as to how enforcement of the choices embedded in TPMs affect the balance of rights between providers and users of content that copyright law seeks to strike. Will enforcement of authors' choices about which uses of a work to permit lead to a balance of rights preferable to the one the copyright statutes seek to achieve? Or does the use of TPMs improperly supplant the law of the state with the "law" of the firm?

Throughout, the authors use the term "technological protection measures" or "TPMs" to refer to the use of technological means to restrict access to the content. These TPMs are sometimes referred to by others as "digital rights management systems", "automated rights management systems", or "copyright management systems". We believe that using a formulation that includes the words "right" distorts the discussion because a crucial part of the debate is whether what is technologically protected is necessarily being protected as a right. Thus, we prefer a more neutral term "technological protection measures". Nevertheless, we have retained the formulations used by other authors when referring to their works.

TPMs as a Fair Supplement to Fair Use

The goal of any copyright statute is the conferment of limited statutory privileges in return for a public benefit on the extinguishment of the term of copyright. However, there exist some limited rights during the statutory period of copyright as well, such as fair use of a copyrighted work during the statutory period of copyright. As mentioned earlier, the 1976 U.S. Copyright Act derives power from the U.S. Constitution. Thus, some in the United States regard the doctrine as an integral part of the constitutional quid pro quo. On such a view, as Prof. Bell puts it, "...fair use provides a public benefit—unbilled access to copyrighted works—to balance the State's grant of a limited monopoly". [14]

As Prof. Bell mentions, automated rights management at first appears to threaten this bargain. It seems as if ARM restricts the public's access to copyrighted works in digital intermedia without offering a benefit in return. He however, strongly advocates that "...friends of fair use should not assume that ARM will leave the public worse off..." [15] To the contrary, it appears to Bell that it is "...likely to provide a net benefit to the public". [16] Prof. Bell argues that by reducing transaction costs throughout the market for copyrighted expressions, ARM benefits the public both directly and indirectly. Having emanated from an intentionally vague statute and developed in various, occasionally contradictory cases, the fair use doctrine necessarily blurs the boundary between valid and invalid copyright claims. High risks of "theft"—here, infringement—increase the insecurity of copyright's protection.

Though the resultant uncertainty obviously harms producers and sellers of copyrighted works, it also harms consumers. Academics, artists, commentators, and other desirous of reusing copyrighted works without authorization must borrow at their peril, consult experts on fair use, or, sadly forgo such use altogether. AMR's clarifying power directly benefits those who would reuse copyrighted works—and through them their public audiences—by creating harbours safe from the threat of copyright litigation. [17]

Moreover, Bell argues that ARM benefits the public indirectly by increasing the transactional efficiency of the market for expressive works. Like other markets, the market for expressive works does not constitute a zero sum game. [18] Bell quotes Coase who observed of markets in general,

"It is obviously desirable that rights should be assigned to those who can use them most productively and with incentives that lead them to do so. It is also desirable that, to discover (and maintain) such a distribution of rights, the costs of their transference should be low, through clarity in the law and by making the legal requirements for such transfers less onerous". [19]

Bell goes on to argue that by its systematic improvement of copyright's transactional efficiency, helps us discover and maintain a distribution of rights to expressive works that will increase net social wealth. ARM thus stands to benefit both producers and consumers. Bell's central theme seems to the authors is that ARMs increase the worth of expressive works and in his assessment devalues the cost of accessing them. This may be clear from this argument where he says,

"In particular, because it increases the *value* of expressive works, ARM will put deflationary pressure on the *price* of accessing them. In general, an asset's current price internalizes the value of its future income stream. Copyrights therefore commonly lose present value because, with the passage of time and their wider distribution, they prove increasingly vulnerable to uncompensated uses. Because it reduces such risks, ARM tends to increase the value of copyrights. But although this windfall might initially accrue to copyright owners, competition among information providers would force access prices downward, toward the marginal costs of obtaining and distributing expressive works. Directly or indirectly, such price pressure would similarly affect the prices that copyright owners can demand. Gains that ARM provides to copyright owners would thus pass on to consumers in the form of reduced access fees". [20]

Bell's hypothesis submits that because ARM will increase the value of copyrighted works, it will encourage their greater production and improved distribution. Consumers will thus benefit from better access to information. Access providers will improve the information itself, too, increasing its quantity and making it better organized, verified, interlinked, diverse, up-to-date, and relevant. Bell believes that, "Although this cornucopia of information may at first come only for a fee, some of it eventually will fall into the public domain". [21]

Prof. Bell, however, takes into the account the present scenario and bases a predication for the future of ARM use. He submits that taking into account the current implementations of ARM, copyright owners might very well offer limited free access to their wares in an attempt to draw more extensive (and expensive) uses. Entrepreneurs will undoubtedly create other services, at present utterly and inevitably unforeseen, to attract and satisfy consumers of information. [22] The authors however believe that this may not necessarily be the case. We believe that as access to copyrighted work would become restricted to paying a fee, samples would in fact become smaller. In any case we believe this is not the problem at all.

Even today, samples of abstracts of intellectual property do not serve any purpose beyond attracting customers to buy the full text. The question which seems more pertinent to us is whether these technological measures which restrict a user's access beyond the protection of copyright statute affords should have the sanction of law? Prof. Bell believes that since TPMs or what he calls ARM, show consumer demand for a product in a free market, such additional protections should have the sanction of law. He states, "Because automated rights management creates well-defined and readily transferable property rights to information, it puts the power of the market in the service of consumer demand. [23] He believes that Prof. Goldstein's explanation is very significant in this regard, "there is no better way for the public to indicate what they want than through the price they are willing to pay in the market place. Uncompensated use inevitably dilutes these signals". [24]

Thus, in Prof. Bell's assessment, "Fared use therefore probably will provide public access to copyrighted works in digital intermedia than fair use does or could. At any rate, no one can plausibly claim that fared use necessarily would serve the public interest any less well than the existing quid pro quo". [25]

In 1998, the U.S. Congress passed the Digital Millennium

Copyright Act (DMCA), [26] which among other things, restricts the dissemination and use of tools that can be used to circumvent access and copy controls that a copyright holder uses to protect his or her work. These provisions make it unlawful to disable or circumvent a TPM of the sort discussed above or to traffic in technology that facilitates such disabling or circumvention. Prof. Bell, writing before the passage of the DMCA, does not argue that TPMs should receive special statutory protection beyond those that the common law provides. [27] However, we believe that an economic defence of applying DMCA protection to enforce a copyright owner's choices about use of a work may proceed differently from an economic defence of applying contract principles to enforce a copyright owner's choices about use of a work. And Bell answers this with the help of what other experts have stated on the matter.

Prof. Neil Weinstock Netanel, for instance, sees in ARM "the spectre of all-consuming copyright owner control". [28] That prospect, he claims, "threatens to upend copyright's already uneasy accommodation of public access with private ownership". [29] Prof. Dennis J. Karjala projects a world where to access a copyrighted work a consumer will have to promise "not to use the underlying ideas to create a competing work, not to further distribute the work or anything contained in the work, not to download any of the factual information contained in the work, not to quote from the work, and so forth". [30] Enforce such promises, he concludes, and "all of the users' rights of copyright will soon disappear". [31] Prof. Michael J. Madison argues that trends in the law and practice of regulating access to information "increasingly mean that no open space exists save that which information producers choose explicitly to provide". [32] Prof. Julie E. Cohen worries that ARM ultimately "will allow content owners to insist on greater protection than copyright law would afford". [33] That result, she claims, would "fundamentally alter the social welfare equation". [34]

TPMs: Dead-bolting Intellectual Property against Fair Use and Permissible Use

Supplanting the Law of Copyright: While the public and the media have been distracted by warning about the evils of "piracy" and lawsuits by the recording and film industries, the enforcement of copyright law in the digital world has shifted from regulating copying to regulating the design of technology. Though it may seem that the development of secure packaging and delivery of software was initially and even today largely designed to prevent purchasers and third party users from making unauthorized uses of digital works that were copyrighted; it may safely be stated that there exists at the very least in its most modest form a spill over effect of unauthorized overprotection that copyright industries and technology experts may be guilty of.

As envisioned by the copyright industries, these "rights management systems" will be capable of controlling, monitoring, and metering almost every conceivable use of a digital work. [35] This increased control, some argue, allows copyright owners to appropriate far more protection than copyright law now provides. For particular significance for this paper, under the doctrine of 'fair use' in the United States, copyright law allows some copying of protected expression under the fair use doctrine (and also under a variety of other exceptions designed to serve the public interest) and allows any after the term of copyright expires. TPMs as we refer to them as; or Rights management systems, in contrast, can insist that permission be sought, and a fee paid, for any use. This is so, moreover, whether or not the underlying information is still (or was ever) protected by copyright.

The development of rights management systems according to Burk and Cohen powerfully demonstrates the ability of technology to regulate behaviour. [36] Much as physical barriers and spatial relations, they argue, constrain behaviour in actual space, technical standards constrain behaviour in cyberspace. They analogize that just as in the physical world, people cannot walk through solid walls, occupy two spaces simultaneously, or carry skyscrapers away in their pockets, similarly, there are certain activities that simply cannot be performed on a particular computer system because the system is not built to accommodate the behaviour—the system may be programmed to deny access without a password, preventing logging on simultaneously from two terminals, or prohibit alteration of a file that is designated "read-only". [37]

Though they point out that at first consideration, the observation that the technology will only do what the technology will do may seem blatantly obvious, they quickly point out that technical standards are within the control of the designer and so confer upon the designer the power to govern behaviour with regard to that system. [38] Burk and Cohen argue that once constraints on behaviour are built into the technical standards governing a technology use of that technology—in essence, the technical standards become a type of law. Such technical rule sets may supplement or even supplant the legal rule sets designed to govern the same behaviour. [39]

In the case of rights management systems, copyright owners determine the rules that are embedded into the technological controls. As Burke and Cohen say, "implementing technical constraints on access to and use of digital information, a copyright owner can effectively supersede the rules of intellectual property law. For example, as described above, the copyright owner may decide that the technological controls will not permit any copying of the controlled content, whether or not the copying would be fair use. They point out that if the integrity of the control is recognized by the state, the legal enforcement of rights also shifts its focus from penalties for unauthorized infringement to penalties for access unauthorized by the rights-holder.

Thus, in a nutshell Burk and Cohen argue that the implications of these developments are harsh: where technological constraints, control over the design of information rights is shifted into the hands of private parties, who may or may not honour the public policies that animate public access doctrines such as fair use. Rights-holders can effectively write their own intellectual property statute in computer code. [40]

Professors Burk and Cohen point out that TPMs can be used not only in connection with works protected under copyright law, but also in connection with works, or portions of works, that never were eligible for or that no longer have copyright protection. For argument sake, we assume that they are correct about these negative effects of TPMs on the public's right of access to copyrighted works. However, the authors have a problem with the solution which Burk and Cohen provide for such negative effects. Burk and Cohen consider a combination of two solutions. [41] First, the government might mandate or encourage the development of TPMs that are specifically designed to allow purchasers to make fair use of content. [42] Second, the government might condition the availability of anti-circumvention protection under the law on the deposit of an access key with a third party, who would issue the key to a party seeking to make fair use (without evaluating the merits of the access application). [43] Without considering whether these approaches are desirable as a policy matter, we believe that these approaches are unworkable and it would be a misunderstanding to believe that they can prove workable under the current copyright law as regards to the doctrine of fair use.

The doctrine of fair use in the United States is codified in Section 107 of the 1976 Act. [44] The examples listed in the Preamble to Section 107 are broad and overlapping. [45] However, the doctrine of fair use is a judicially created 'defence' to copyright infringement that allows a third party to use a copyrighted work in a reasonable manner without the copyright owner's consent. As Leaffer puts it, "Although codified in the 1976 Act, the doctrine of fair use has retained its nature as an equitable rule of reason to be applied where a finding of infringement would either be unfair or undermines 'the progress of science and the useful art'. [46] Productive use supports the underlying goal of copyright law by increasing our fund of knowledge and information. Accordingly, a productive use should be impeded only when it is so excessive as to undermine the incentive to produce copyrighted works. [47]

Thus, on a first glance, it may become clear that fair use can never be claimed as a right. No person can state that he or she has a right to make a fair use of the copyrighted work. In fact, fair use may only be pleaded as a defence in a court of law when a person stands accused of infringing another's copyright and this doctrine has no application elsewhere. Thus, we believe that the solution put forward by Burk and Cohen is incompatible with the current copyright law of fair use. Though, the judicially created doctrine of fair use has been defined as a privilege in others than the owner of a copyright to use the copyrighted material in a reasonable manner without consent, notwithstanding the monopoly granted to the owner. [48]

However, one must be careful not to confuse this privilege with a right to do so. Under the current copyright law, no person can demand access to a copyrighted work in order to make 'fair use' of it. The defence of fair use only comes into play after the plaintiff has made out a *prima facie* case for copyright infringement by showing copying of the original work and substantial similarity between the works. Once this occurs, the defendant bears the evidentiary burdens of production and persuasion that the infringing use of the copyrighted work was privileged as a fair use. [49]

Thus, if Burk and Cohen's example is to be workable at all, first and foremost we would have to realize that we are dealing from a very different 'fair use' than the one codified under the 1976 Act. Burk and Cohen too somewhat realize this when they state, "each of the two possible mechanisms for preserving fair use in a digital rights management environment has advantages and drawbacks. Automatic fair use functionality does not require human intervention but is unlikely to afford the full spectrum of fair uses allowed by law. The use of a trusted third party intermediary to mediate access, in contrast, potentially allows the full spectrum of uses but is less responsive to anonymity and spontaneity concerns. The optimal result, we suggest, is an infrastructure that combines the two". [50]

However, now there is more beyond copyright protection, TPMs and other statutory protection for such TPMs. Now, content providers are employing technological self-help to combat online copying in a less prominent albeit aggressive manner. For instance, the music industry has developed software programs that would sabotage the computers and internet connections of people who download pirated music. [51] The authors believe that this is something which goes beyond any protection that should or ought to be provided. We question whether this is an appropriate and commensurate response under the law to online file-sharing, or a problematic escalation in an unhealthy technological arms race in order to achieve supremacy between content providers and infringers?

We believe that passing a statute such as the DMCA may well be within the power of Congress, however, sometimes self-help is not the best thing and the law should not allow content providers to take the onslaught to the infringers. This would be akin to citizens taking law into their own hands and providing vigilante justice. On the other hand, even as a personal defence, such an action is debatably beyond the value of the property sought to be protected and is not an equal and commensurate force.

However, before we jump to conclusions about protecting one's property, building fences and classifying intellectual property as property capable of being properly analogized, personal defence a statement of Matt Jackson should remind us something very important and which lies at the core of this debate:

"One cannot overemphasize that the Constitutional purpose of copyright is to stimulate content creation for the public benefit, not to create a private property right based on a moral notion of ownership". [52]

Moreover, we believe that though there may be a number of potential justifications for copyright statutes, the basic core of any copyright law is that the individual's right of ownership is necessarily, for good or bad, attached to a societal goal i.e. to encourage the formation of creative works. Thus, we believe that such a right cannot be treated as a "natural right" at all. Rather such a right is by its very nature engineered to spark further intellectual progress.

TPMs and Free Market Regulation: A Misplaced Belief? Julie E. Cohen believes that the "...cyber economists' belief in the superiority of contract for allocating usage rights in digital works rests on two points. First, they argue that granting more control to the purveyors of digital works will make creative and informational works accessible in the long-run (which, it is assumed, will result in more progress) as the natural result of competition in the consumer market. Second, they assert that the legislative process is comparatively unsuited to accomplish these ends because it is coercive and controlled by special interests. [53]

Neither of these points, she argues, survives more thorough scrutiny. Even assuming that a market based on voluntary, informed bargaining over rights in digital works would work as the cyber economists say it would, the conditions for such bargaining do not exist in the market we have. As a result, it is impossible to say with certainty that the market would be better at promoting access and progress than the existing system of pubic ordering via legislative process. [54] Cohen pronounces that "two fundamental requirements of the neo-classical model of social ordering through private exchange are knowledge of contract terms and meaningful (i.e., voluntary and fully informed) assent". [55] Both, she says, are necessary (though not sufficient) requirements for an "unregulated" market to reach the efficient equilibrium point; the absence of either or both may signal a market failure justifying some form of adjustment. The authors agree with Cohen that under the proposed digital [copyright management system (CMS)] regime, however, consumer transactions relating to digital works will bear little resemblance to the paradigmatic bargained-for exchange.

Instead, she says, much like the typical software purchase today, they will be governed by standard form of "licenses" that include provisions regarding permissible and impermissible uses. Digital CMS enable the use of such "click-through" contracts to require acceptance of usage restrictions for any type of work that is made available online. [56] Cohen poses a critical question, whether this sort of transaction, in aggregate, can or will produce the near-perfect, self-equilibrating market that, for the neo-classically grounded economists, constitute the pinnacle of social ordering. [57] Cohen also believes that cyber economists have been guilty of evading this question in the past. She believes that, "They argue that...copyright law...constitutes the onerous standard form contract and market ordering...constitutes the flexible, policy sensitive instrument". However, she points out that, [T]he cyber economists compare the legislative process with the market-generated collective licensing institutions, and find the market superior. Both legislative and market actions reflect the pursuit of self-interest, but the self-interest manifested in the market is (so the appears to go) uncomplicated by distorting interest-group effects, undiminished by administrative costs, and subject to the market's wealth-maximizing power of correction. But that is disingenuous, and far too simple. [T]he comparison is misdirected. The legislative process may (indeed must) be imperfect, but it does not follow that the market is always preferable". [58]

Cohen is probably right in reminding us and the 'cyber economists' in particular that all real-world institutions are subject to flaws and lobbying and influence of interest groups. One may argue that in a market-based economy this is more so. Large corporations are able to influence market flows and the like. This is, in fact, a primary lesson of institutional economics. Cohen rightly points out that the market in which we live today is not the pure neo-classical model that the cyber economists posit. But we pose a few questions of our own: "Even if the market in which we live and supposing that this is the model which our successive generations are going to inherit from us are any different from the market and economy that we inherited from our ancestors? Have such standard form contracts not proved workable even in an imperfect economy and market? May a customer who is not satisfied with the standard form of the contract not try and strike a deal more agreeable to him with the owner of copyright?" [59]

Extent of the Threat and Legal Responses

Race to the Bottom between Content Providers and Infringers: We believe that the debate boils down to this: "what does a content provider gain through use of TPMs which he may not be so able to gain through copyright law? It seems to us that some take objection to such a system of technological protection as an addition to copyright protection. One plausible solution may be the removal of the blanket copyright protection for such digital works which employ TPMs. This is not to suggest that such works will not have any remedy under law if used in an unauthorized manner. But just as in instances of trespass over real tangible property, damages may be collected, similarly, unauthorized use of a TPM protected work may make the offender liable for damages, however, not for damages for infringement of copyright.

Yet, such an argument presupposes that the objection to TPMs is because they make certain digital works 'favoured children of intellectual property' as they are afforded both copyright protection as well an additional protection by self-employed technological measures. This may not be the case. Even in cases of real property though the law of trespass provides a remedy against unauthorized admission and like; yet people have been known to build fences on their properties so as to further ensure that a trespasser does not tread where he is not wanted and the law sanctions such self-employed protection measures as advisable and wise".

Having debated the pros and cons of TPMs, it is worth asking whether they are really as much of a threat to the availability of online content as critics fear. Consider this argument: [60]

The notion that code is law under, girds a powerful theory, but some of its most troubling empirical predictions about the use of code to restrict individual freedom have not yet come to pass. To be sure, since the DMCA's passage, a number of unobtrusive rights management schemes have entered wide circulation. Yet, only a handful of cases have been brought against those who have cracked such schemes, and there had been little, if any, decrease in consumers' capacity to copy digital works, whether for fair use or for wholesale piracy. Programmers have historically been able to crack nearly every PC protection scheme, and those less technically inclined can go to the trouble of generating a fresh copy of digital work without having to crack the scheme, exploiting the "analog hole" by, for example, filming a television broadcast or recording a playback of a song. Once an unprotected copy is generated, it can then be shared freely on the internet file-sharing networks that run on generative PCs at the behest of their content-hungry users.

However, we believe that such an argument would have us relying on programmers to circumvent TPMs much too heavily. Moreover, the DMCA's threat of criminal prosecution would probably not change the calculus so heavily. But Zittrain goes on to say: [61]

Thus, the fears of digital lockdown through trusted systems may seem premature or unfounded. As a practical matter, any scheme designed to protect content finds itself rapidly hacked, and the hack (or the content protected) in turn finds itself shared with technically unsophisticated PC owners. Alternatively, the analog hole can be used to create a new, unprotected master copy of the protected content. The fact remains that so long as code can be freely written by anyone and easily distributed to run on PC platforms, [TPMs] can serve as no more than speed bumps or velvet ropes—barriers that the public circumvents should they become more than mere inconveniences.

Apple's iTunes Music Store is a good example of this phenomenon: music tracks purchased through iTunes are encrypted with Apple's proprietary scheme, and there are some limitations on their use that, although unnoticeable to most consumers, are designed to prevent the tracks from immediately circulating peer-to-peer networks. But the scheme is easily circumvented by taking music purchased from the store, burning it onto a standard audio CD, and then re-ripping the CD into an unprotected format, such as MP3. [62]

Courts: A Techno-Legal Approach to the Technological Restrictions: Thus, having taken into account how the deployment of technology can undermine or supplant the balances struck by law, we would not be doing justice to this task if we were to take it for granted that law is simply powerless in the face of technological change. To the contrary, legal rules can privilege some technological innovations over others, they can influence what sorts of technologies become widely distributed, and they can help to generate social norms that affect how technology is developed and used.

We attempt to study the legal responses to technological innovation in terms of two judgments handed down by courts in the United States, which we believe adequately demonstrate the debate being generated by the technological revolution and concerns regarding its proper scope.

The first case we consider is *Storage Tech. Corp. vs. Custom Hardware Eng'g and Consulting, Inc.* [63] The court in Storage Technology explored the concept of authorization, and the use of the DMCA to enforce contractual provisions. There, defendant was a repair company that fixed data storage libraries built by the plaintiff. [64] To perform its work, the company had to intercept maintenance error codes sent by plaintiff's data storage software embedded in the system. [65] To successfully intercept the codes, however, defendant's computers had to "override a password protection scheme", which defendant accomplished simply by having its software guess at the key until it found the right one. [66] Plaintiff argued this was foreclosed by the DMCA because it violated the initial sales contract. [67]

The Storage Technology court noted that "'uses' that violate a license agreement constitute copyright infringement only when those uses would infringe in the absence of any license agreement at all". [68] The plaintiff sold physical tape libraries but only licensed the necessary software. [69] That license covered only the "functional code portions of the software", which "specifically excludes the maintenance code. However, both the functional and maintenance code are automatically loaded into the RAM upon start-up, and copying the entire code is necessary to activate and run the library". [70]

Storage Technology argued that even if its customers were authorized to access the maintenance codes, its customers could not in turn authorize defendants, because customers were not permitted to "sub-license, assign, lease or permit another person to use" the codes. [71] The court disagreed, noting that other portions of the license agreements demonstrated "the authorized use is tied to a particular machine, rather than a particular person". [72] This is not dissimilar from the notion that a legitimately issued password, even in the hands of someone other than to whom it was originally issued, may use it without committing circumvention under Section 1201(a).

Proceeding to Storage Technology's DMCA claim, the court argued that even when circumvention is found under the DMCA, "[a] court must look at the threat that the unauthorized circumvention potentially poses in each case to determine if there is a connection between the circumvention and a right protected by the Copyright Act". [73] Noting the lack of copyright infringement here, and perhaps agreeing with defendant that "it [was] implicitly authorized to copy the maintenance code", [74] the court held that "[t]he activation of the maintenance code may violate [Storage Technology's] contractual rights vis-à-vis its customers, but those rights are not the rights protected by copyright law. There is simply not a sufficient nexus between the rights protected by copyright law and the circumvention of the [plaintiff's] system". [75]

Similarly, in the case of *Ticketmaster L.L.C. vs. RMG Technologies Inc.*, [76] plaintiff website operator and copyright owner maintained a website with internal pages protected by a lock-out screen, provided the authorized password to access these pages on the lock-out screen itself, freely permitted the use of those internal pages by individuals who accepted the terms of service (ToS) agreement and only forbade its use by automated "robots" through that ToS. [77] Defendant created and sold a device that allowed customers to navigate the pages automatically, facilitating faster ticket purchases than ordinarily possible with a single person encountering the "Captcha" system. [78]

The court took a creative route to imputing both Sections 1201(a) and (b) [79] liability to RMG, finding that because users of the device violated the ToS, when the users of RMG's program subsequently navigated the webpages (necessarily copying them to RAM), they then committed copyright infringement. [80] The court further found that the Captcha device protected this right of reproduction, which defendant primarily intended his device to circumvent. [81] Though defendant asserted that "Captcha is designed to regulate ticket sales, not to regulate access to a copyrighted work" (or the right of reproduction), the court rejected this argument without explanation. [82]

Arguably, the purpose of Ticketmaster's site is indeed to sell tickets, not to provide exclusive access to its copyrightable descriptions of upcoming performances. [83] We believe that there is a flaw in the decision, as many others before it, that the court did not adequately examine the issue of authorization in its Section 1201(a) analysis. For the purposes of the DMCA, where should the court have looked for "authority"? The ToS explicitly said that automated devices were prohibited, but that is a tenet of contract law, the violation of which should not necessarily trigger revocation of authorization or DMCA liability. Moreover, the ToS applied only after the lockout screen was passed and Ticketmaster made the password publicly available, which essentially authorized anyone who could read it. While click-wrap agreements like the ToS here are valid contracts in theory, any user would glean an implicit authorization to use the website from the free availability of the password. [84]

However, it is also important to recall the Federal Circuit's holding in Storage Technology, [85] which reiterated that because the DMCA is intended to help protect rights of copyright, and not of contract, the DMCA should not be used to enforce contractual restrictions. [86] Furthermore, in Chamberlain, [87] the court noted the need to avoid a construction of the DMCA that would "allow any copyright owner, through a combination of contractual terms and technological measures, to repeal the fair use doctrine with respect to an individual copyrighted work". [88] Otherwise, copyright holders can enforce their will, through increasingly complicated licenses and technological measures, and have it supported by the DMCA. And this we believe is a very real threat.

Moreover, as a passing comment, it may be stated that the duties of Western-world internet service providers (ISPs) to police or pre-empt undesirable activities are still comparatively light, even after such perceived milestones as the Digital Millennium Copyright Act and the Supreme Court's decision against file-sharing promoters in the case of *Metro-Goldwyn-Mayer Studios Inc. vs. Grokster Ltd*. [89] Although there is more regulation in such countries as China and Saudi Arabia, where ISPs are co-opted to censor content and services that governments find objectionable, [90] regulatory efforts are still framed as exceptions to the rule that where the internet goes, freedom of action by its subscribers follows.

Conclusion

In 1976, when copyright law was most recently overhauled, the internet was not really a major cause for concern. Gillespie tells us why:

The ARPANET was only a research project run by the military and a few universities, and the traditional supporters of copyright (publishers, studios, producers, and the like) had not yet discovered why they would eventually care about its copyright implications. Congress was only beginning to tackle the question of whether computer software should be granted the same copyright protection enjoyed by print and other analog works. There was no need to deal with the nascent question of online distribution. Later, when the internet did appear as a public and potentially commercial medium, legislators began fleeing pressure to revise the rules they have written back in the 1970s, to once again keep pace with the new technology. [91]

However, it seems that once the U.S. government began to consider how copyright law should apply to the new information medium, [92] there seems to be some evidence that it shared the vision of the major movie studios, even leading one to believe that it may have been influenced by their lobbying—that the relentless piracy made possible by the internet meant that copyright law would need to be stronger and more rigorously enforced.

The Working Group on Intellectual Property Rights' White Paper [93] proposed what it claimed were minor adjustments, sufficient to protect content owners and make internet a safe place to release their work without fear of piracy. But these adjustments, we believe redefined the scope of copyright, in anticipation of a digital marketplace for cultural expression. [94] Most prominent among the proposals was an anti-circumvention statute: If a copyright owner were to distribute a digital work with some kind of technological barrier built in (password security, watermarking, encryption, anti-copying codes, etc.), it would be illegal for a user to gain unauthorized access by breaching that barrier. Furthermore, it would be illegal to make or distribute any tool that assisted others in doing so. This was justified as preparation for an impending arms race between beleaguered copyright owners and determined hackers, as described in the NII White Paper. [95]

Congress was aware that American law was for the first time adding rules about technology to a copyright doctrine that had long prided itself on being "technology neutral". Prof. David Nimmer, while quoting the House Committee on Commerce Report, argued that historically, Congress has achieved the objectives of the Constitution's Copyright Clause "by regulating the use of information—not the devices or means by which the information is delivered or used by information consumers". [96] Copyright law had always restricted certain activities and ensured certain rights, without regard to the techniques and tools with which they were accomplished. [97] But, as Congress thought, it was time that a beast of its own in the form of a legal regime be established to take on the beast that was the internet.

The Digital Millenium Copyright Act became law on October 28, 1998, [98] and arguably represents the most dramatic change in the history of U.S. copyright law. However, it is not without precedent. Scrambling content has been the primary means to protect cable and satellite broadcasts from being pirated (here "pirated" means gaining access without subscribing, rather than copying). [99] The law protects against the theft of cable television service not only by making the act of theft illegal but also by making it criminal to "assist" by producing or distributing the devices that unscramble the signal. [100] The DMCA also borrows from "shrinkwrap" licenses, which grant the owner technical control of both the software in the abstract and the particular copy purchased, dictating largely at the owner's whim what the user is and is not permitted to do. All of these, we agree, help shift copyright law from its traditional attention to delimiting copying to a new emphasis on regulating access. [101]

Some in the legal community have described the DMCA as "paracopy-right", to emphasize that it is not so much an alteration or expansion of the copyright doctrine, but rather a companion law that straddles it, staking claim on different though overlapping legal territory. [102] But some believe that even this is misleading, for the DMCA shares neither the logic nor the strategy of copyright. [103] It anticipates a new technological regime, where control depends upon blending of technology, law, and license, which share the task of not just copying, but access, use, and purchase. [104]

It remains to be seen whether the DMCA is here to compliment the law of copyright and whether it is here as a mere gatekeeper at the door of copyright owners. However, there can be no doubt that the window has been opened, as small as it may seem, thus allowing the entry and sanction of technological restraint methods and also allowing them to merge together with the law and other elements together.

Endnotes

1. Margaret Jane Radin (2004), "Regulation by Contract, Regulation by Machine", *Journal of Institutional and Theoretical Economics*, 142, 152.
2. Margaret Jane Radin (2004), "Regulation by Contract, Regulation by Machine", *Journal of Institutional and Theoretical Economics*, 142, 152.
3. The authors use the term 'law in cyberspace' rather than 'cyber law' as the authors are of the opinion that there exists no comprehensive body of law worthy of being referred to as 'cyber law'. Rather, the authors are of the opinion that there are a number of different laws which regulate behaviour in cyberspace.
4. U.S. Constitution, Article 1, Sec 8, Cl.8.
5. 17 U.S.C., Section 102.

6. 17 U.S.C., Section 102(b).
7. More likely to be termed 'fruits of his or her labour' in India taking into account the different levels at which an author may achieve copyright protection in India and the contrast in U.S. law. It may be noted that U.S. courts have taken exception to the 'sweat of the brow' theory for copyright protection and a detailed analysis does not form part of this paper.
8. 17 U.S.C., Section 106.
9. 17 U.S.C., Section 107.
10. 17 U.S.C., Section 109.
11. United States Patent and Trademark Office, available at: http://www.uspto.gov/web/offices/com/doc/ipnii.
12. Tom W. Bell (1998), "Fair Use vs. Fared Use: The Impact of Automated Rights Management on Copyright's Fair Use Doctrine", 76 N.C.L. Rev. 557, 566-67.
13. Patricia L. Bellia, "Cyber Law: Problems of Policy and Jurisprudence in the Information Age", 230.
14. Tom W. Bell (1998), "Fair Use vs. Fared Use: The Impact of Automated Rights Management on Copyright's Fair Use Doctrine", 76 N.C.L. Rev. 557, 585.
15. *Id.*
16. *Id.* at 586.
17. *Id.* at 587.
18. *Id.* at 588.
19. Ronald H. Coase (1994), "The Institutional Structure of Production", in Coase (ed.), 'Essays on Economics and Economists, 3, 11.
20. Tom W. Bell *at.* 588.
21. *Id.* at 61.5. However, Prof. Merges would state otherwise: Compare Bonito Boats, Inc. vs. Thunder Craft Boats, Inc., 489 U.S. 141, 155 (1989) (holding that a state law protecting boat hulls from copying was pre-empted by federal law), and Compco Corp. vs. Day-Brite Lighting, 376 U.S. 234, 237 (1964) (holding that a state unfair competition law was pre-empted by patent law), and Sears, Roebuck and Co. vs. Stiffel Co., 376 U.S. 225, 231 (1964) (same), with Aronson, 440 U.S. at 266 (holding that a contract affecting rights to a patent was not pre-empted). Prof. Merges notes that pre-emption, which has been applied almost exclusively to overturn state legislation, has in theory been available as a limit on the terms that parties can

include in a private contract; but no court so far as I can determine actually has ever used this principle to render unenforceable a particular licensing agreement. Robert P. Merges, "Expanding Boundaries of the Law: Intellectual Property and the Costs of Commercial Exchange: A Review Essay", 93 MICH. L. REV. 1570, 1610 (1995) (footnote omitted) (reviewing Peter A. Alces and Harold F. See, The Commercial Law of Intellectual Property [1994]). Bell responds: Professor Merges argues that contract offers scant competition to copyright as a means of protecting proprietary information in digital media. "[T]he argument for the dominance of contract has one serious flaw: it fails to address the problem of rights against those who are not in contractual privity". Merges, supra note 21, at 19. He does not, however, address the impact of advanced ARM on this problem. If access to works could be obtained only through the information provider (directly or through an authorized online distributor) no 'third parties' to the contract would exist". Professor Lemley observes of the contract option in the analogous case of shrinkwrap license, "I suspect that copyright owners would find this an unattractive alternative, however, and that in fact they would prefer to 'pick and choose' only the copyright rules that benefit them". See: A. Lemley (1995), "Intellectual Property and Shrinkwrap Licenses", 68 S. CAL. L. Rev. 1239, 1278. All contracts "affect" third parties, however. Under common law, only very few such as contracts to kill generate sufficient negative externalities to merit invalidation.

22. Tom W. Bell (1998), "Fair Use vs. Fared Use: The Impact of Automated Rights Management on Copyright's Fair Use Doctrine", 76 N.C.L. Rev. 557 at 595.
23. *Id.* at 595.
24. Paul Goldstein (1994), "Copyright's Highway", 217.
25. Tom W. Bell at 590.
26. "The Digital Millennium Copyright Act of 1998", U.S. Copyright Office Summary, available at: http://www.copyright.gov/legislation/dmca.pdf.
27. Tom W. Bell (2001), "Escape from Copyright: Market Success vs. Statutory Failure in the Protection of Expressive Works", 69 U. CIN. L. Rev. 741, 749-50 (distinguishing between common law protection and DMCA protection of TPMs).

28. Neil W. Netanel (1996), "Copyright and a Democratic Civil Society", 106 Yale L.J. 283, 285.
29. *Id.*
30. Dennis S. Karjala (1997), "Federal Pre-emption of Shrinkwrap and On-Line Licenses", 22 U. Dayton L. Rev. 511, 513.
31. *Id.*
32. Michael J. Madison, "Legal-Ware: Contract and Copyright in the Digital Age", 67 Fordham L. Rev. 1025, 1031.
33. Julie E. Cohen (1998), "Lochner in Cyberspace: The New Economic Orthodoxy of Rights Management", 97 Mich. L. Rev. 462, 472.
34. *Id.* at 550.
35. Patricia L. Bellia et al. (2006), "Cyber Law: Problems of Policy and Jurisprudence in the Information Age". 231.
36. Dan L. Burk and Julie E. Cohen (2001), "Fair Use Infrastructure for Rights Management Systems", 15, Harv. J.L. and Tech. 41, 51.
37. *Id.*
38. Lawrence Lessig (1998), "Code and Other Laws of Cyberspace", Joel R. Reidenberg, "Lex Informatica", 76 Tex. L. Rev. 553.
39. Dan L. Burk at 51.
40. *Id.* at 52.
41. *Id.* at 56, 59.
42. *Id.* at 56.
43. *Id.* at 59.
44. The Preamble to Section 107 reads: Notwithstanding the provisions of Section 106, the fair use of a copyrighted work, including such use by reproduction in copies or phono records or by any other means specified by that section, for purposes such as criticism, comment, news reporting, teaching (including multiple copies for classroom use), scholarship, or research, is not an infringement of copyright.
45. They are meant to be illustrative, not exhaustive, allowing for other contexts in which the fair use defence might arise. For example, the preamble does not specifically mention parody, but the categories of criticism and comment are broad enough to include parody.
46. Marshall Leaffer (2005), "Understanding Copyright Law", 469.
47. See, e.g. Twin Peaks Prods. Inc. v. Publ'ns, Int'l, Ltd. (finding

defendant's detailed report of the plots of a popular television program went far beyond merely identifying their basic outline for the transformative purposes of comment or criticism).

48. Rosemont Enters. Inc. vs. Random House Inc., 366 F. 2d 303, 306 (2d Cir. 1996), cert. denied, 385 U.S. 1009 (1967) (citing H. Ball, Copyright and Literary Property 260 (1944).
49. Leaffer, at 470.
50. Dan L. Burk and Julie E. Cohen (2001), "Fair Use Infrastructure for Rights Management Systems", 15 Harv. J.L. and Tech. 41, 66.
51. See, e.g., Andrew Ross Sorkin (2003), "Software Bullet is Sought to Kill Musical Piracy", N.Y. Times, May 4.
52. Matt Jackson, "Using Technology to Circumvent the Law: The DMCA'a Push to Privatize Copyright", 23, Hastings Comm./Ent. L.J., 607.
53. Julie E. Cohen (1998), "Lochner in Cyberspace: The New Economic Orthodoxy of Rights Management", 97 Mich. L. Rev. 462.
54. *Id.* at 483.
55. *Id.*
56. *Id.* at 484.
57. *Id.*
58. *Id.* at 492.
59. This in fact has been done in the past. See: Jacobsen v. Katzer, No. 2008-1001, 2008 WL 3395772 (Fed. Cir. Aug. 13, 2008). The United States Court of Appeals for the Federal Circuit recently issued an opinion that bolsters the enforceability of open source software licenses. In Jacobsen vs. Katzer, the Court held that a licensor providing free open source software properly can limit the further distribution of the software through terms in the open source software license requiring attribution credits to the original author. The decision is important because the Court held that the party failing to provide credit required under the license violated copyright law. One of the provisions in the license agreement was that, if the license agreement was not agreeable to any person; that person should contact the licensor in order to work out an alternative.
60. Jonathan Zittrain (2006), "The Generative Internet", 119 Harv. L. Rev. 1974, 1997-2000.
61. *Id.* at 2001.

62. *Id.* [Where in late 2005, Sony BMG Music produced audio CDs that included software that could run if the CD were inserted into a PC for playback. See: Tom Zeller Jr., "The Ghost in the CD", N.Y. Times, November 14, 2005, at C1. The software installed a DRM system onto the PC and then copied the CD's music in a protected format not compatible with the popular Apple iPod. Sony suggested that users employ the "indirect" method of burning and re-ripping in order to produce music that could be played on an iPod. See Sony BMG Music Entertainment, Frequently Asked Questions, available at: http://cp.sonybmg.com/xcp/english/faq.html#ipod (encouraging users to write to Sony BMG for instructions on this method); see also Zeller, supra (noting that Sony BMG provides instructions for how to load FairPlay-incompatible tracks onto an iPod).]
63. 421 F.3d 1307, 1310 (Fed.Cir. 2005).
64. Storage Tech., 421 F. 3d at 1310.
65. *Id.*
66. *Id.*
67. *Id.*
68. *Id.* at 1316.
69. *Id.* at 1310.
70. *Id.*
71. *Id.* at 1316 (Internal quotation marks omitted).
72. *Id.* at 1316-17 ("[Storage Technology's] argument, however, ignores the rest of the license agreement. The prohibition on third-party use of the code is modified by a later provision stating that equipment owners 'may transfer possession of internal code only with the transfer of the equipment on which its use is authorized'. Additionally, the license grants the customer the use of the code for 'the sole purpose of enabling the specific unit of equipment for which the internal code was provided...' The clear implication of those sections is that the license is tied to the piece of equipment on which the software resides. Thus, the authorized use is tied to a particular machine, rather than a particular person" (alteration in original).
73. *Id.* at 1319.
74. Id. at 1311.
75. *Id.* at 1319.
76. Ticketmaster L.L.C., 507 F. Supp. 2d at 1111-12. The court's interpretation of Ticketmaster's copyright infringement claim

has staggering implications. The court held that viewing plaintiff's webpages in a browser (and thus storing a copy in RAM), consisted of making copies of those webpages within the copyright right of reproduction. Id. Next, Ticketmaster's ToS grants a license to users who want to view (and thus, according to the court, copy) its copyrighted pages. Id. Finally, the court held that when users violated the terms of service and continued to navigate the webpages, it committed copyright infringement. Id. This implies that anyone who violates a similar ToS and continues to browse is liable for copyright infringement; a shocking proposition in the Internet age.

77. 507 F. Supp. 2d 1096, 1102 (C.D. Cal. 2007).
78. *Id.* at 1102-03. Captcha is an application that presents "a box with stylized random characters partially obscured behind hash marks". The user is required to type the characters into an entry on the screen in order to proceed with the request. Most automated devices cannot decipher and type the random characters and thus cannot proceed to the copyrighted ticket purchase pages.
79. 17 U.S.C. Section 1201 of the DMCA provides for Circumvention of copyright protection systems. Available at: http://cyber.law.harvard.edu/openlaw/DVD/1201.html.
80. Ticketmaster L.L.C. Id. at 1105-10; See also MAI Sys. Corp. vs. Peak Computer Inc., 991 F.2d 511, 519 (9th Cir. 1993).
81. *Id.*
82. See *Id.* at 1112.
83. Lexmark Int'l, Inc. vs. Static Control Components, Inc., 387 F.3d 522, 549 (6th Cir. 2004) ("Nowhere in its deliberations over the DMCA did Congress express an interest in creating liability for the circumvention of technological measures designed to prevent consumers from using consumer goods while leaving the copyrightable content of a work unprotected").
84. See Ticketmaster L.L.C., 507 F. Supp. 2d at 1102, 1107, 1112.
85. Storage Tech. Corp. vs. Custom Hardware Eng'g and Consulting, Inc., 421 F.3d 1307, 1310 (Fed. Cir. 2005).
86. See 421 F.3d 1307, 1319 (Fed. Cir. 2005) ("The activation of the maintenance code may violate [Storage Technology's] contractual rights vis-à-vis its customers, but those rights are not the rights protected by copyright law. There is simply not a sufficient nexus between the rights protected by copyright law

and the circumvention of the GetKey system").

87. Chamberlain Group Inc. vs. Skylink Techs.,Inc., 381 F.3d 1178, 1201 (Fed. Cir. 2004).
88. *Id.*
89. 125 S. Ct. 2764 (2005).
90. See: OpenNet Initiative, Documenting Internet Content Filtering Worldwide, available at: http://www.opennet.net/modules.php?op =modload&name=Archive&file=index&req=viewarticle&artid= 1; Jonathan Zittrain and Benjamin Edelman, Documentation of Internet Filtering Worldwide, available at: http://cyber.law.harvard.edu/filtering.
91. Tarleton Gillespie (2007), "Wired Shut: Copyright and the Shape of Digital Culture", 174.
92. See: Debora Halbert (1999), "Intellectual Property in the Information Age: The Politics of Expanding Ownership Rights", Westport, CT, 28, 29, 32-33.
93. NII White Paper.
94. Dan Burk (2003), "Anti-Circumvention Misuse", *UCLA Law Review,* 50, 1095-1140; Julie Cohen (1996), "A Right to Read Anonymously: A Closer Look at 'Copyright Management' in Cyberspace", *Connecticut Law Review*, 28, 981-1039.
95. NII White Paper.
96. David Nimmer (2000), "A Riff on Fair Use in the Digital Millennium Copyright Act", 148 U. Pa. L. Rev. 673, 683.
97. Tarleton Gillespie (2007), "Wired Shut: Copyright and the Shape of Digital Culture", 175. Gillespie writes: "In a display of sheer tautological bravado, the House Committee on Commerce tried to reassure themselves by adjusting their bill so that it would be a free-standing law rather than an amendment to Title 17 of Copyright Act; without changing any of the bill's language, which clearly worked to regulate copyrighted work and its use, they felt that writing it as a separate law would preserve copyright law as "technology neutral". This separation was not continued as the DMCA made it into law. See: HR 105-551:25.
98. Digital Millennium Copyright Act (DMCA), Pub. L. No. 105-304, 112 Stat. 2860 (1998) (codified at 17 U.S.C. 512 and in various sections of Chapters 12 of Title 17 of the U.S.C.).
99. Tarleton Gillespie, *Id.*

100. 47 U.S.C. SS 553, "Unauthorized Reception of Cable Services".
101. Tarleton Gillespie, at 177.
102. For the idea of "paracopyright," see Burk, "Anti-Circumvention Misuse".
103. The DMCA includes an explicit stipulation intended to ensure that its legal domain would not impinge on fair use protections: "Nothing in this section shall affect rights, remedies, limitations, or defences of copyright infringement, including fair use, under this title". Digital Millenium Copyright Act, 1201 (c)(1).
104. Tarleton Gillespie, at 177, 178.

5

Trade Secrets Law and Economic Development in India

Faizanur Rahman

Introductory Remarks

The world is in a knowledge age. Ideas and information are an increasingly important part of the economy. Intellectual property, data and other similar information, which are intangible, are often the most valuable assets owned by a business, even more so than the physical assets. [1] Most of the value of health care products, entertainment material, and other high technology products is a result of creation, invention, innovation, research, design or testing. Fashion clothing, books, know-how, computer programs, computer games, recorded music, movies, videos clips and online services are traded for the content, information or creativity and not for the fabric, plastic, metal or paper on which they are housed. Many of these assets are statutorily protected, subject to certain limitations, as copyrights, trademarks, patents designs or other intellectual property. Trade secrets are also a form of intellectual property but are not statutorily protected in many jurisdictions. Trade secrets may prove to be ephemeral, because once lost, are like the proverbial horse that once leaves the barn, is impossible to put back. In the present digital era of information, including the way trade secrets are being stored and disseminated in electronic format, the ease with which trade secrets are lost is daunting. [2]

The importance of trade secrets in the ambit of intellectual property has gained widespread recognition so much so that trade secret protection of working technologies has taken precedence over protection through patents. [3] North Atlantic Free Trade Agreement (NAFTA) and Agreement on Trade Related Aspects of Intellectual Property (TRIPS Agreement, Article 39) include specific provisions directed towards increasing the protection of trade secrets. Prior to these agreements, Article 10*bis* of the Paris Convention (covering Unfair Competition) provides support for international standards of trade secrets protection but there is lack of a comprehensive international treaty on the lines of patent, copyright and trademark law.

Trade secrets are one of the problematic areas in the sphere of intellectual property simply because the modern IPR laws are tuned to bring transparency and probity in knowledge management. Trade secrets still shroud in secrecy and had exacting demands for the IP protection. [4] The nature of trade secrets is too obscure to define in subtle terms and comprehension. In this sense, the trade secrets are perhaps the most difficult form of intellectual property to protect due to prolonged secrecy and confidentiality. Owners of trade secrets maintain the confidentiality of their trade secrets under legal protection and claims for injunctive relief for unauthorized use and dissemination of trade secrets and recovery of damages. The person who leaks trade secrets can face criminal charges for the break of confidentiality.

The procedural gametes entail some steps that can be taken to protect (i.e. to maintain the confidentiality of) trade secrets including disclosure within the organization. It also requires that all information disclosed is subject to a non-disclosure agreement which restricts the use of that information as a trade secret. In some cases, a company's employees manual themselves by prohibiting the disclosure of proprietary information by labelling all proprietary information as confidential—even restricting access to research facilities.

Thus, a company can protect its confidential information through non-complete and non-disclosure contracts with its employees within the framework of employment law and restraint of trade under the contract law. This is justified on the ground that it is reasonable in geographic and time scope for overall economic vitality.

A company typically invests money, time and energy into generating information regarding refinements of processes and operations to maintain its market dominance. The creator of such knowledge regarded as "trade secret" is entitled to "special knowledge" named as intellectual property. The present paper takes a legal stance of trade secret laws besides underlining the major hiccups and hurdles in the application of IP management [5] and also highlighting the scope trade secrets law in new economic perspective.

Trade Secrets: A Conceptual Overview

Trade Secrets under TRIPS Agreement: Article 39.1 of the TRIPS provide that "in course of ensuring effective protection against unfair competition as provided in Article 10*bis* of the *Paris Convention*, 1967 says that members shall protect undisclosed information" of the sort which is described in paragraphs 2 and 3 of Article 39. Paragraph 2 describes the general category of confidential information, which is protected in common law countries through judge-made law, rather through statute. Article 10*bis* contains no reference to the protection of confidential information as an aspect of unfair competition. Article 10*bis* (2) defines as an act of unfair competition "any act of competition contrary to honest practices in industrial and commercial practices". Article 10*bis* lists three particular practices which are to be prohibited. The TRIPS Agreement negotiators were anxious to preserve the confidentiality of test data submitted to government approval agencies.

Given the long approval process, particular for pharmaceutical products, the opportunity for wrongful appropriation of such data by competitors was self evident. This concern is accommodated by Article 39.3 which provides that, "Members, requiring as a condition of approving the marketing of pharmaceutical or of agricultural chemical products which utilize new chemical entities, the submission of undisclosed test or other data, the origination which involves a considerable effort, shall protect such data against unfair commercial use. In addition, Members shall protect such data against disclosure, except where necessary against unfair commercial effort shall protect such data against unfair commercial use.

It should be noted that Article 39.3 contains three limitations. *First*, it applies only to pharmaceutical products and chemical agricultural products; *secondly*, the protection is extended only against unfair competition uses; and *thirdly*, the government authority is exempted from the requirement of confidentiality in the public interest. Thus, it has been held that a government accrediting agency may use the confidential test data of an applicant when considering applications by other applicant in respect of similar products. [6]

Where, the specifications of an invention relatable to an article substance covered under sub-section (2) of Section 5 have been recorded in a document or the invention has been tried or used, or, the article or the substance has been sold, by a person, before a claim for a patent of that invention is made in India or a convention country, then, the sale or distribution of the article or substance by such person, after the claim referred to above is made, shall be deemed to be an infringement of exclusive right to sell or distribute under sub-section (1):

Provided nothing in this sub-section shall apply in a case where a person makes or uses an article or a substance with a view to sell or distribute the same, the details of invention relatable thereto was given by a person who was holding an exclusive right to sell or distribute the article or substance. [7]

Definition of Trade Secrets: As all IP laws are generally territorial in character by definition, the trade secrets vary by jurisdiction, particular types of information and subject of trade secret protection. A trade secret is commonly defined as any formula, pattern, device or compilation of information which is used in one's business, and which gives human opportunity to obtain an advantage over competitors who do not know or use it. Broadly speaking, there are *three* factors that are common to all such definitions of a trade secret. Trade secret is information that: [8]

- Is not generally known to the public.
- Confers some sort of economic benefit on its holder derived specifically from it not being generally known and not just from the value of the information itself.
- All trade secrets are the subject of reasonable efforts to maintain their secrecy and confidentiality.

North American Free Trade Agreement (NAFTA) defines trade secret as "information having commercial value, which is not in the public domain, and for which reasonable steps have been taken to maintain its secrecy".

The Trade Related Aspects of Intellectual Property Rights (TRIPS) lays down three essential conditions which are to be fulfilled by any information before it can be considered undisclosed information (trade secret). They are:

- such information must be secret, i.e., not generally known or readily accessible to "persons within the circles that normally deal with the kinds of information in question".
- the information must have commercial value because it is secret, and
- the information must be the subject of reasonable steps by its owners to keep it secret.

The Uniform Trades Secrets Act, 1970 also provides for the definition of trade secrets, which is as follows:

"Information, including a formula, pattern, compilation, program device, method, technique, or process, that: (i) derives independent economic value, actual or potential, from not being generally known to, and not being readily ascertainable by proper means by other persons who can obtain economic value from its disclosure or use, and (ii) is the subject of efforts that are reasonable under the circumstances to maintain its secrecy".

After reviewing all the above definitions, we can say that a trade secret refers to data or information relating to the business which is not generally known to the public and which the owner reasonably attempts to keep secret and confidential. Trade secrets generally give the business a competitive edge over their rivals. Almost any type of data, processes or information can be referred to as trade secrets so long as it is intended to be kept as a secret, and involves an economic interest of the owner. For example, a business may have certain internal business processes that it follows for its day-to-day operations that give it an edge over its competitors. This could be regarded as a trade secret. [9]

Categories Recognized as Trade Secrets

The following section provides examples of circumstances where trade secret protection was approved or denied. Courts have provided trade secret protection to: [10]

- Formula.
- Patterns.
- Plans.
- Designs.
- Physical devices.
- Processes.
- Software.
- Know-how.

Please keep in mind that different courts may reach contrary conclusions concerning trade secret status with respect to what may appear to be identical matters.

Formula: Formula is a group of symbols that make a mathematical statement or a conventionalized statement expressing some fundamental principle or a representation of a substance using symbols for its constituent elements. It establishes a right direction for making something worthwhile or lucrative. A formula (i.e., a recipe that allows one to create a product) can be a trade secret.

Common formulas found to be trade secrets in food, drug,

and cosmetics industry include formulas for butter flavouring, cheese, breakfast cereal, seasoning for fried chicken, special diet rations for dogs, mixed alcoholic beverages, lipstick, and hair conditioner. The Coca-Cola Company has put numerous security measures in place to keep its formula a secret. In fact, the formula gives the Coca-Cola Company a significant business advantage in the soda market, as there is no other soda that tastes the same.

Pattern: A pattern is a form, template, or model (or, more abstractly, a set of rules) that can be used to make or to generate things or parts of a thing. If the things that are generated have enough in common for the underlying pattern to be inferred or discerned—in which case the things are said to exhibit a pattern. The detection of underlying patterns is called pattern recognition.

Plan: A plan is a proposed or intended method of getting from one set of circumstances to another. They are often used to move from the present situation, towards the achievement of one or more objectives or goals. An inventor my seek protection for an article to be effectively manufactured/ prepared through a process that he has discovered/rediscovered under this category if he is not in a position to reveal it fully (patenting).

Design: Design is a decorative or artistic work. It may also be termed as an arrangement scheme. Following categories of goods/inventions may be protected under designs:

- Circuitry for an advanced minicomputer.
- Colour TV circuitry.
- Schematics for an analog circuit.
- Plans and specifications for gears and rollers of a photo-processing machine for drilling equipment.
- Plans and designs for a veneer dryer.
- Moulds for the manufacture of street markers.

Physical Devices: Physical device is a device that has some physical implementation. It is an actual piece of hardware, not an emulated device. It is used in manufacturing.

These devices include:

- A device for manufacturing radio parts.
- Machinery and equipment used to manufacture polyethylene.
- Machinery and equipment used to manufacture saw grade diamonds.
- A computer tool used to service microprocessor-based elevators, a tool for making a pressure-sensing mechanism.
- A machine for inking carbon paper and ribbons, and an adhesive-tape machine.

Process: Process is a generalized method of doing something, generally involving steps or operations that are usually ordered and/or are interdependent. A process, method or technique used to make the final end product can also be a trade secret. Examples of processes found to be trade secrets include:

- A process to manufacture foam crash pads.
- A process to treat metal.
- A process to manufacture fibreglass.
- A method and procedure to manufacture epoxy resin rods.
- A process to manufacture potassium sulphate.
- A process for an environmentally sound method to manufacture coated paper.

Know-how: Know-how is information that enables a person to accomplish a particular task or to operate a particular device or process. Information and experiential expertise related to using formulas or processes, know-how etc. can be a trade secret. Examples of trade secrets in this area include:

- Know-how pertaining to the construction of plant chemicals.
- Methods for testing procedures to assure the quality of raw material.
- Know-how to ascertain whether CAT scanning equipment and components are operating according to specifications and to identify malfunctions.
- Methods to manufacture typewriters.

Tools of Trade Secrets

Trade secrets are by definition not disclosed to the world at large. Instead, owners of trade secrets keep their special knowledge out of the hands of competitors through a variety of civil and commercial means, non-disclosure agreements (NDA) and non-compete clauses. [11] It is important to bear in mind that a trade secret need not be something that is novel nor should it have any real or intrinsic value to be protected. The only requirement is that it must be a secret. [12] Tools to protect trade secrets ensure against any misappropriation, sabotage, or piracy. Therefore, businesses must ensure that they protect their trade secret by adopting some tools which are outlined below:

- *Employment Agreement:* Depending upon their needs, business should include suitable confidentiality, non-disclosure and non-compete clauses in agreements with employees. These may include the type of information that is likely to be disclosed, the manner in which it should be used and restrictions on disclosure post-termination.
- *Trade Secret Policy:* Such a policy is a must for businesses that heavily rely on their trade secrets. A basic step to develop such a policy is to identify and prioritize the business secrets based on their value and sensitivity. Employees must be informed about the policy and consequences of its breach before they agree to abide by the policy and sign an acknowledgement to that effect.
- *Non-disclosure Agreements (NDAs):* Business can also enter into NDAs with third parties while discussing any business prospects and ventures. In this way, the third parties can be precluded from divulging any trade secrets.
- *Adequate Documentation:* It is important for businesses to keep a track of the trade secrets that are developed and have sufficient records to shows that the trade secret was developed by them and belongs to them. These records would be of evidentiary value in case of a dispute. It would also be useful for such business to conduct a trade

secret audit at regular intervals to keep up to date with any changes.

- *Security Systems:* Access to trade secrets and confidential information may also be restricted to only select personnel who have to undergo proper security checks. In case of an electronic environment, the businesses should use adequate software programs, virus scans, firewalls and other security and authentication technologies to safeguard their trade secrets.

Trade secret protection can, in principle, extend indefinitely and this may offer an advantage over patent protection, which lasts only for a specifically limited period of time. Historically, trade secrets took the form of keeping advanced military technology from one's enemies and formidable foes but in a contemporary society, technological innovation has universalized trade secrets. [13] Discovering of trade secrets can only be possible through lawful methods of reverse engineering and industrial espionage.

Significance of Protection of Trade Secrets

Trade secret acts as an incentive to develop incremental innovation of technology by not meeting the non-obviousness standard of patent law, or where patents and copyrights are unavailable, ineffectual or unattractive. Right in trade secret, in certain circumstances, can cast longer than patents. Scientific discoveries, which are of increased importance, also face difficulties of patent protection. They can be protected by trade secrets. Moreover, where a technology does not fall clearly within the traditional IPRs, viz. patents or copyright, trade secrets come handy. Furthermore, inventions (protected as utility model or as patents), trademarks, industrial designs, artistic or literary works, where they have not yet been made public, are kept as trade secrets until used or published as such, or during the process of registration or grant of the relevant intellectual property rights. A substantial part of economically meaningful technology, particularly new and high technology (cutting edge technology) which is prone to reverse engineering, such as biotechnology, computer program microchips, computer-aides designs, is kept as trade secrets. [14]

Trade secrets or know-how may consist of the complementary information obtained through the exploitation of patented technology that, while not being patentable, allows a more efficient use of the patented product or process. Exclusivity of the protection allows innovation, invention and imitation, by offering to the owner an opportunity to discourage free riders and to recoup his investment. Product life cycle in some IPR-sensitive industries has shrunk dramatically. The time-compression, in turn, reduces the period in which R&D and innovation costs can be recouped and puts a premium on strong and rapid protection of innovation through trade secret.

There are many other reasons for increasing reliance on trade secrets such as:

- A patent means publicity, and enterprises wish to avoid publicity in connection with industrial property;
- A patent may be questioned after it is granted;
- The process of obtaining a patent is long and uncertain;
- There are difficulties in discerning and proving infringement of patents;
- There is possibility of compulsory licensing of a patent;
- Patent gives protection only for a limited period, but trade secrets can prolong it;
- In copyright, though it protects expression and not ideas, but by trade secrets, the ideas can also be protected so long as those ideas are not published in some way. It is more vital if the publication contains technical knowledge.

There are substantial differences between others IPRs and trade secrets. The other IPRs are defined by statute and limited in duration. Trade secrets are protected not by registration but by contractual restrictions on use, disclosure etc. There is no limitation in time for trade secrets. It will be protected by *de facto* circumstances beyond the control of the owner of the secret, who can prevent third parties from developing independently, or engaging in conduct which leads to the disappearance of the secrecy, i.e., "*reverse engineering*". Thus, know-how has been characterized as monopoly *in fact.* Furthermore, unlike other IPRs, whose holders enjoy the exclusivity of the right during its tenure, i.e., patent or copyright, in the case of trade secret, if the information is disclosed by accident or uncovered through legal means by third parties, the law does not provide any remedy. Trade secrets that are voluntarily revealed, insufficiently guarded or reverse engineered, lose all protection and become subject to free competition.

Producers/manufactures who attempt contractually to limit the reverse engineering of unpatented innovation run the risk that courts will hold such restrictions as unenforceable.

The originator of trade secrets obtains no exclusive rights to make, use, sell or reproduce it in the manner of patents or other statutory IPRs. Furthermore, contractual protection of trade secrets is limited to the parties to the contract. Rather, third-party acquisition of secret knowledge becomes actionable only when obtained by improper means. Moreover, where the "owner" proves to the satisfaction of the court the misappropriation of his trade secrets, it generally limits the injunctive relief to the estimated period for reverse engineering.

In the case of *Northern Office Micro Computer (Ply) Ltd. vs. Rosenstein*, [15] in United Kingdom, in recognizing that computer programs which are not common place should be eligible for protection as trade secrets, Marais, J. said that the protection given by the law of trades secrets in the context of ex-employees should be of a limited nature and the employer's "lead-time", the time to develop the program, should be all that was protected. Even a potential transferee of trades secret may develop the technology himself or acquire from other source. An obligation on the transferee not to exploit the licensed know-how after the termination of the agreement is also considered to be effective only in so far as the know-how is still secret.

The economic rationale behind the protection of confidentiality is to offer an incentive to invest in the creation of information. A strong IPR system, along with the protection of trade secrets, is considered to be conducive for further R&D. Industrial property law is general, and trade secrets in particular, provide an incentive for innovations and the development of new technology by granting certain exclusionary rights resulting from the rules that prevent third parties having an access to the secret technology without the owner's authorization. By excluding the third parties, the technology would have a market value which would lack without such a protection. [16]

However, trade secrets have the potential of adversely affecting the economic development of a country and create serious challenges for competition law by keeping information secret. As long as disclosure does not take place, and barring widespread independent development by third parties, know-how is unavailable for competitors and for the general public. This leads to an accumulation of high technology by a small number of enterprises, and thus to a concentration of economic power which implies risks for a free competition. Hence, trade secrets, clubbed with strong patent protection, can have their portent effects on the economy of the country, which will be deprived of all the knowledge and information kept as trade secret. As scientific and technological discoveries and inventions are quite often built on already existing knowledge, and many economically significant research developments can be conceptualized on already existing, cost-effective sequences, trade secrets hold back this knowledge from those engaged in intellectual pursuits.

Since research results are available to be added to the general pool of knowledge on which further research can be based and new knowledge can be generated, it leads to duplication of research. Trade secrets, thus, have the potential of adversely affecting trade competition and research and development (R&D) of a country. Such lost benefits to society will thus be the "dead weight burden" of the new IP regime, which will also affect the consumer interests. The more secure the possession of a trade secret, the less a patent-holder or copyright owner has to worry that charging a high royalty rate will induce others to seek to avoid paying it by investing in his/her creation. With less risk of entry of close substitutes to worry about, the owner of the trade secret can extract a high royalty income from the customers at artificially high prices and limit the output of the product. [17]

As the secret information cannot become the source of new developments, the concentration of basic information would end up to a situation of monopoly. In this scenario, small and medium sized entrepreneurs would be hard hit world-over. As the multinational corporations (MNCs) are holders of most of the technology related trade secrets, they will determine the direction of future trade, with longer patent protection (under the TRIPS Agreement, it is 20 years) and privatization of research.

Trade secrets have their foreseeable effect on transfer of technology and competition as well. As their economic value is comparable to patents, not only in terms of the investment required for obtaining them but also the competitive advantages they allow to its owner, it is, therefore, not surprising that trade secrets have become an important element in the technology transfer process. Unpatented technology plays a significant role in contemporary economic activity compared to patented technology.

Trade secrecy is quite often maintained to extend the monopoly over the technology beyond the patent period. In fact, unpatented and secret technology has become an important component of patent licensing. In order to guard against accidental disclosure or reverse engineered technology of trade secrets, the owners generally insert restrictive clauses to know-how transactions to preserve the market value of such a technology and limitations on the availability of the pertinent know-how. This makes such technology expensive and many a time out of reach.

Since transfer of technology may involve the leakage of proprietary information, licensing contracts may include provisions in which the licensee promises the confidentiality of the licensor. The trade-secret protection is designed to guarantee the licensor, rights to its technology. But in trade secret and know-how licenses, the licensor and licensee can become potential rivals. There are no international rules on the breach of such covenants, except governmental agreements. To protect his interests, the licensor may insert restrictive clauses and charge a high premium to counter such eventuality. This will further restrict the transfer of technology to the licensee. It is also noticeable that domestic R&D in developing countries can be a lengthy process and clearly lacks the certainty that licensing provides. Licensing, on the other hand, is often less effective in building a base of technical capability; with trade secret, it is even more so. The cost factor is also a constraint for foreign technology, if it comes with restrictive clauses for trade secrets.

Trade Secrets and Competition Laws

Members countries of the TRIPS in Article 40 took note of and deplored the practices and conditions prevalent in the licensing of IPRs which restrain competition, have an adverse effect on trade and which can impede the transfer and dissemination of technology. The member countries are authorized by Article 4(2) to prevent or control the practices or conditions that may constitute an abuse of the IPRs having an adverse effect on competitors in the relevant market. Each member is entitled to specify practices or conditions associated with IP licensing which may, in particular cases, constitute an abuse of IPRs. [18]

When IP right holders fix unreasonably high prices compared to the cost of production resulting into large monopoly profits, necessarily it is a case of unjust enrichment; and an abuse of IPR. There is a 'carte blanche' for the government to make any legislation necessary to prevent the abuse of IPRs.

It states: "Nothing in this agreement shall prevent members from specifying in their legislation, licensing practices or conditions that may in particular cases constituted an abuse of IPRs..." [19]

Article 8(2) is more explicit than Article 40 in saying that IP right holders engage in practices which unreasonably restrain trade. This provision clearly establishes that the TRIPS do not interfere with measures taken by governments against anti-competitive, dominant or monopolistic conduct of right-holders.

The Competition Act, 2002 [20] was passed to provide economic development, prevent practices having adverse effect on competition in order to promote and sustain competition in markets, to protect the interests of consumers and to ensure freedom of trade carried on by other participants in markets, in India, and for matters connected therewith or incidental thereto.

The major purposes of the Competition Act, 2002 or MRTP Act, 1969 laws were control of monopoly, monopolistic or dominant power, control of predatory practices, restrictive business practices or unfair trade practices, promoting competition, honesty and fair play in commercial activities, truthful advertising and overseeing the interests of consumers. The Act directs all enterprises not to enter into an agreement which causes or is likely to cause an appreciable adverse effect on competition within India. [21] The agreement may be with regard to production, supply, distribution, storage, acquisition or control of goods or provision of services. All such anti-competitive agreements are declared to be void. [22] It also lays down the agreements which are presumed to have an appreciable adverse effect on competition.

The law gives limited exemption [23] to IP right holders from the provisions of Section 3, to take all or any steps to vindicate any of the IP rights granted through six named enactments. It permits IP right holders: (a) to engage in a conduct including entering into anti-competitive agreements to restrain any infringement of IP rights, or (b) to impose reasonable conditions as may be necessary for upkeep of the rights which are conferred on the IP right-holder, under six statutes named therein. It reads as under:

"Nothing in this section shall restrict:

1. The right of any person to restrain any infringement of, or to impose reasonable conditions, as may be necessary for protecting any of his rights which have been or may be conferred upon him under:
   - The Copyright Act, 1957 (14 of 1957);
   - The Patent Act, 1970 (39 of 1970);
   - The Trade and Merchandise Marks Act, 1958 (43 of 1958) or now the Trade Marks Act, 1999 (47 of 1999);
   - The Geographical Indications of Goods (Registration and Protection) Act, 1999 (48 of 1999);
   - The Designs Act, 2000 (16 of 2000);
   - The Semi-conductor Integrated Circuits Layout-Design Act, 2000 (37 of 2000).
2. The right of any person to export goods from India to the extent to which the agreement relates exclusively to the production, supply, or control of goods or provision of services for such export.

In relation to the conflict between IPRs on the one hand and the norms of competition policy and law, on the other, there was sufficient clarity in the High Level Committee on Competition Policy and Law, known as the *Raghavan Committee*, which stated as follows: [24]

"All forms of IP have the potential to raise competition policy/law problems. IP provides exclusive rights to the holders to perform a productive or commercial activity, but this does not include the right to exert restrictive or monopoly power in the market or society…But at the same time there is a need to curb and prevent anti-competition behaviour that may surface in the exercise of IPRs.

There is, in some cases, a dichotomy between IPRs and competition policy/law. The former endangers competition while the latter engenders competition. There is a need to appreciate the existence of a right if any anti-competitive trade practice or conduct is visible to the detriment of consumer interest or public interest, it ought to be assailed under the competition policy/law". [25]

The exercise of IPRs has to be in a manner which promotes competition as also upholds reward in the form of IPR for human creativity, effort and investment in the subject matter of IPRs. The exclusive rights granted under IPRs should not be allowed to become tools to justify anti-competition behaviour or trade practices that are clearly detrimental to public interest.

Under the MRTP Act, 1969, Section 33(3) was somewhat parallel to present Section 3(5), but the whole purpose of CA, 2002 was to strengthen competition and remove the difficulties experienced in MRTP Act, 1969.

The CA, 2002 has to fulfil the aspirations of consumers from operations of anti-monopoly legislation or curbing unjust enrichment or curbing predatory practices that are particularly allowed to the governments against IP right-holders. [26]

The idea is that the IP right-holder should not abuse the dominant or monopolistic position resulting from exclusive rights vested by virtue of any IP laws. The IPRs on one hand and the competition right on the other, are separate rights having equal value; the competition right would not give way to IPRs and both would hold ground. [27] This has a major implication on trade secrets laws and necessitated to be explored in subtle term because right vs. property and right of tenant are separated. Therefore, both cannot be subsumed under monopoly law, competition law and IP law.

Trade Secrets Law in India

There is no specific law in India that protects trade secrets and confidential information. Nevertheless, Indian courts have upheld trade secret protection on the basis of principles of equity, and at times, upon a common law which in effect amounts to a breach of contractual obligation.

Trade Secrets under Contract Law: Trade secret is rather administered under Indian Contract Act, 1872, with provisions relating to restraint of trade. [28] An agreement to restraint a servant from competing with his employer after the termination of employment may not be allowed by the courts. [29] Thus, in *Brahmaputra Tea Co vs. E. Scarth*, [30] where an attempt was made to restrain a servant from competing for five years after the period of service, the court observed:

"Contracts by which persons are restrained from competing, after the term of their agreement is over, with their former employers within reasonable limits, are well known in English law, and the omission to make any such contract an exception to the general prohibition contained in Section 27 indicates that it was not intended to give them legal effect in this country". [31]

The principles thus established have been approved by the Supreme Court in *Niranjan Shanker Golikari vs. Century Spinning and Manufacturing Co. Ltd.* [32]:

"A company manufacturing cord yarn was offered collaboration by a foreign producer on the condition that the company shall maintain secrecy of all the technical information and that it should obtain corresponding secrecy arrangements from its employees. The defendant was appointed for a period of five years, the condition being that during this period he shall not serve anywhere else even if he left the service earlier".

Shelat, J. held the agreement to be valid. The defendant was accordingly restrained from serving anywhere else during the currency of the agreement.

"The evident is clear that the appellant has torn the

agreement to pieces only because he has been offered a high remuneration. Obviously, he cannot be heard to say that no injunction should be granted against him to enforce the negative covenant which is not opposed to public policy. The injunction issued against him is restricted as to time, the nature of employment and as to area and cannot therefore be said to be too wide or unreasonable or unnecessary for the protection of the interest of the respondent company".

One of the principles is that a master is not entitled to restrain his servant after the termination of employment from offering competition, but he is entitled to reasonable protection against exploitation of trade secrets. [33]

Indian Contract law besides putting trade secrets under breach of contract offers remedies for encouragement of creative and innovative abilities. [34] The principle on which the protection afforded by law is exemplified in the following statement in Charlesworth: [35]

"Intellectual property rights overlap, protecting different facets of a product. For example, the product itself may be patented, its method of manufacturing may be protected as a trade secret; sales literature and software used to run the product, may be protected by copyright; its shape or configuration may be protected by new design right; and its name by a trademark.

The usual remedies for breach of confidence are: action for an account of earnings from the use of the information; action for damages and an injunction for prevention of misuse. For an action to succeed, it would be necessary to show that the information was of confidential nature which was shared under an obligation of confidence with the person who proceeded against the terms and there was an actual or threatened use or disclosure of the information. If the information has already become a part of public knowledge, no action may lie. [36]

Since the information alleged to be confidential may be of value to the plaintiff only for a certain period, interim injunction will ordinarily be granted only for a specified period depending upon the circumstances and the nature of the confidential information.

In regard to balance of convenience, the following factors are considered:

1. Whether the effect of an injunction would be a disclosure disastrous to the defendants,
2. Whether the terms of injunction are such that it is extremely difficult for the defendants to know what they may do and what they may not do,
3. Whether it is certain upon the material before the court that even if they were successful at the trial, the plaintiff would obtain an injunction rather than damages. [37]

Damages or compensation is determined on the basis of the market value of the confidential information based on a notional sale between a willing seller and a willing purchaser. This method may be more appropriate for confidential information relating to industrial designs or processes or business secrets. Trade secrets are protected forever if kept confidential. If the confidentiality of the information is breached it is no more a secret.

The TRIPS agreement recognizes different forms of intellectual property. The Agreement intends to recognize and protect the intellectual property rights across the world. The agreement brought uniformity in the intellectual property laws throughout the world. The Agreement is a blueprint on intellectual property rights and regulation. All the member states of the TRIPS Agreement have adopted the provisions of the Agreement either by amendments to the existing laws or by enacting new legislations. India, being a member state, did follow the suit by amending its patent law, copyright law and by enacting new legislations on trademarks, geographical indications, industrial designs and integrated circuits. However, still there is no law on the trade secrets and confidential information. It is the only area where India is lagging far behind as far as intellectual property rights are concerned. [38]

Draft National Innovation Act, 2008

In response to this, the Indian Government has taken a step ahead by releasing a draft National Innovation Act, 2008 to boost research and innovation. [39]

The draft Act proposed by the Department of Science and Technology, has a three pronged approach. Firstly, it undertakes to encourage innovation through an innovation support system facilitated by the public-private partnership. The second approach is evolving into a National Integrated Science and Technology Plan. The third objective includes codifying and consolidating the law of confidentiality to protect confidential information, trade secrets and innovations.

The draft NI Act is widely speculated to be modelled on *America's Creating Opportunities to Meaningfully Promote Excellence in Technology, Education, and Science Act* (Competes Act). The Preamble of the Competes Act puts the objective of the law as to invest in innovation through research and development, and to improve the competitiveness of the United States. It focuses on three primary areas of importance of maintaining and improving United States' innovation in the 21st century:

1. Increasing research investment,
2. Strengthening educational opportunities in science, technology, engineering, and mathematics from elementary through graduates school, and
3. Developing an innovation infrastructure.

The draft NI Act through codification and consolidation of the law of confidentiality demonstrates the significance of trade secrets and confidential information within the realm of innovation. Innovative ideas, products and business practices help enterprises to maintain competitive superiority in the market alongside furthering their economic interests. [40] It is for this reason that there is a need to prevent others from taking advantage of the breakthrough ideas and knowledge or in ordinary parlance the confidential information or trade secrets.

It may be recalled that under the TRIPS Agreement 'trade secrets' are referred as 'undisclosed information'. [41] Any information prevented from being disclosed so long as such information: (a) is secret in the sense that it is not, as a body or in the precise configuration and assembly of its components, generally known among or readily accessible to persons within the circles that normally deal with the kind of information in question; (b) has commercial value because it is secret; and (c) has been subject to reasonable steps under the circumstances, by person lawfully in control of the information, to keep it secret.

Conclusion and Summation

Traditionally, oriental societies, including India, as such did not favour the idea of monopoly over knowledge and information. At the time of Independence, 85 percent of the Indian population was dependent on agriculture directly or indirectly. Now after seven decades of Independence, this figure has come down to 58 percent of the population. India is fast metamorphosing from being an agrarian economy into a "*knowledge based economy*". [42] India is emerging as a hub of software technology and information technology enabled services (ITES). It is becoming the most sought after destination for contract research and manufacturing and for conducting clinical trials. In the present era of knowledge and information technology and with globalization and liberalization of trade policies, the attitude of the Indian public, judiciary and the government towards effective protection and enforcement of intellectual property rights is changing for the better. More so, legal policies relating to intellectual property rights have undergone dynamic reforms. [43]

Intellectual property rights have garnered strong impact on the modern day life. TRIPS has mandated its member states to implement the provisions of the agreement in order to promote and protect intellectual property rights. Member states have been asked to provide protection to different intellectual property rights by making necessary adjustments in their existing laws or by enacting new laws. In order to fulfil such obligations under the Agreement, member states have amended their laws or have brought up new legislations. India, being a member state to the TRIPS Agreement, brought changes in its intellectual property laws in fulfilment of its obligations under the Agreement. [44] However, still there is no law on the trade secrets and confidential information. It is the only area where India is lagging behind as far as intellectual property rights is concerned. [45]

Protection of trade secrets is a neglected and under privileged issue. Protection is offered for trade secrets basically under the common law. There was no statutory mechanism to offer protection to trade secrets. However, after the coming into being of TRIPS Agreement mandating the protection to trade secrets there were definite attempts all over the world to offer protection to trade secrets. States now protect trade secrets either under unfair competition laws or under economic espionage law along with contract laws and common law. But unfortunately, in India, there is no statutory breakthrough in this regard. In the absence of statutory measures for the protection of trade secrets, protection is offered under common law and contract. India is lagging behind in the protection of trade secrets. [46]

Prior to 1991, the policy of the Government of India was to demand from business entrepreneurs to disclose their trade secrets and technology before undertaking any business. This was considered as a major hurdle in the industrialization process of the country since industrialized countries offer protection to trade secrets instead of compelling their disclosure. However, after 1991, with the adoption of liberalization policies and economic reforms, India changed its stand on trade secrets. Further, the coming into being of the TRIPS Agreement has mandated to offer protection to trade secrets all over the world. India is also obligated to offer protection to trade secrets but could not come across major breakthroughs in this regard. Currently, trade secrets are protected either under contract law or under the common law in India.

In response to the TRIPS Agreement, the Indian government has taken a step ahead by releasing a draft National Innovation Act, 2008 to boost research and innovation. [47] The draft Act proposed by the Department of Science and Technology, has a three pronged approach. Firstly it undertakes to encourage innovation through an innovation support system facilitated by the public, private or public-private partnership. The second approach involves evolving a National Integrated Science and Technology Plan. The third objective underlines codifying and consolidating the law of confidentiality to protect confidential information, trade secrets and innovation.

Under the draft NI Act, trade secret and confidential information are elucidated in Chapter VI titled as "Confidential and Confidential Information and Remedied and Offences". The chapter explicates on obligations of confidentiality and remedies to protect and preserve confidentiality. The obligation to maintain confidential information, under the draft statute, rests on the contractual terms and conditions and government recommendations. The remedy under the draft NI Act include preventive or mandatory injunction restraining misappropriation of confidential information [48] besides the mandatory damages. [49]

Nonetheless, the draft Act has many salubrious provisions including the provisions compelling the Ministry of Science and Technology to present an annual national integrated science and technology plan to the government, tax and fiscal incentives for innovation and the creation of designated special economic zones for innovations. The management of intellectual property and trade secrets under the NI Act is dubbed absurd by many IP practitioners in the country.

Pavin Anand, a leading advocate of IPR, criticized Chapter VI which deals with trade secrets and confidentiality, providing an exception to the offence of breaching trade secrets. It says that disclosure of the confidential information can be held to be in public interest by a court of law. The ground for criticism is the term "public interest" which in the Act is too vague. 'Public interest' is not defined anywhere in the draft which gives rise to ambiguity as to what situation would be treated as apt for disclosure of such information. [50]

Moreover, Section 12(4) is also controversial. It says that an injunction restraining uses of confidential information "may stipulate conditions for future use upon payment of a reasonable royalty for no longer than the period of time for which use could have been prohibited". The proposed exception from infringement tantamounts to introducing a compulsory license in trade secrets. To buttress this point, one may say that these provisions would make it possible for someone to steal the recipe for making Coca-Cola and to manufacture a drink using this recipe at a cheaper price, while paying a 10 percent royalty fee.

With an increasing number of "*trade secrecy*" cases coming up before the Indian courts, this promises to be a welcome development for the IP community. So far, courts have protected trade secrets under the common law "breach of confidence" doctrine. With a statutory enactment, there is bound to be more clarity and certainty in the law. However, the question that needs to be asked is: Do we want the American statutory model of trade secrecy (where trade secrecy norms are codified into a statute) or do we want to retain the flexible case law (judicial) approach that is currently endemic to the UK and India. Both approaches come with their respective *pros* and *cons*.

Manisha Singh Nair of Lex Orbis IPR firm opined that the court's application of common law approach to protect trade secrets had been inconsistent. Therefore, a statutory law on trade secrets and confidentiality within the framework of IPR is not only a good idea but a necessity.

The draft has suitably identified the performance metrics for building up an innovation-based competitive economy, but the parameters and roadmap for their execution have to be designed. [51] The draft is open to public suggestions and debate following which it shall become a final legislative enactment. The final Act should reflect the plans and measures to be undertaken in furtherance of the broad goals, the corpus to be set aside to realize them and should also identify the various authorities responsible for clearances, infrastructural support, participation and benefit sharing. It needs to be furnished with sound provisions for different sectors for execution of the goals. The enforcement mechanism and the infrastructural set up to effectuate the substantive provisions have to be stated clearly. There is a need to integrate planning by building linkages across different sectors to spur innovative activity. [52]

The concluding para of the paper focuses on the needs of the concrete statutory legislation on the protection and regulation of trade secrets. Legislation may actually create awareness among legal persons about the importance of confidential information, which they may own. This might also have a serious impact when the confidential information of a company has been misappropriated and the process of calculation of damages would start.

In this era of globalization, multinational corporations want assurances that the national law will protect their secrets in order to invest in India; and legislation in this regard may also specify how a court must conduct its proceedings because litigation in this aspect is a delicate act which might either kill the plaintiff's economic benefits derived from the secret or his prospects of competition if the information is leaked even by mistake to some other person.

Endnotes

1. Poorvi Chothani (2007), "Trade Secrets", *Manupatra Intellectual Property Reports (MIPR)*, Vol. 2, August 4, p. A-33.
2. Id.
3. Manisha Singh Nair, "India: Protection of Trade Secrets", available at:

http://www.mondaq.com/article.asp?articleid=52466.

4. Gaurav Wahie, "Evaluating Trade Secret under the IPR Paradigm: The Hypothesis of Trade Secrets as Rights Analyzed in the Pure Hohfeldian Sense", available at: www.legalserviceindia.com.
5. http://en.wikipedia.org/wiki/Trade_secret.
6. M.P. Bhatnagar (2004), "Country Report: TRIPS Implementation in India", in S.K. Verma and Raman Mittal (eds.), 'Intellectual Property Rights: A Global Vision', pp. 518-521.
7. Id.
8. http://en.wikipedia.org/wiki/Trade_secret.
9. Kunal Arora, "Trade Secrets As An Intellectual Property and its Protection", available at: www.legalserviceindia.com.
10. http://www.annauniv.edu/ipr/tradecatagories.php.
11. http://en.wikipedia.org/wiki/Trade_secret.
12. Aashit Shah (2002), "Protecting Your Trade Secrets", available at: www.indlegal.com/ProtectingYourTrade.htm.
13. Cynthia M. Gayton (2007) "Commercial Satellite Imagery: Confidential Information Knowledge Management and Trade Secret Law", *Journal of Information and Knowledge Management Systems*, 37(2), pp. 192-206.
14. S.K. Verma (2002), "Legal Protection of Trade Secrets and Confidential Information", *Journal of the Indian Law Institute*, Vol. 44, No. 3, July-September.
15. [1982] FRS 124.
16. Ibid. at p. 345.
17. *Id.*
18. Ashwani Kr. Bansal (2006), "Economic vs. Morality of IPRs: Strengthen Competition Act, 2002", *Journal of Constitutional and Parliamentary Studies,* Vol. 40, July-December, pp. 243-251.
19. See Article 40(2) of TRIPS.
20. The legislation is based on then recommendations of High Level Committee on Competition Policy and Law (Raghavan Committee, May 2000). It was passed with fanfare but government has been lack luster in furthering the same, after the Supreme Court objected to usurping the jurisdiction normally

vested in legal/judicial officers in favour of administrative services officers.

21. Section 3(1) of CA, 2002.
22. Section 3(2) of CA, 2002.
23. Section 3(5) of CA, 2002.
24. Ibid. at p. 248.
25. Id.
26. See Article 8(2) or 40 of TRIPS.
27. Akin to right to property and right of tenants not be evicted; both rights are of equal value.
28. Pollock and Mulla (2004), "Indian Contract Act and Specific Relief Acts", pp. 818-822.
29. Avtar Singh (2002), "Law of Contract", 8th edition, pp. 260-261.
30. (1885) 11 Cal 545.
31. Madonnel and Mac Pherson JJ at pp. 549-550.
32. (1967) 2 SCR 378: AIR 1967 SC 1098.
33. See the judgement of Younger, L.J. in *Attwood vs. Lamont*, (1920) 3 KB 571: (1920) All ER Rep 55.
34. Ibid. at pp. 422-423.
35. Charlesworth's (1991), "Business Law", 5th edition, p. 637.
36. Sir Robert Megarry in *Thomas Marshall vs. Gunile,* (1978) 3 All ER 193, 203.
37. P. Narayanan (2007), "Intellectual Property Law", 3rd edition, pp. 323-331.
38. N.S. Sreenivasulu and M.S. Sowmya (2007), "TRIPS Compliant Intellectual Property Regime in India: Implications of TRIPS in Modifying the Cantors and Canons of Our System', *Manupatra Intellectual Property Reports (MIPR),* Vol. 3, Part 2, October, pp. A-79-80.
39. Kamakhya Srivastava, "Indian Innovation Act: Trade Secrets and Confidentiality", available at: www.ipfrontline.com.
40. Malathi Lkshamikumaran et al. (2004), "Utility Models: Protection for Small Innovations", 46(2), *Journal of Indian Law Institute*, pp. 322-332.
41. M.D. Nair (2001), "Protection of Trade Secrets, Undisclosed Information", *The Hindu*, November 22.
42. Sunil B. Krishna (2007), "Enforcement of Intellectual Property Rights in India", *Manupatra Intellectual Property Reports*

(MIPR), Vol. 3, Part 2, October.

43. *Id.*
44. N.S. Sreenivasulu and M.S. Sowmya (2007), "TRIPS Compliant Intellectual Property Regime in India: Implications of TRIPS in Modifying the Cantors and Canons of our System", *Manupatra Intellectual Property Reports (MIPR),* Vol. 3, Part 2, October, p. 71.
45. *Supra* note 40.
46. N.S. Sreenivasulu and M.S. Sowmya (2007), "TRIPS Compliant Intellectual Property Regime in India: Implications of TRIPS in Modifying the Cantors and Canons of our System", *Manupatra Intellectual Property Reports (MIPR),* Vol. 2, Part 4, August, p. A-47.
47. *Supra* note 41.
48. Article 12, Draft National Innovation Act, 2008.
49. *Id* Article 13.
50. Peter Ollier, "Managing Intellectual Property: India Trade Secrets Law Dubbed Absurd", available at: www.tradesecretsblog.info/2008/10/managing_intellectual_property.html.
51. Tanushree Sangal (2008), "Unfurling the Proposed National Innovation Act", *Manupatra Intellectual Property Reports (MIPR)*, Vol. 3, Part 3, November, p. A-47.
52. *Id.*

6

Legal Protection to Kashmiri Shawls

Farooq Ahmad Mir, Mir Farhatul Aen and Mir Junaid Alam

The valley of Kashmir, surrounded by high range of snow clad mountains with temperature ranging from sub-zero to 20°C during two-thirds of a year, make it a most ideal place for indoor handicrafts. These handicrafts, especially shawls and carpets, have traditionally helped inhabitants of Kashmir to eke out their living. Two varieties of shawls have earned GI that has cropped up new issues of maintaining quality through certification, rewarding creativity of artisans. The issues together with the blending of Geographical Indication of Goods (Registration and Protection) Act, 1999 with other local laws have been discussed in this paper.

Intellectual property rights have proved to be an indispensable tool in different sectors of development both in developed and developing countries. The economic development of any country depends upon affluent natural resources, adequate skilled and unskilled manpower, adequate tangible assets, superior innovations, adequate intellectual property protection and proper utilisation of available resources. Intellectual property facilitates entry of new comers to a market by helping to attract venture capital and enabling production to be licensed to incumbents, allowing the customers to distinguish the products and services of one producer from those of another thereby enhancing profit margin of an organisation, developing customer loyalty and helping a particular country to increase incomes of its inhabitants. Intellectual assets such as intellectual property, knowledge of human capital, capabilities of an organisation play a key role in business improvement and economic growth.

An increasing market share and profitability of an organisation purely based on intellectual assets and capabilities may further help it in enhancing its value creation. [1] This holds true in case of geographical indications. It is widely believed that an effective protection of a GI product, by way of preventing loss of value through copying, free riding or usurpation, could facilitate an increase in the inflow of cash income to the community involved in its production. Hence, GI is often cited as a tool that has the potential to contribute to rural development, although indirectly, through reduction in poverty of the rural people. In the developed world, especially in European Union, a consumer survey revealed that they highly appreciate origin-guaranteed products and generally 40 percent of the consumers are ready to pay a 10 percent premium price for such products. [2]

Geographical Indication

The Geographical Indication of Goods (Registration and Protection) Act, 1999 (hereinafter referred to as the GI Act, 1999) is the first Act in India to provide for registration and better protection of GI to goods. The definition of GI as per the Act is: "Geographical indication in relation to goods means an indication that identifies such goods as agricultural goods, natural goods or manufactured goods as originating or manufactured in the territory of a country, or a region or locality in that territory, where a given quality, reputation or other characteristics of such goods is essentially attributable to its geographical origin and in case where such goods are manufactured goods, one of the activities of either the production or of processing or preparation of the goods concerned takes place in such territory, region or locality, as the case may be". [3]

The goods eligible for GI registration thus, may be agricultural goods, natural goods, manufactured or man-made goods, handicrafts, industrial goods and food stuff. Each of these items may belong to one or more classes of the Fourth Schedule—Classification of goods—Name of the classes of the GI Act, 1999. The goods mentioned in the Fourth Schedule provide for a speedy identification of the general content of numbered international classes. They correspond to the major content of each class and are not intended to be exhaustive in accordance with the international classification of goods. [4]

Identification of Geographical Indication

Any candidate for possible GI should be one of the items with territorial/regional or local geographical characteristics. Such geographical characteristics in items are to be the manifestation of:

- weather/climate or environment of a locality.
- soil or water induced products.
- biological attributes of the locality.
- cultural attributes of the locality.
- bio-cultural attributes of the locality.
- traditional age-old practices of the locality.
- traditional expression having local bindings.
- social/environmental/spiritual/religious beliefs or practices.

The steps for identifying a possible GI are:

1. Attributes of a GI candidate should be categorized into one or many of the above geographical characteristics. This happens to be the first step towards identification of a GI candidate.
2. The second step is the marketing and production feasibility assurance of the good(s). There are standard procedures of survey of samples for both feasibility studies and experimental marketing.
3. The third step is to consolidate an organized effort through 'any association of persons or producers or any organization or authority, established by or under law, representing interest of producers of the concerned goods'. This is required to fulfil the 'need to ensure equitable treatment to producers of the goods concerned, that consumers of such goods shall not be confused or misled

in consequence of such registration'. GI, being a collective right, identification of an association is must.

Heritage of Kashmir

The people of Kashmir rose to great heights of art, culture and economic prosperity primarily when the influences came from outside rather than from within. Kashmir is home to numerous artefacts in which shawls, woodcraft products, *papier machie* products, scarves, stoles, silk sarees, *khatambandh*, hand-knotted carpet, *sozni* embroidered crafts are worth mentioning.

Documents produced by UNCTAD, [5] WTO, [6] and UNESCO [7] have argued that crafts form a substantial part of a country's cultural heritage. Skills related to such crafts must be protected in the areas of their origin as well as their affiliation to a community. The economic argument spelt out in such documents is that when crafts are copied or exported without the consent of the crafts people, they are deprived of earnings that are rightfully theirs. Imitated crafts also give a bad name to the original crafts much to the detriment of the economic validity of original craft activities.

Kashmiri Shawl

Soft, attractive and elegant, Kashmiri shawls are the result of the weaver's skill in colouring, designing, embellishing and the use of fine fabrics. The geographical position of the Kashmir valley, the North-West region of India, is also vital in providing the finest and softest fleece, the main source of wool. After cleaning and processing, the fleece is used for creating woollen items. [8] The principal source of wool is a Central Asian species of the mountain goat (*Capra hircus*).The quality of wool usually depends on the climate and the altitude at which the animal is found. The shawl goat which lives on a higher altitude and a colder climate has the finer fleece and a thicker coat. The natural habitat of such wool-producing species is on a very high altitude, nearly above 4,500 metres

(14,750 ft.). The wool used for *pashmina* shawls made in Kashmir comes mostly from Tibet. Wool from Tibet is called *chokul.* Largely, wool is derived from two kinds of sources—the domesticated shawl goat, *capra hircus*, and from a variety of non-domesticated animals. Wool obtained from the domesticated shawl goat is called "*pashm*", widely used by Kashmiris for making the *pashmina* fabric.

Types of Shawls Accorded the GI Status

Kashmiri *Pashmina:* Kashmiri *pashmina* was filed for registration as GI under Application Number 46. The application was filed by the Craft Development Institute, Srinagar which is a registered society under the Jammu and Kashmir Societies Registration Act, 1998. [9] Application was made for the registration of *pashmina* in Class 24 of Schedule Fourth appended to GI Act, 1999. [10]

Kashmiri *pashmina* is the woven form of *pashm.* It is made in three qualities which are largely assessed on the fineness of the yarn and tension of the weave. During the weaving process the fabric is woven in three basic weaves, viz.

1. Twill or *Sade Bunai*;
2. Diamond or *Chash-m-e Bulbul Bunai;*
3. Herring Bone or *Gada Kond Bunai.*

Among the three, diamond weave is produced in large quantities and considered special to Kashmir while herring bone is made on specific orders only.

Specifications which Led to GI Protection of *Pashmina* Shawl:

1. Made of undergrowth of fleece from the mountain goat "*Capra hircus*", having a fineness of 12-16 microns,
2. Made of delicate, fine woollen yarn that is spun out of this fleece by the hand spinning process,
3. Hand woven using warp and weft yarns,
4. Woven in three weaves: (a) the twill weaves, (b) the diamond weave, and (c) the herring bone weave,
5. Have dyed/un-dyed yarn for weaving, and

6. Rendered/un-rendered with fine hand embroidery in different proportions.

***Kani* Shawl:** Application for registration of *kani* shawl as GI was made by the Craft Development Institute. It was GI Application Number 51 and falls in Class 25 of the Fourth Schedule appended to the GI Act, 1999. [11]

A *kani* shawl has a distinct antiquity. It has proved its worth and has enticed the aesthetic buds of the craft lovers since ages. The intricate patterns, splendid weaving and the exotic colours of this shawl have smitten its admirers across the globe. A small hamlet kanihama, located on the Gulmarg road, 20 kms from Srinagar has monopoly over the weaving of this age old craft. But with the passage of time, many villages in district Budgam started working on this craft.

Specifications which Led to GI Protection of *Kani* Shawl:

1. Long documented history of more than 300 years of traditional practice from Mughal Empire,
2. Wool as a material with a unique quality of fineness directly linked with the local climate and geographical conditions,
3. Highly celebrated and easily recalled product reputation directly associated with the region,
4. Distinctive process of production with unique method of articulating weaving sequence through "*taleem*" singing, [12] and
5. Localised terminology of weaves and process as a part of vernacular vocabulary.

Apart from *pashmina* and *kani* shawls, other important variety of Kashmiri shawls include *amli* or *amlikar* shawls. Entire *pashmina* and *tus* shawls are embroidered with *pashm*, silk or *zari* threads and became popular in the beginning of the nineteenth century. It is submitted that *amli* shawl involves the techniques of both the *pashmina* weaving and then *sozani* embroidery done on them. Both *pashmina* and *sozani* embroidery are registered GIs, therefore *amlikar* shawl is also a fit candidate for GI registration. Though it has been put forth before the GI Registry, has not yet been accorded the GI status.

Like other handicrafts, Kashmiri shawl is more labour and less capital intensive in nature, therefore, having scope for employment generation at a large scale. Moreover, as an export oriented sector, it is instrumental in foreign exchange earnings.

Post-GI Challenges

Protection of Traditional Knowledge (TK): India has introduced and modified its IPR laws to take care of traditional knowledge—largely biodiversity and medicinal knowledge. Crafts have not been given much consideration.

The different crafts in Kashmir are carried on professional lines by the inhabitants of particular area(s) generation after generation. These are based on skill, knowledge and experience. Some of these crafts are based on what in local language is known as *taleem.* This *taleem* is based on traditional knowledge and is a copied script which can be prepared by a trained professional and read by trained persons only. It consists of precise instructions that are to be strictly followed by the weavers during the weaving process. This coded script is in real form a weaver's technical language.

The *taleem* cannot be accorded copyright protection as it is already in public domain and no individual is entitled to claim exclusive copyright protection over it. It cannot be protected under the Designs Act as it does not satisfy the requirements of originality, novelty and no prior publication. The TK needs protection and it is to be protected under the GI Act itself. However, there are some writers who deny the suitability of GIs to protect TK on the ground that GI protection is of assistance only where the knowledge is associated with a defined geographical area.

Thus, if the knowledge is scattered, as in the case of Ayurvedic system of medicine, a GI cannot be used. [13] Further, the goods must enjoy a commercial reputation. This is because a GI merely signifies the true source of the goods, and if the source is not important to the consumer, protection by means of a GI is immaterial. It has been suggested that the representatives of interested local communities must first survey the industry and consumer groups regarding the market demands for various indigenous products because a significant market for the product is an essential criterion for the use of a GI. [14]

A large portion of TK is currently being documented, but GI cannot be used to protect all of it because knowledge underlying a GI remains in the public domain, and hence its misappropriation (qua biopiracy) is not protected against. As such, GIs should be considered as a part of a wider set of policy measures that seek to protect and reward indigenous knowledge. This raises the possibility of complementary, though overlapping, IPRs covering similar subject matter. By way of example, consider handicrafts: the technical content may be protected as a technical idea, while the cultural value as a form of expression and its distinctive characteristics through marks or indications of geographical origin. [15] Keeping in view the inadequacy of GIs for the protection of TK, some countries have devised *sui generis* systems to protect their indigenous knowledge.

There are, however writers, who argue that GIs may be better than *sui generis* system for the protection of that TK which has been in the public domain for so long that it is difficult to assign it to a specific right holder. [16]

As already pointed out that in case of handicrafts, the requisite knowledge is in the public domain and distinctiveness of the product is dependent on human factors, therefore, the product may be manufactured anywhere. However, when produced in a particular area, the product enjoys a unique reputation. In such cases, a GI affords considerable protection because consumers are willing to pay a premium in the market for products manufactured in that region, and using that region's traditional methods. GI seems to be one of the best ways of protecting such products because they cannot receive patent-like protection, nor do they derive their uniqueness from any natural factor available only in that area.

Lack of Adequate Enforcement Mechanism: Kashmiri

pashmina is renowned for its delicacy and the weave has attracted attention of the nations from all over the world since times immemorial. The use of this aesthetically crafted apparel has been the pride of oriental royalty and European Lords. Despite upheavals of times, the Kashmiri *pashmina* is being threatened by the influx of similar looking sub-standard counterfeit products sold in the name of original Kashmiri *pashmina*. It is the artisans of Kashmir who have protected and sustained this traditional practice through difficult times. The same practitioners are now up against every country and community who are not only imitating these crafts but are also claiming ownership over these practices. In these times, many main woollen production centres like Amritsar and Ludhiana have also started production of cheap jacquard woven woollen shawls copying the traditional *pashmina* designs and marketing the same as "*pashmina*".

These shawls are largely manufactured and are of inferior quality. [17] Apart from these attempts, the other countries producing machine-made *Pashmina* products are also marketing their produce with the same "Kashmiri *pashmina*" brand even though they do not meet the quality standards. [18] *Pashmina* type products are also being manufactured by China. [19] These machine-woven shawls are competing with the hand-woven Kashmiri *pashmina* and driving it out of business. This leads to the loss of traditional skills of the craftsmen and an erosion of their profits as the high cost genuine (handmade) work is forced to compete with the low quality product.

All this is being done in spite of the fact that the name "*pashmina*" is inextricably attached to the region of Kashmir. In fact, when a product has the *pashmina* tag attached to it, it signifies two things: one that the product has been made in Kashmir, and two, that the product possesses certain characteristics which are owed to the unique method of manufacture followed by the people of that region. Both these factors which make *pashmina* unique, are being misappropriated and abused, by the use of the name in loose sense by these other manufacturers. This rampant misuse of Kashmiri *pashmina* demonstrates the urgent need for an effective enforcement mechanism.

Production of Raw *Cashmere*: Of the estimated 16 MT (metric ton) annual production of raw *cashmere,* [20] China produces an estimated 12 MT per year, Mongolia just over 3 MT, Afghanistan around 1 MT, and Iran and other countries like India, Nepal, Pakistan, Tibet, Kazakhstan, Tajikistan and Kyrgyzstan produce smaller quantities. China is a major *cashmere* shawl producing country followed by Nepal, Europe and India. In respect of Kashmir, the wool is known as *pashmina* and due to inadequacy of raw material, Mongolian or Chinese *cashmere* wool is used in the manufacture of *pashmina* Shawls, therefore, Kashmir does not have monopoly in raw material segment. [21]

However, in respect of *pashmina,* Kashmir has monopoly and exclusivity to the extent of hand embroidery done on these shawls. These embroidered *pashmina* and *kani* Shawls are mainly and mostly consumed in the domestic market. It therefore, emerges that strategy for international market for *pashmina* "*cashmere*" needs to be revisited in the face of the fact of this competition which deserves recognition. [22]

Establishment of *Pashmina* De-hairing Plant: Changpas is a nomadic schedule tribe leading a pastoral life in the mountains of Ladakh and Tibet regions. Historically, they have been the principle suppliers of the soft wool to Kashmir where it underwent a number of processes before getting on to the loom. The traders in Kashmir region used to procure raw *pashmina* produced by *pashmina* goats which was distributed to middlemen in Kashmir. The middlemen had an identified network of women, scattered across the valley, who processed the raw *pashmina* on spinning wheels to make a fine thread out of the wool. The thread was then sent to manufacturing units where artisans manually weaved it to make fine quality *pashmina* products.

In 2004, *pashmina* de-hairing plant was installed in Leh. It was jointly funded by Ladakh Autonomous Hill Development Council, Union Textile Ministry and the United Nations Development Programme (UNDP). The plant is run by a cooperative group called All Changthang *Pashmina* Growers Marketing Society. The cooperative group sells the processed *pashmina* directly without involving any middlemen. The dehaired *pashm* could be supplied to wool companies such as Oswal and Raymond. The National Conference government in Jammu and Kashmir had proposed ban on the de-hairing plant, arguing that *pashm* dehaired in machines was of inferior quality. [23]

The market experts and *pashmina* dealers also blame the introduction of mechanical dehairing units for creating the *pashmina* divide. The dealers argue that the chemicals and machines have reduced the durability and quality of *pashmina.* It is also possible that the people in Ladakh may start manufacturing this craft on a large scale like China and Nepal in the name of Kashmiri *pashmina shawl*. This issue needs to be addressed at the earliest possible time. Same will be the situation if the people in Tibet start practising the same craft because Tibet is the main centre of raw material procurement for this traditional Kashmiri craft.

Reaping Benefits: Reaping of benefits by the stakeholders is yet another challenge. Main stakeholders in this craft include a chain of persons like women involved in de-hairing and spinning, clippers (*purzgar*), weaver (*vover*), washermen (*chalungar*) and dyers (*rangur*). It is their labour and skill which is being reaped by the traders. They toil hard but receive less. It is their haplessness which is being exploited by the moneyed people who have access to global market. Those with the superior bargaining powers in the supply chain appropriate a disproportionate share of the economic benefits out of GI protection.

Thus, benefits do not get percolated down to the weaker sections of the chain downstream, thereby nullifying to a large extent, the development implications of GI protection. It is essential to ensure that any benefits accruing out of the GI status of a product percolate down to the actual producers/artisans, not only because it is their legitimate right, but also to ensure the survival of the age-old products in future. The artisans have kept these handicrafts tagged with GI alive. In absence of adequate returns, new generations will prefer to move to alternate professions, which is already visible. [24]

In valley, more than 80 percent weavers/artisans work under job work arrangement with the manufacturers called "*wustkar*" who himself may or may not be a skilled weaver. The broker intermediates between the weaver/artisan and retailer/exporter and negotiates the price depending on quality, look and furnish. The payment to artisan is not instant and can stretch for months, which is a common practice. This may overtime make the traditional knowledge (TK) based products extinct. [25]

A number of middlemen actively involve themselves in various places of the supply chain. The involvement of these middlemen is responsible for the fluctuations of the prices of both the raw materials as well as the end products. Those artisans who make their own product do not find it easy to have direct access to the raw materials and believe that it is only the upper class of the *pashmina* segment that has control over the raw material. The middle men buy the raw material from the suppliers of Ladakh and supply it to the machine owners.

Therefore, there is a scarcity of raw material in the market and the local artisans requiring the raw material in smaller quantities do not find it accessible. Some people also buy raw material in bulk and dump it and sell it at higher prices to the local artisans thereby making it difficult for them to be cost effective in manufacturing their own products. Further, they cannot sell manufactured products directly to the customer because of the involvement of the middlemen. They have to sell their products to the middlemen (known as *dalaals*) at a little lower rate. The middlemen then sell it to other people higher up in the hierarchy who have the customers as the terminal point. It is these middlemen who reap the benefits for the hard work which is being done by the artisans in manufacturing these products.

The problem is compounded by the fact that the GI Act, 1999 defines registered proprietor in relation to a GI as meaning any association of persons or producer or any organisation for the time being entered in the register as the registered proprietor of the GI. The term "producer" in relation to handicrafts means any person who trades or deals in such production, exploitation, making or manufacturing, as the case may be, of the goods. [26] This definition does not distinguish between a real producer, retailer or dealer. As a result of this discrepancy, the benefits of the GI Act may not percolate down to the real producer.

Quality Control: In State of Jammu and Kashmir, there is Jammu and Kashmir Handicrafts (Quality Control) Act, 1978 (Q.C. Act) for the improvement of quality of handicrafts and every manufacturer who is registered as such shall be allotted a quality control mark which shall be stamped on a handicraft manufactured by him and the dealers who deal in such handicrafts should bear such quality control mark (Q.C. Mark). [27] It is observed that Kashmiri crafts including shawls which are put forth for sale in different retail outlets of the State are not bearing this quality control mark and consumers are seldom getting the real value of their money for lack of authenticity.

The GI Act, 1999 and the Q.C. Act may apparently appear to contradict each other but the deeper analysis of the provisions of these two enactments reveal that they are complementary to each other and should be implemented and enforced in combination with each other in order to maintain competitiveness and quality of the products in market, the former guaranteeing the origin of the goods and the later maintaining the quality. The quality standards cannot be established, met, complied and certified through law alone. It is to be supplemented by accredited testing laboratories and efforts like brand building and positioning these as high value products with historical background. It is to be further augmented with certification and labelling conforming to the international standards.

As an initiative towards building an international brand for Kashmir crafts, specially the world renowned *pashmina*-based textiles, a detailed project report (DPR) for setting up a testing and quality certification facility at Srinagar was submitted to the State government so that the due share of Kashmir *pashmina* may be reclaimed in the global market through its standardisation and hallmarking. [28] The unique project involved identifying real *pashmina* shawls and tagging them with a radio frequency identification chip (RFID). The chip would be coded with information about the manufacturing source as well as product specifications. To undertake these functions, a quality control officer has been appointed at Craft Development Institute (CDI), Srinagar.

Unfair Trade Practices Associated with the Shawl: Unethical practices are common in this craft activity and these are carried out at production level as well as marketing level and no support is available to the shawl industry to survive or negate the stiff unfair competition both at the national level as well as the international level. At production level, because of non-availability of indigenous raw material and therefore, high dependency for raw material on competitors, use of cheaper variety of yarn or finer count yarn mixed with coarser variety during spinning is resorted to. Wool blends are used in case of woollen shawls to cut input costs.

In case of *pashmina,* Mongolia wool imported by spinners outside the State and mill spun is used which has greatly affected indigenous hand spun *pashmina.* Various synthetic yarns are used to produce *pashmina* imitations and is sold under fancy names. Though "Kashmiri *pashmina*" has been brought under the GI Act, 1999 but manufacturers and traders are not using this as a certification mark. In case of "Kashmiri shawls" handloom mark or wool mark could also be used for quality certification but the traders/exporters do not utilize this certification as well.

There is a lack of direct contact between the craftsmen and the customers. Even though the market price of Kashmiri shawl is very high, the weavers as already pointed out, are literally paid peanuts for their efforts. Intermediaries try their best to impoverish the poor weavers. Apart from this, the brokers pocket enormous profits by resorting to certain malpractices. They purchase the masterpieces at rock bottom prices and later sell them in the market at skyrocketing prices to the foreigners who are ignorant of their actual price. [29] Further, there are vendors within the valley who sell machine-made shawls in the name of Kashmiri *pashmina* shawls. [30] Such practices are in no way less detrimental to the reputation of Kashmiri shawl trade.

It is pertinent to note that handicraft sector is closely linked to tourism and any tourist visiting the valley is attracted to have a look at fascinating varieties of Kashmiri handicraft and takes back with him a variety of these gifts. [31] Here, the tourism department has an important role to play. Under the Jammu and Kashmir Registration of Tourist Trade Act, 1978, [32] the tourism department is vested with powers to check the menace. The Act empowers the Commissioner of Tourism to black-list any trader involved in any malpractice. [33] For this purpose, malpractice *inter alia* includes dishonesty, cheating, touting, impersonation, charging a price higher than that displayed on the label or remuneration higher than that fixed under the Act. [34] Where the reasonability of the labelled price is in dispute, the opinion of the Director of Handicrafts, J&K shall be final. [35]

No Financial Support: Majority of artisans are from poor economic background and therefore they mainly face economic problems. A larger group of artisans do not have resources to setup their own looms. There are artisans who have setup their own looms but they still find it hard to work for their own product. They require a substantial amount to start working for their own product because they have to pay for the raw materials in cash and also they get the payment for the shawl only after completion of the shawl and that too in instalments. As a result, their money gets blocked in the market with traders thereby making it necessary to have more money with them to start working on next product because if they wait for the money of the finished product, they will be losing a number of working days. The compulsion to quickly sell the product due to poor financial conditions makes it very difficult for the artisan to take a risk of working on their own products and sell them on their own.

Skill and Dedication Trade-offs: Since the daily expenses of the modern times are very high and the income of the artisans is very low, the artisans are found to compromise on the grounds of skill. Sometimes the real skill of craft is not delivered because the artisans are not working with the same dedication since they are being underpaid. Therefore, they want to work on products which would be easier to work on.

However, the market demand for the skill is ever increasing and the present day customers demand innovative designs every time but the artisans are not ready for those masterpiece skill works for the income they are being paid. The perception built over the years for the Kashmiri *pashmina* products is getting a hammer as the customers are not ready to buy the same products every time and the artisans are not willing to show their skills for the feeble incomes.

Inaccessibility to Market for Independent Artisans: Working for their own products invites a number of problems and risks for the artisans and one of them is the inaccessibility to the market for their products. There exists a near absolute disconnect between the individual artisans and the market. The artisan who often works for the master craftsman or cooperative has no information for whom the product is produced and how it is marketed.

Artisans working for their own products have to look for the customers in the vicinity or domestic market in order to make the efforts of making their own product cost effective. Financial conditions do not allow them to collect their manufactured products and then look for customers. Hence, it is very difficult for them to get better customers for their products. The result is that they prefer to work for their master where they face no problems of market since in that case they are bothered about their labour and have no concern about the utilisation of the product being manufactured.

There are artisans who have sufficient resources on manufacturing side but are facing the problems of market. They demand the support of the government in making outlets available at tourist spots in peak tourist season on lease or on rental basis in order to make it possible for them to come in direct contact with the customers.

Time Specific Export Trade: In order to compete with the manufacturers across the globe, export orders are to be completed in a specific period of time and the traders are looking to get orders of higher magnitude. This compels the manufacturers to compromise on the grounds of quality.

Registration Problems: Majority of artisans are not registered with any group/association/government departments and they are being deprived from the privileges given by the State or Central Government to artisan groups. Artisans want the process of registration to be made easy for them. Artisans find it difficult to fulfil the formalities of registration as it is a time consuming process and it not possible for a local artisan to lose his working time in completing these formalities.

Use of New Designs: The artisans work for their masters and they provide the designs to be made to the artisans. The artisans have no say in the designs and they are only concerned about their labour after the making of the product. The designs are mostly the older ones and they make new designs only when an order is received. There is a lot of hesitation on the part of masters in experimenting new designs.

Many artisans who make their own products also lack awareness about the modern market preferences for designs and as such repeatedly use old designs.

Women Folk Abandoning Spinning: One of the big setbacks to the *pashmina* craft has been the women folk giving up on the spinning of *pashmina* . The raw material procured is given for spinning to women folk who use traditional charkhas (*yeinders*). The women folk use spinning wheel for spinning the *pashm* to obtain the yarn from the *pashm*.

Presently, spinning can fetch a woman about ` 10-15 a day and as such women find it better to do something else other than spinning. Consequently, hand spun yarn is becoming scarce which makes it easy for machine spun yarn to overtake the market.

Consignment Basis Trade of Arts Emporium: The J&K Arts Emporium was established with the purpose of giving a cushion to the traders where they would be selling their products. But now the goods are delivered to the emporium with the understanding that payment for the goods is made only once the goods are sold. The traders do not find it useful and are hence very hesitant in delivering their goods because as per the traders they cannot afford to keep their costly goods in the custody of the emporium where they themselves cannot play any role in selling those goods. There have been cases where the traders were returned the goods at the end of the season with the justification of lesser demand for the products and the goods being returned were not in a good condition and it incurred extra expenses to give them finishing again for selling them in the market.

Need for Wider Governmental Measures

The production of a variety of handicrafts in J&K means that there is a vast potential for employment in this sector. Realising this vast potential for employment, the J&K government has during the last more than twenty years undertaken large-scale training programmes for the youth in learning and creation of new designs and new products while conserving the past. This is being done with the hope that these trainees after the completion of the said courses could become craftsperson and will not only have their source of living but would utilize their efforts for modernisation and revival of traditional handicrafts particularly *kani* shawl.

Unfortunately, the dreams did not come true. Since these trainees are from poor families, they are not in a position to erect their own looms and bring warps for weaving. The result is that these boys and girls after receiving the training either go for other jobs or are sitting idle and waiting for some financial assistance. The Jammu and Kashmir Handloom Development Department is running production centres in the Kanihama area, but each is having a limited capacity of ten looms only. So they can accommodate only 60 workers. [36]

Further, in case of *kani* shawls and *pashmina* shawls, the number of training centres is very less. Besides, there are *amli* shawls also and government altogether has ignored them while establishing the training centres at the district level. There is a need for enhancement of the number of training centres in all districts in respect of all types of shawls.

Scant welfare schemes from the government had also been forcing the artisans to leave this age-old trade. [37] On papers, some health and group insurance schemes, that provide the family of the artisans a free treatment cover, were introduced. But these benefits were never passed on to them as the schemes were never implemented. [38] Majority of the artisans do not have any awareness regarding various activities affecting their craft directly or indirectly. They are unaware about the various artisan schemes.

There are artisans who had some knowledge about the various schemes being provided to them and they had applied for the schemes but the lengthy procedures and the poor response being showed to them by the authorities had made them disinterested in any such activity. They considered every such activity as sheer wastage of their time. A number of artisans had been asked to pay bribe in order to get their cases forwarded for the allotment of funds. The poor artisans found it miserable to pay bribe for the loans which they were supposed to repay with interest.

Conclusion

Kashmiri shawls are world renowned for their intricate designs and smooth weave. They involve the traditional ways in their making. They are being imitated both outside and within the country. This is evident by passing off Chinese, Nepali Woollen products and Amritsari jacquard loom woven shawls in the name of Kashmiri *pashmina*. These are going to deteriorate brand image of Kashmiri *pashmina* and *kani* shawls in the international market. These should be branded and certification marks should be applied to them so that there is a genuine demarcation between hand-made and machine-made *pashmina* shawls. The latter should have a considerable price concession as compared to the former. [39]

It is submitted that authorities should allow competition but at the same time quality should also be maintained. It should be ensured that shawls of other origins should not be sold under the Kashmiri brand name but rather under their own name such as Amritsari, Nepali, and Chinese etc. The technology can be put to use to trace origin of these Kashmiri shawls. Each GI product should mandatorily under law maintain a bar code. The bar code should enable the prospective buyer to trace the origin. It is further suggested that Jammu and Kashmir Handicrafts (Quality Control) Act, 1978 and the GI Act, 1999 should be implemented together. The result would be an improvement in quality and maintenance of international standards and prevention of unauthorised use. The handicrafts and tourism departments have a big role to play to check the unfair trade practices in trade of Kashmiri shawls. It is the high time for the government to launch massive skill development programs as also special welfare schemes for the benefit of artisan community.

The present paper is the part of the Major Research Project titled "Legal Protection of Kashmiri Handicrafts: A Case for Geographical Indications" sanctioned by UGC. The financial assistance received for undertaking this Project is acknowledged.

Endnotes

1. Akash S.B. and H.Y. Kamble (2010), "Intellectual Property Rights and Economic Development", in Talwar Sabanna (ed.), 'Intellectual Property and Economic Development with Special Reference to India', Serial Publications, New Delhi, pp. 1-3.
2. World Trade Organization (WTO), "World Trade Report 2004: Exploring the Linkage between the Domestic Policy Environment and International Trade, WTO, Geneva, p. 72.
3. Section 2(a) of the GI Act, 1999.
4. "Halsbury's Laws of India, Intellectual Property-II", 20(2), Lexis Nexis Butterworths, New Delhi, 2005, pp. 341-342.
5. www.un.org/../6_session_wipo.pdf.
6. www.wipo.int/edocs/mdocks/Lac/en/omp.
7. www.unescobkk.org/../Glossary.pdf.
8. Anamika Pathak (2008), "Pashmina", Roli Books, New Delhi, p. 27.
9. Registration Number 4332 S/2003.
10. Class 24 includes textiles and textile goods, not included in other classes; bed and table covers.
11. Class 25 deals with clothing, footwear, headgear.
12. *Taleem* refers to the language of shawl weaving. Each line of the *Taleem* is a clear representation of each stage (*raftar*) of weaving or the pick of the weaving. The increase or decrease of colours, or changes in their places necessary to produce the required flowers, is exactly represented through *Taleem.*
13. Shivani Singhal (2008), "Geographical Indications and Traditional Knowledge", *Journal of Intellectual Property Law and Practice*, Vol. 3(11), p. 733.
14. Downes (2000), "How Intellectual Property Could be a Tool to Protect Traditional Knowledge", 25, *Columbia Journal of Environmental Law*, p. 253.
15. D. Rangnekar (2004), "The Socio-economics of Geographical Indications: A Review of Empirical Evidence from Europe", UNCTAD-ICTSD Project on IPRS and Sustainable Development, Geneva, Switzerland, p. 3.
16. M. Pannizon and T. Cottier (2005), "Traditional Knowledge and

Geographical Indications: Foundations, Interests and Negotiating Positions in EU", in Petersmann (ed.), 'Developing Countries in the Doha Round: WTO Decision-making Procedures and WTO Negotiations on Trade in Agricultural Goods and Services", Robert Schuman Centre for Advanced Studies, European University Institute, Florence.

17. William Moorcroft and George Trebeck (2000), "Travels in India", Low Price Publications, p. 110.
18. For instance, due to wide publicity by the Nepal shawl industry, a misconception has now become widespread that Pashmina is originally a product of Nepal and not of Kashmir. Even a Google search reveals that there exist a number of web portals associated with the sales of pashmina that refer to it as originating from Nepal. In fact, this so-called "pashmina" industry in Nepal is a major foreign currency earner for the country. There are over a hundred "pashmina" producing units in Nepal, out of which 95 percent are in Kathmandu valley alone. Over 90 percent of Pashmina manufactured in Nepal is exported and only 10 percent is consumed locally. Nepal "pashmina" is exported to around 40 countries, mainly in Europe, America and Asia. As per media reports, of late, Nepal "pashmina" has earned a bad name in the international market. Even, polyester and woollen mixed materials are being exported in the name of pashmina recently. Nepali "pashmina" entrepreneurs say that it is also due to the breakneck competition in the international market, *The Himalayan Times*, 2007.
19. *The Scotsman,* Edinburgh, February 7, 2005, available at: http://thescotsman.
20. *Pashmina* fabric is commonly referred to as *cashmere* in the West and it comes in various forms such as, shawls, stoles, etc. *Pashmina* is the highest form of *cashmere* made in Kashmir.
21. As per J&K State Wool Board, there is a demand of around one lakh kgs. of *pashmina* per year in Kashmir region but the traders are able to procure only 15,000-20,000 kg. from Ladakh.
22. "Diagonostic Study: Kashmiri Shawls: Kani, Pashmina, Raffal", J&K Entrepreneurship Development Institute, 2011, p. 22.
23. "*Pashmina:* The Future is Warm", Down To Earth, available at: www.downtoearth.org, May 24, 2012). See also, *The Tribune,* Chandigarh, India, March 29, 2004.
24. Kanihama, a small village in Budgam District, was once known for

its *kani* shawls. But now members of the families, who have been engaged in shawl weaving for generations, are turning to other professions due to economic reasons (Firdous Hassan, "*Kani* Shawl Faces Extinction", *The Kashmir Monitor,* November 24, 2011).

25. The process of *kani* shawl weaving for instance is complex and needs high degree of skill and patience. One shawl may take more than six months for completion and for these six months an artisan supports his family on meagre resources.
26. Section 2(n) and Section 2(k) of the GI Act, 1999.
27. Section 7 of the Q.C. Act.
28. Proposal for establishment of Testing and Quality Certification Centre for promotion of "*Pashmina*" exports at Bagh Ali Mardan Khan by Craft Development Institute, Srinagar, 2009.
29. At one occasion, a customer from Bulgaria informed that she purchased a shawl from a reputed shop in Srinagar for ` 5 lakhs but its actual price was ` 50,000 only (Arshi Javid, "Wanning Art of Weaving *Kani* Shawls", *GreaterKashmir,* June 3, 2007).
30. Mukeet Akmali (2012), "Handicraft Traders Protest Malpractices by Vendors", *Greater Kashmir,* May 4, 2012.
31. "Kashmir Handicraft Boom", *Daily Exclesior,* May 29, 2011.
32. Act No. IX of 1978.
33. Section 7 (1).
34. Section 2 (g).
35. Proviso (3) to Section 2(g).
36. Farooq Ahmad Mir and Farhatul Ain (2010), "Legal Protection of Geographical Indications in Jammu and Kashmir: A Case Study of Kashmiri Handicrafts", *Journal of Intellectual Property Rights,* Vol. 15, May, p. 226.
37. Nissar Bhat (2011), "Bad Guys Crafting Fake Kashmir", *Greater Kashmir*, June 11.
38. Sajjad Bazaz (2011), "Of Endangered Community", *Greater Kashmir,* October 29.
39. This view was also expressed by Controller General Patents, Designs and Trade Marks, P.H. Kurian in one day seminar-cum-workshop on 'Geographical Indications for Awareness and Registration of GI Authorised Users' organised by Registrar of Geographical Indications held in June 2011 at J&K Entrepreneurship Development Institute, Sempora Srinagar.

7

Political Economy of TRIPS Agreement

Mohammed Saheb Hussain and Mutakyahwa Charles

"Thus we recognise that the rules and practices of intellectual property, and how they evolve, are the product of political economy. Developing countries—and in particular poor consumers of products which may be protected by IP rights—negotiate from a position of relative weakness. There is a fundamental asymmetry in relationships between developed and developing countries, based ultimately on their relative economic strength". [1]

Introduction

The agenda leading to the Agreement on Trade-Related Aspects of Intellectual Property Rights (TRIPS) and the subsequent discussion on the same was a belated agenda in the Uruguay Development Negotiations. However, no sooner as it was introduced, it captured the attention of the negotiators to the extent of developing an agreement on intellectual property rights.

This paper discusses the situation leading to the introduction and ultimately the coming into force of the TRIPS Agreement. Chief among them is the developing countries' expectations of economic gains which came as a lobbying factor to secure their acceptance, which had not been realized till date.

The paper further discusses the source of discontent on part of developing countries towards the limitations set under Article 3 for strict observance of IPRs in relation to the unenthusiastic developed countries' measures on technology transfer to developing countries. Importantly, this part creates a basis for the political economy of the TRIPS Agreement.

Since complying with the TRIPs Agreement, though with reservations, has not heeded to developing countries' expectations of establishing technological base for economic advancement, this paper chats out recommendations for a better future.

Genesis of TRIPS Agenda to the Uruguay Round Negotiations and Reaction from the Developing Countries

The Uruguay Round of multilateral trade negotiations which was launched at Punta del Este, Uruguay in 1986,.took place in the background of the claim by American industries that they were suffering from heavy losses from the absence of adequate protection of their intellectual property rights abroad. The industries in such sectors as computer software and microelectronics, entertainment, chemicals, pharmaceuticals, and biotechnology, had become concerned about the loss of commercial opportunities abroad and wanted notable changes.

In 1987, a survey [2] by the United States International Trade Commission (USITC) confirmed, on the basis of public hearings held and questionnaires administered, that firms in the United States were losing some 50 billion dollars, owing to lack of protection abroad of the intellectual property. [3] In this regard, US found the idea of taking up the issue of protection of intellectual property rights (IPRs), within the General Agreement on Tariffs and Trade (GATT) framework—it being more useful and practical. [4]

There was consequently a general feeling, [5] among the developing countries, that the concern with the protection of IPRs was being expressed by the American government on behalf of the industries. Therefore, all such efforts towards the establishment of an effective regime for the protection of IPRs were aimed at furthering the interest of the American and Western industries and not those of the developing countries. [6]

This feeling was not without reasons. As observed, the US private sector, in particular the pharmaceutical industry, was already leading in the effort to establish a trade-based approach. Thus, their argument was to the effect that: 'We must also work to get more broad-based economic organizations, such as the OECD and the GATT, to develop intellectual property rules, because intellectual property protection was essential for the continued development of international trade and investment'. [7]

As already presented before, the developing countries were vehemently opposed to the idea of including intellectual property issues in the discussion under the multilateral trade negotiations with such strong industry influence and specific agenda. The developed countries, considered intellectual property a matter that exclusively belonged within the competence of the World Intellectual Property Organization (WIPO).

However, in 1970s, the developing countries had already initiated their own initiatives to revise the Paris Convention on the Protection of Industrial Property. [8] The developing countries were worried on the link that would be established between the TRIPS Agreement under GATT Forum and the existing intellectual property rights conventions such as the Berne Conventions for the Protection of Literary and Artistic Works, [9] the Rome Convention for the Protection of Performers, Producers and Broadcasting Organizations, [10] and the Treaty on Intellectual Property in Respect of Integrated Circuits. [11]

Not only the developing countries were unenthusiastic in linking intellectual property protection with the GATT Forum but even the European Countries too were.

US, on the other hand, was also unhappy with the protective measures taken under WIPO for the protection of intellectual property rights. This was mainly for the fact that WIPO lacked the enforcement mechanism, thus US referred to it as an administrative body. This was because imitations were being carried out with impunity much to the detriment of industrialized countries.

As such, US pioneered the inclusion of the TRIPS Agreement in the Uruguay Negotiations. It was also contended that the lack of adequate protection and enforcement of IPRs in the developing countries had led to serious distortions and increasing damage to world trade. [12]

For example, it was estimated by the US International Trade Commission that the percentage of international trade involving IPRs had grown dramatically, and had more than doubled since the Second World War. It was also claimed that the US had lost between US$ 43 to US$ 61 billion in 1986 due to foreign counterfeiting and product piracy. [13]

Stressing the above point home, Adede [14] opined: Counterfeiting and copyrights piracy increased in the 1980s because of the desire of the developing countries to catch up in the industrialization process and to have access to printed educational material which they needed in that context. The situation was accelerated by the following factors: the advent of copy-prone electronic-based technologies and products; the growing competitiveness of newly industrialized developing countries in the manufacturing sector; the increasing globalization of the market-place; and the growing perception of intellectual property by the enterprises of the developed countries as a strategic asset. Thus, there was tension between the quest for tighter protection of IPRs for the promotion of creativity being pursued by the industrialized owners of the property and the policy of maximization of social welfare arising from an impeded diffusion of that creativity, being pursued by the developing countries, through more relaxed protection of IPRs.

The first move by the US to introduce TRIPS in the Uruguay Negotiations was during the Tokyo Round [15] on the Anti-Counterfeit Code (ACC). However, the said Anti-Counterfeit Code was not adopted at that time. Thus, when the GATT Ministerial Conference was convened in Punta del Este, Uruguay [16] to discuss the mandate for the next round of negotiations, with a view also of adopting the said Anti-

Counterfeit Code, US mounted pressure to include IPRs beyond the question of counterfeiting and piracy, among the issues of discussion under the Uruguay Round of Multilateral Trade Negotiations.

Thus, because the meeting was primarily on trade-related economic measures, the Trade Ministers at Punta del Este coined the IPR agenda in the same expression to read as "Trade-related Aspects of Intellectual Property Rights—TRIPS" and included it in the agenda of the Uruguay Round.

Various intellectual property experts have been concerned with the US abruptly and seriously fighting for inclusion of the TRIPS in the GATT Forum. According to them, the fact is that the fight for TRIPS aimed at enhancing technological transfer to developing countries is far fetched, if at all.

Frederick Abbott [17] for instance is of the view that "the decision by the United States government to use its economic power as a weapon against developing countries fighting a battle against a deadly plague plausibly leads developing country government officials and common citizens to question the economic, social and political foundation of the TRIPS Agreement". [18] However, the inclusion of the TRIPS agenda in the Uruguay Round, Adede puts it, came as "a political compromise whose legal foundation was yet to be clarified". [19] It is because the TRIPS agenda on the table was so trivial and featured as a footnote on the list of the proposed agenda for further discussion.

According to the Ministerial Declaration of [20] September 20, 1986, the mandate of the Uruguay Round on Trade Negotiations, included the following issues for discussion: tariffs, non-tariff measures, tropical products, natural resource-based products, textile and clothing, agriculture, subsidies and countervailing measures, safeguards, GATT articles, MTN (Multilateral Trade Negotiations) agreements and arrangements, dispute settlement, trade-related investment measures, and trade-related aspects of intellectual property rights including trade in counterfeit goods.

The negotiating objectives [21] aimed at reducing the distortions and impediments to international trade. Further, it also considered the need to promote effective and adequate protection of intellectual property rights, so that enforcement measures and procedures do not themselves become barriers to legitimate trade.

It was an express term of the negotiations that the same would aim at developing a multilateral framework of principles, rules and disciplines dealing with international trade in counterfeit goods, taking into account work already undertaken in the GATT. These negotiations would be without prejudice to other complementary initiatives that may be taken in the World Intellectual Property Organization and elsewhere to deal with these matters. [22]

To convince the opposing forces—the developing countries in particular—the US [23] raised an argument that: under the GATT Forum, the developing countries may have opportunities to use a bargaining power and secure trade-offs in negotiating favourable terms on issues such as textiles and clothing, agriculture, tropical products and safeguards as part of the package that include the IPRs.

In this way, the presentation of the above opportunities seemingly indicated tangible gains for the developing countries, if they accept the proposed package deal, the latter were convinced and ultimately accepted the proposal. This was because of their weighing the positiveness and negativeness of their continued rejection of the IPR inclusion in the GATT Forum. So, the developing countries accepted the inclusion of the IPR issues in the GATT Forum as a *quid pro quo* to transfer of technology and developmental policies.

In 1990s, serious discussions on the inclusion of TRIPS into the GATT commenced, leading to the TRIPS Agreement but after taking into consideration the shadow proposal prepared and presented by fourteen developing countries.

Thus, in 1993, the TRIPS Agreement was adopted and came into force in 1994. The developing countries had three reasons in support of the TRIPS. One was the expectations of gains in other trade areas by way of trade-offs; protection against unilateralism envisaged by US under Section 301; possibilities for benefits from improved market access in general and from market-based policies for attracting foreign investments.

In short, as presented above, the protection of intellectual property rights under the GATT, [24] faced a number of problems, mainly because the US Congress rejected the charter proposal for the establishment of the International Trade Organisation (ITO) and as a counter measure, by devising legal measures [25] in her domestic legislation, the enforcement of which would render the provisions of GATT absolutely obsolete. [26]

As such, desirous of reducing distortions to international trade and promoting adequate and effective protection of intellectual property rights so that there should not be any barriers to international trade, members designed and brought into effect an international Agreement on Trade-related Aspects of Intellectual Property Rights, i.e. the TRIPS.

The main objective [27] of the TRIPS was, among others, the protection and enforcement of the intellectual property rights that should necessarily contribute to the promotion of technological innovation and transfer and dissemination of technology, to the mutual advantage of producers and users of technological knowledge and in a manner conducive to social and economic welfare, and to the balance of rights and obligations.

TRIPs Agreement came into force therefore, specifically [28] for creating better environment where new rules and discipline concerning the basic principles of GATT 1994 and other international intellectual property agreements or conventions would take roots in applicability.

Hammering the point home, Article 2 of the TRIPS states, *inter alia*, that the implementation of the TRIPS Agreement must comply with the existing obligations upon members under the provisions in the Paris, Berne and Rome Conventions and on the Treaty on Intellectual Property Related to Integrated Circuit.

The Articles 1 through 12 cited for compliance under the Paris Convention relate to patents, industrial design, trade and service marks, national treatment and global administrative organ of patents in general. Article 19 of the Paris Convention gives powers to Member States to enact separate laws for patents provided that the same does not contravene with the Convention.

TRIPS incorporated cognisance of the fact that least developed [29] countries needed special attention by allowing some flexibility in their domestic legislations so that they could create a sound and viable technological base. In this regard, least developed countries were to put the Agreement into effect 15 years after the commencement date. This was intended so as to give room for creating a sound and viable technological base for the developing countries.

TRIPS Agreement Coverage

Under the TRIPS, a number of intellectual property rights are being protected. Section 1 of the Agreement provides for the protection of the copyright and related rights. In this regard, however, the protection of the copyrights was in tandem [30] with Articles 1 through 21 of the Berne Convention [31] and the Appendix thereto. The Berne Convention provides for protection of copyright and related rights and rental rights.

Trademark, as a specific component of intellectual property rights, is also covered under the TRIPS. [32] In this regard, any sign or any combination of signs, capable of distinguishing the goods or services of one undertaking from those of other undertakings, is capable of constituting a trademark.

TRIPS also provides for the geographical indications, [33] for the purpose of identifying the originality of goods from the territory of a member or a region or locality in that territory, where a given quality, reputation or characteristic of the good is essentially attributable to its geographical origin.

In this regard, members are obliged to provide the legal means for interested parties to prevent the use of any means in the designation or presentation of a good that indicates or suggests that the good in question originates in a geographical area other than the true place of origin in a manner which misleads the public as to the geographical origin of the good; or any use which constitutes an act of unfair competition within the meaning of Article 10*bis* of the Paris Convention. [34]

Other types of intellectual property rights covered by the TRIPS Agreement include the industrial designs, patents layout designs (topographies) of integrated circuits, undisclosed information and control of anti-competitive practices.

Economic Implications of TRIPS Application to Developing Countries

The effect of TRIPS on technology diffusion, according to Linda, [35] holds significant implication for economic growth. As argued herein above, the justification for intellectual property rights generally relates to the need to protect the incentive to innovate weighed against the social cost of allowing monopoly profits to accrue and the loss to society of not having free access to the protected goods.

According to the empirical study made by Kumar, [36] the intellectual property rights regime is likely to affect economic growth indirectly by encouraging the innovative activity that in turn is the source of total factor productivity improvements. The IPR regime therefore could also affect the inflows of FDI, technology transfer and trade that might impinge on economic growth. The relationship between IPR and development could be subject to the causality problem as developed countries are likely to have a stronger IPR regime than poorer ones. In this regard, the study suggests, that the relationship between IPR protection and development are non-linear. [37]

In other words, this means that patent protection for

instance, will tend to decline in strength as economies move beyond the poorest stage into a middle-income stage. The reasons advanced to this effect, has always been that middle income countries, have greater abilities to imitate new technologies. That is why Falvey says that providing stronger IPR protection to foreign firms could cripple domestic industry of emerging states or economies previously relying on pirated technologies.

The preference of imitation over innovation has got significant acceptance in China which of late, is referred to as the world's factory. Kevin Zheng Zhou, [38] a Chinese scholar and professor at the School of Business University of Hong Kong says that: Innovation, however, is not the only choice for a product introduction. Because there can be only one pioneer in any product market, imitation remains a viable and more common strategy than innovation. Imitation can take different degrees, from pure clones, which represent "me-too" products to creative imitation, which takes an existing product and improves upon it. And product development accordingly can take a mixed form between two extremes of a continuum from brand new innovation to pure imitation.

Principally, Kevin Zheng [39] encourages the developing and least developed countries to broaden their technological base through imitation. This is due to the fact that, according to Kevin Zheng, pure innovation takes effect after the country has heavily invested in research and development (R&D) strategies, which bearing in mind the economic position of a country in question, may prove futile.

As such, basing on the findings of other scholars, like Lieberman and Schnaars, [40] Kelvin Zheng further presents that unlike imitators, innovators have the potential to create markets, shape consumer preference, and even change consumer's basic behaviour. He says that a consumer's behaviour can change fundamentally to the effect that the consumer cannot imagine living any other way.

But what drives Kevin Zheng [41] to opt for imitation as

the best strategy for technology advancement in the developing countries, is found in his conclusion on this argument saying that: An imitation strategy may also lead to better new product performance. Imitation costs often are much lower than innovation costs because an imitator, for example, need not spend as many resources on research; the existing products already provide the imitator with information for its product development

As such, *one- size-fits-all* [42] concepts advocated by the TRIPS under Articles 3 [43] and 4 [44] has received significant discontentment specifically from developing and least developed countries.

Their argument has been founded in Article 7 of TRIPS that defines the objectives of the TRIPS Agreement. It clearly establishes that the protection and enforcement of intellectual property rights do not exist in a vacuum. They are supposed to benefit the society as a whole and do not aim at the mere protection of private rights.

During the Doha Ministerial Conference, [45] the developing and least developed countries, commonly known as Group of 14 [46] were of considered argument that TRIPS cannot place limits (in terms of Article 3 of the TRIPS) on health priorities. The best example advanced by developed countries in favour of access to medicines by developing countries was compulsory licensing of drugs, (like anti-retroviral drugs for instance) by developing and least developed countries. The argument by the developing countries mainly was that while the need for drugs was of utmost urgency, there existed none of their own pharmaceutical industries and necessary infrastructures, thus rendering the TRIPS provisions on compulsory licensing nugatory.

According to Servaas Van Thiel, [47] the 2000 study commissioned by WIPO also established that access to affordable drugs in developing countries, involves numerous and complex issues, including healthcare infrastructure, international pricing mechanisms, financing and debt, tariffs and patents. The study also found out that patent protection, though an important issue that can be addressed in the context of public health and AIDS crisis cannot possibly be an important factor impeding access to AIDS medicines in sub-Saharan Africa. To cement the finding, the study cited the TRIPS Agreement which extended the compliance to it by developing countries up to 2016.

It can be noted that even the developed countries are still divided on the issue of compulsory licensing. To some, it is seen as a set back to economic progress. Justine Charles Ward [48] says that: Mandatory licensing need not be economically destructive, but if and only if carried out in a controlled manner. However, there is no free lunch here either—the royalty fees generated by the mandatory licensing scheme must be sufficient to offset the planned-for level of revenue (for cost repayment and for return to the investor) which is being set aside in favour of anticipated revenues from the mandatory licensee. The cost to the consumer may indeed be reduced, but if and only if the total costs to the generic licensee are sufficiently low to generate an adequate profit for a non-innovator/licensee while at the same time paying the necessary royalty to the pioneer innovator who did have such expenses.

Justin's argument above means that immediate mandatory licensing does not give an opportunity to the patent holder to work on the patent for profit. Thus, due regard should be given to matters of genuine emergency and for a limited time. Failure to this, may result in the damage to subsequent investor's confidence and other innovation destroying results.

By necessary implication, the motive by developing and least developed countries in objecting to the TRIPS "one-size-fits-all" approach, was quite different from economic gain but society welfare in general.

According to Chon, the developed countries discontent towards compulsory licensing in respect of drugs for instance, during the Doha Ministerial Conference, was based on further argument that the language referencing development to TRIPS is not mandatory but rather hortatory [49] and is placed within parts of the treaty that are not in the main treaty body.

However, this position has received a rebuttal from developed countries, advancing Articles 31(1) and (2) of the Vienna Convention [50] which provides for interpretation of treaties in good faith according to ordinary meaning given to the terms of the treaty in their context and in the light of its object and purpose.

The WTO was developed as the intellectual property law enforcer and the WIPO remained as the administrative body for the major multilateral intellectual property institutions such as the Paris Convention for the Protection of Industrial Property and the Berne Convention for the Protection of Literary and Artistic Works. But during the Doha negotiations, the developing countries remained vocal, calling for WIPO to change its outlook from high protectionism to flexibility. [51]

In this regard, scholars [52] have established that WIPO had been historically more receptive to producers than to users' interests. This was mainly due to the fact that WIPO's operating budget is largely derived from Patent Cooperation Treaty filing fees, most of which come from applications filed by developed country members.

In order to clear its image and make members have faith in WTO and WIPO, Article 68 of the TRIPS set out the framework in which WIPO and TRIPS Council would work for the interests of all members and an agreement to this effect was executed. [53]

In this regard, the extension of time in applying TRIPS provisions given to least developed countries, under Article 66 [54] of TRIPS, remained meaningless to these countries, including Tanzania, mainly because there was no apparent efforts to let them access necessary technology.

That is why, in recent years, heeding to the concerns by the developing world, the World Health Organization (WHO) has tried to reshape the focus of the TRIPS equation of minimum standards, so that the intended innovative purpose of TRIPS can be achieved. Thus, the WHO states:

The need is greater than ever for innovation in healthcare products, including medicines, pharmaceuticals, diagnostics, and medical devices.

The above WHO's finding of 2003 was in support of the former UN Secretary General's [55] observation in 2001 when he said that:

Intellectual property protection is key to bringing forward new medicines, vaccines and diagnostics urgently needed for the health of the world's poorest people.

For instance, Article 66(2) urges developed countries to provide incentives to enterprises and institutions in their countries as a way of promoting and encouraging technology transfer to least-developed country Members. This would enable the latter to create a sound and viable technological base. But the Convention sets no framework on how this can be achieved and thus remains illusory to developing countries. Besides developing and least developed countries, various scholars and academicians have argued extensively as to whether the TRIPS was designed to encourage technology transfer (leading to economic growth) to these countries.

Developing Countries' Expectations

A major development of potentially great significance took place at the General Assembly of the World Intellectual Property Organisation (WIPO), held in Geneva from September 27 to October 5, 2004. This was the presentation of a proposal [56] by several developing countries to establish a "Development Agenda" for WIPO.

The proposal [57] presented by developing countries was divided into two parts. Part I entitled "Intellectual Property and International Trade", dealt mainly with the norms and principles to be applied to trade in counterfeit and pirated goods. It provided for the establishment of certain procedures and remedies to discourage such trade, while trying to ensure an unimpeded flow of trade in legitimate goods. Part II, entitled "Standards and Principles Concerning the Availability,

Scope and Use of Intellectual Property Rights", set out the objectives and principles underlying an agreement on such standards and specified the basic standards relating to different categories of IPRs, i.e. patents, marks, industrial designs, geographical indications, copyrights and neighbouring rights and integrated circuit layout designs.

By separating the proposed text of a TRIPS agreement into two parts, as proposed by Adede, the developing countries wanted, in the first instance, to signal their determination to emphasize the part dealing with trade in counterfeit goods while minimizing the part relating to substantive standards on IPRs.

Secondly, with regard to the latter part, the developing countries wanted to highlight the importance of the public policy objectives underlying national IPR systems, the necessity of recognizing those objectives at the international level and the need to specify some basic principles which could subsequently elucidate the application of any standards established in the TRIPS Agreement.

Thirdly, they insisted on the need to respect and safeguard national legal systems and traditions on IPRs, in view of the diverse needs and levels of development of States participating in the IPR negotiations.

As such, the following are the specific issues and the advanced proposal by developing countries, as Martin Khor [58] summarises them, if at all, the International Community was committed to fully and adequately address development challenges [59] on an equitable basis.

Development Dimensions and Agriculture

It was a factual issue that agriculture had become the most important and controversial issue. Agriculture is particularly important for developing countries, because around 75 percent of the population in developing countries lives in rural areas, and the vast majority is dependent on agriculture for their livelihoods. The first proposal in Qatar, in 2001, called for the end agreement to commit substantial improvements in market access; reductions (and ultimate elimination) of all forms of export subsidies; and substantial reductions in trade-distorting support.

Before the Uruguay Round (1986-1994), agriculture was largely exempt from multilateral trade disciplines. The GATT of 1994, the multilateral trade framework that prevailed until the creation of the WTO, had rules for agricultural trade, but at the same time it contained many loopholes that allowed contracting parties to use non-tariff barriers and subsidies.

Over the years, agricultural trade became more and more distorted with OECD countries, for example, increasingly making use of subsidies to promote their agricultural sectors. In the Uruguay Round, agriculture was brought back to the multilateral trading system, with new rules and commitments in the areas of market access (trade restrictions affecting imports), domestic subsidies and export subsidies. The short-term results of these disciplines in terms of effective liberalization of agricultural trade was limited, and paid dearly to the developing countries.

Agriculture is at the heart of realizing the development promise of the Doha Development Round. With more than half of the population in developing countries residing in rural areas and much higher poverty in rural than in urban areas, growth in agriculture could have a disproportionate effect on reducing poverty.

Thus, the Doha Round proposed for the elimination of export subsidies, significant cuts in domestic support and in tariffs (both in developed and in developing countries). But the developing countries came up with their own proposal on agriculture which in effect was organized around three pillars: market access, export subsidies and domestic support.

The developing countries are in accord [60] with the fact that technological innovation, science and creative activity in general are rightly recognized as important sources of material progress and welfare. However, despite the important scientific and technological advances and promises of the 20th and early 21st centuries in many areas, the developing countries noted [61] that a significant "knowledge gap", as well as a "digital divide", continue to separate the wealthy nations from the poor. In this context, the impact of intellectual property has been widely debated in past years.

As such, the developing and least developed countries proposed to WIPO that intellectual property protection is intended as an instrument to promote technological innovation, as well as the transfer and dissemination of technology. Intellectual property protection cannot be seen as an end in itself, nor can the harmonization of intellectual property laws leading to higher protection standards in all countries, irrespective of their levels of development.

Therefore, the developing countries further stated that the role of intellectual property and its impact on development must be carefully assessed on a case-by-case basis. Intellectual property protection is a policy instrument, the operation of which may, in actual practice, produce benefits as well as costs, which may vary in accordance with a country's level of development. On this alone, the developing countries proposed further that a Programme of Action is needed to ensure that, in all countries, the costs do not outweigh the benefits of IP protection.

Intellectual Property Norm-Setting

Martin Khor [62] says that WIPO is currently engaged in norm-setting activities in various technical committees. Some of these activities would have developing countries agree to IP protection standards that largely exceed existing obligations under the WTO's TRIPS Agreement, while these countries are still struggling with the costly process of implementing TRIPS itself.

Khor argues further that the current discussions on a draft Substantive Patent Law Treaty (SPLT) in the Standing Committee on the Law of Patents is of particular concern. The proposed Treaty would considerably raise patent protection standards, creating new obligations that developing countries would hardly be able to implement.

As such, in the course of discussions, developing countries have proposed amendments to improve the draft Substantive Patent Law Treaty (SPLT) by making it more responsive to public interest concerns and the specific development needs of the developing countries.

That is why, during the Doha Ministerial Conference, the developing and least developed countries advanced arguments that TRIPS cannot place limits (in terms of Article 3 of the TRIPS) on health priorities for instance. The best example advanced by developed countries in favour of access to medicines by developing countries was compulsory licensing of drugs, (like antiretroviral drugs for instance) by developing and least developed countries. The argument by the developing countries mainly was that while the need for drugs was of utmost urgency, there existed none of their own pharmaceutical industries and necessary infrastructures, thus rendering the TRIPS provisions on compulsory licensing nugatory.

Their argument went further to the effect that the provisions of any treaties in this field must be balanced and clearly take on board the interests of consumers and the public at large. It is important to safeguard the exceptions and limitations existing in the domestic laws of Member States. In other words, the developing countries were seeing the developed countries as furthering the IPR proposal for their own economic benefit and at the detriment of the developing countries. To hammer this point home, the Commission Report [63] on intellectual property rights, makes a finding that:

The process of implementing TRIPS has not resulted in a shrinking of the gap that divides these two sides; rather it has helped to reinforce the views already held. Those in favour of more IPRs and the creation of a "level playing field" hail TRIPS as a useful tool with which to achieve their objectives.

On the other hand, those who believe that IPRs are bad for developing countries believe that the economic playing field was uneven before TRIPS and that its introduction has reinforced the inequality. So firmly and sincerely held are these views that at times it has appeared that neither side has been prepared to listen to the other. Persuasion is out, compulsion is in.

Finally, developing countries proposed that the potential development implications of several of the provisions of the proposed Treaty on the Protection of Broadcasting Organizations that the Standing Committee on Copyright and Related Rights is currently discussing should be examined taking into consideration the interests of consumers and of the public at large.

Transfer of Technology

According to Articles 7 and 8 of the TRIPS Agreement, the transfer of technology has been identified as an objective that intellectual property protection should be supportive of and not run counter to. Yet, many of the developing countries and LDCs have taken up higher IP obligations in recent years simply due to the lack of necessary infrastructure and institutional capacity to absorb such technology.

Even in developing countries that may have a degree of absorptive technological capacity, higher standards of intellectual property protection have failed to foster the transfer of technology through foreign direct investment and licensing. In effect, corrective measures are needed to address the inability of existing IP agreements and treaties to promote a real transfer of technology to developing countries and LDCs.

As such, the developing countries proposed for, a new subsidiary body within WIPO which could be established to look at what measures within the IP system could be undertaken to ensure an effective transfer of technology to developing countries, similarly to what has already been done in other fora such as the WTO and the UNCTAD.

Among these measures, the developing countries noted with particular interest the idea of establishing an international regime that would promote access by the developing countries to the results of publicly funded research in the developed countries. Such a regime could take the form of a Treaty on Access to Knowledge and Technology. Thus, they proposed that it is also important that clear provisions on transfer of technology be included in the treaties currently under negotiation in WIPO.

Intellectual Property Enforcement

Intellectual property enforcement should also be approached in the context of broader societal interests and development-related concerns, in accordance with Article 7 of TRIPS. The rights of countries to implement their international obligations in accordance with their own legal systems and practice, as clearly foreseen by Article 1(1) of TRIPS, should be safeguarded.

According to Khor, [64] in setting up the Advisory Committee on Enforcement (ACE) 2002, the WIPO General Assembly clearly rejected a "TRIPS-plus" approach to enforcement matters, by deliberately deciding to exclude all norm-setting activities from the Committee's mandate. In undertaking any future work under its mandate, the ACE should be guided by a balanced approach to intellectual property enforcement. The ACE cannot approach the issue of enforcement exclusively from the perspective of right holders, nor have its discussions focus narrowly on curbing the infringement of IP rights. Such discussions are important, but the ACE must also give consideration to how best to ensure the enforcement of all TRIPS-related provisions, including those that would impute obligations to right holders as well.

In this regard, the developing countries proposed that particular attention should be paid to the need to ensure that enforcement procedures are fair and equitable and do not lend themselves to abusive practices by right holders that may unduly restrain legitimate competition. In this regard, they noted that Article 8 of TRIPS states that corrective measures may be necessary to curb practices that may adversely affect trade and the international transfer of technology. One should also bear in mind the related provision of Article 40 of TRIPS, which addresses anti-competitive practices in contractual licenses. All of these provisions of the TRIPS Agreement should be adequately brought into WIPO's framework for effective implementation.

Technical Cooperation and Assistance

In this proposal, the developing countries noted with appreciation that WIPO is the main multilateral provider of technical assistance in the field of intellectual property. By virtue of the 1995 agreement with the WTO, it plays an important role in providing developing countries with technical assistance to implement the TRIPS agreement. Further, that as a United Nations specialized agency, WIPO has an obligation to ensure that its technical cooperation activities are geared towards implementing all relevant UN development objectives, which are not limited to economic development alone.

Thus proposed that these activities should also be fully consistent with the requirements of UN operational activities in this field—they must be, in particular, neutral, impartial and demand-driven.

Furthermore, programs for technical cooperation in IP related matters should be considerably expanded and qualitatively improved. This is important to ensure that in all countries the costs of IP protection do not outweigh the benefits thereof. In this regard, national regimes set up to implement international obligations should be administratively sustainable and not overburden scarce national resources that may be more productively employed in other areas. Moreover, technical cooperation should contribute to ensuring that the social costs of IP protection are kept at a minimum.

The proposal went further to the effect that WIPO's legislative assistance should ensure that national laws on intellectual property are tailored to meet each country's level of development and are fully responsive to the specific needs and problems of individual societies. Thus, they finally proposed that it must be directed towards assisting developing countries to make full use of the flexibilities in existing intellectual property agreements, in particular to promote important public policy objectives.

TRIPS Agreement and Public Health

Article 8 of the TRIPS Agreement, confers right to the member states to adopt measures for public health and nutrition, but the said measures must be in compliance with the TRIPS provision.

The compliance referred to under Article 8 of TRIPS for strict observance by every member state, is well elucidated under Article 3 of TRIPS which states that in observing the Agreement, every member state shall accord treatment to foreigners no less than it is favourable to its own nationals. In effect, this came to be the most problematic part of implementation of the TRIPS Agreement, especially when it came to public health issues. The strict compliance under Article 3 of TRIPS was totally eroding its main objective as stipulated under Article 7.

But as elaborated above, this has been a source of discontent, especially, during the Doha Ministerial Conference where, the developing and least developed countries were of considered argument that TRIPS cannot place limits (in terms of Article 3 of the TRIPS) on health priorities.

The efforts by developing countries yielded results on November 14, 2001, when the Doha Ministerial Conference issues a Declaration which in effect recognized all concerns raised by the developing and least developed countries on matters of public health. For instance, Clause No. 4 of the said

Declaration sates that:

We agree that the TRIPS Agreement does not and should not prevent Members from taking measures to protect public health. Accordingly, while reiterating our commitment to the TRIPS Agreement, we affirm that the Agreement can and should be interpreted and implemented in a manner supportive of WTO Members' right to protect public health and, in particular, to promote access to medicines for all.

Conclusion

Based on the foregoing, it is true that the TRIPS Agreement was so designed as a yardstick for all matters pertaining to the protection and promotion of intellectual property matters globally. Although it passed through a number of rounds or negotiations, the parties to the said negotiations had no consensus *ad idem* during the discussions.

Principally, each party was suspecting the other. While the developed countries found the TRIPS a founded security for their innovations, industrial products and markets, the developing countries and least developed countries together took the question of intellectual property as a threat to their technological advancements.

It was after the introduction of the favourable packages for developing and least developed countries, especially market access to their agricultural inputs that the latter came to give in. It is very unfortunate that the proposed favours for the developed and least developed countries, as Adede puts, have not been realised till date.

Recommendations

The following recommendations are made by the authors after going through this research paper as discussed below.

Call for Reform of TRIPS to Bring a Practically Balanced Application: The Uruguay Round, as a matter of history, was undoubtedly the most far reaching of all multilateral trade negotiations and agreements. However, the voice of discontent from the developing countries, on the benefit to be derived from the consequential agreements, has been louder than ever.

Various scholars still insist that the all arrangement for TRIPS, as abruptly as it was introduced into the Round agendas, hold developing countries to lose which strongly signals for reforms, in order to make it beneficial for the developing countries.

For instance, when assessing the Uruguay Round, Wayne [65] opines: When viewed from the standpoint of its list of objectives, some hold the view that the Uruguay Round was an unqualified success. Others hold the view that it was successful from the point of view of developed countries and that the developing countries were left to ponder the fruits of the trade agreement.

The conclusions on intellectual property rights made during the negotiations clearly indicated that the developing countries are bound to lose. The new standards that guarantee royalties to holders of patents and copyrights require more payments to the developed world by developing countries. This is also in a context where the automatic patenting of some products has been subject to strict limits by the Uruguay Round.

The above argument still holds water, notwithstanding the fact that the net outcome on the intellectual property product depends heavily on the type of technology appropriated by developing countries and the use to which they are put. The technological base appropriated by developing countries from developed countries is very minimal if any at all.

Compulsory Transfer of Technology from Developed to Developing Countries: The developing countries, under Articles 65 and 66 of the TRIPS, were given a grace period of suspending the enforcement of the Agreement, until they created a sound technological base.

Article 66(2) of the TRIPS, obliges developed countries to encourage their respective enterprises and institutions to transfer technology to the developing countries with a view to enhancing technological base to the latter. Reports on the implementation of Article 66(2) must be submitted annually by the respective developed countries to TRIPS Council, since its commencement in 1999.

The available findings, however, indicate that there hasn't been mandatory technology transfer as per Article 66(2), but on the basis of *quid pro quo* offers—that is, technology transfer in exchange for other concessions—in other treaty negotiations.

The big problem associated with this lackadaisical approach on part of developed countries in transferring technology to developing countries, is the lack of a clear definition of what constitutes developed countries in the TRIPS Agreement.

Most of the scholars have been defining developed countries basing on the classifications by the Organization for Economic Cooperation and Development (OECD) and World Bank which classified developed countries as high-income countries [with annual gross national income (GNI) per capita (Atlas method) greater than US$ 11,116].

As such, there is a lack of clarity as to which countries are legally obliged to encourage technology transfer to others under Article 66(2).

Secondly, neither WTO nor TRIPS states what constitutes technology transfer as a term. Most of them have been relying on the relatively broad definition used in the TRIPS Council submissions of New Zealand, [66] which states that:

Technology transfer is interpreted in this report broadly to include training, education and know how, along with any capital component. [67]

Using the United Nations definition, New Zealand sees four key modes of technology transfer: (i) physical objects or equipment; (ii) skills and human aspects of technology management and learning; (iii) designs and blueprints which constitute the document-embodied knowledge on information and technology; and (iv) production arrangement linkages within which technology is operated.

Lack of clear definition as to what constitutes technology transfer, has created room for developed countries to interpret and stretch whatever activity is carried out to constitute technology transfer at the detriment of the developing countries. Thus, a call is made that TRIPS should be more eloquent on defining who are developing countries and what constitutes a technology transfer.

Strengthening the TRIPS Council with Formal Rules, Procedures and Sanctions: The report submission on the implementation of Article 66(2) of TRIPS is not governed by any common format.

As such, reports may be adversely impacted by bias and overstatements. As a result, it has been difficult to establish, based on the report data, as to what extent are policies specifically targeted towards developing country members and whether the programmes encourage the transfer of technology to developing country members.

It is, thus, suggested that TRIPS Council need be strengthened with formal rules, procedures and sanctions for state reporting on technology transfer by developed countries.

Endnotes

1. Abbott, F.M. (2002), "The TRIPS: Legality of Measures Taken to Address Public Health Crises", in 'The Political Economy of International Trade Law', Kennedy and Southwick, J.D. (eds.), Cambridge University Press.
2. Adede, A.O. (2001), "The Political Economy of the TRIPS Agreement: Origins and History of Negotiations", Acts Press, Nairobi, Kenya, p. 6.
3. Collier, T. (1991), "The Prospects for Intellectual Property in GATT", *Common Market Law Review*, No. 4, pp. 383-385.
4. Coller, T., supra note 3.
5. Adede, A.O., supra, p. 8.
6. Ibid.
7. Cottier, T. (1991), "The Prospects for Intellectual Property in the GATT", *Common Market Law Review*, No. 9, p. 385.

8. Adopted on March 20, 1883, as revised at Stockholm on July 14, 1967, in 828 United Nations Treaty Series (UNTS) 305 (hereinafter referred to as the Paris Convention).
9. Adopted September 9, 1886, as revised at Paris on July 24, 1971, in 1161 UNTS 31 (hereinafter referred to as the Bern Convention).
10. Adopted October 26, 1961 in 496 UNTS 43, (hereinafter referred to as the Rome Convention).
11. Adopted May 26, 1989, reprinted in 28th International Legal Materials, (ILM) 1477, 1989 (hereinafter referred to as the Washington Treaty).
12. GATT (1985), "Report on the Group of Experts on Trade in Counterfeit Goods", L/5878, October 9, p. 3.
13. Slaughter, J. (1990), "TRIPS: The GATT Intellectual Property Negotiations Approach their Conclusion", 11 EIPR 418. See also USITC (1988), "Foreign Protection of Intellectual Property Rights and the Effect on US Trade and Industry", Pub. 2065, Inv. No. 332-TA-245.
14. Adede supra quoting Slaughter, J., supra note 13.
15. Agreement on Measures to Discourage the Importation of Counterfeit Goods, GATT Doc. L/4817, July 31, 1979.
16. From September 15-20, 1986.
17. Abbotte, M.F., supra note 1, p. 312.
18. Ibid.
19. Adede, A.O., supra, p. 7.
20. The last day of the Ministerial Conference that convened at Punta del Este from September 15-20, 1986.
21. Sandiford, W., "GATT and the Uruguay Round", available at: www.eccbcentralbank.org/Rsch_papers/Rpmr94.pdf.
22. The Uruguay Round Ministerial Conference Declaration made on 20th September 1986, in *GATT, Basic Instruments and Selected Documents* [BISD] reprinted in 25 ILM 1623, 1626 (1986).
23. Adede, Ibid., p. 9.
24. http://news.bbc.co.uk/2/hi/europe/country_profiles/2430089.stm.
25. Section 301 and special Section 301 included in the Bilateral Trade Agreements (BITs) and in the Bilateral Intellectual Property Agreements (BIPs).
26. The Panel's holding on the Canada's complaints against USA, supra.

27. Article 7 of TRIPS.
28. See the Preamble to the TRIPS Agreement.
29. Articles 64-65 of TRIPS.
30. Article 9 of TRIPS.
31. The Berne Convention of 1974.
32. Article 15 of TRIPS.
33. Article 22 of TRIPS.
34. Article 10 Article 10*bis* of the Paris Convention, 1967.
35. Linda, Y.Y. (2007), "Global Intellectual Property Rights and Economic Growth", *North-Western University Law Journal of Technology and Intellectual Property*, Vol. 5:3, p. 437.
36. Kumar, N. (1998), "Intellectual Property Rights Technology and Economic Development: Experiences of Asian Countries", Research and Information System for Developing Countries, New Delhi.
37. Ibid.
38. Zheng Zhou, K. (2006), "Innovation, Imitation and New Product Performance: The Case of China", *Industrial Marketing Management*, Elsevier Inc., 35, pp. 394-402, available at: www.sciencedirect.com.
39. Zheng Zhou, K. supra note 45.
40. Schnaars, S.P. (1994), "Managing Imitation Strategies: How Late Entrants Seize Marketing from Pioneers", The Free Press, New York.
41. Schnaars, S.P. supra note 45.
42. Chon, M. (2006), "Intellectual Property and the Development Divide", *Cardozo Law Review*, Vol. 27, pp. 2821-2912.
43. Article 3 of TRIPS.
44. Article 4 of TRIPS.
45. World Trade Organization (2002), "Declaration on the TRIPS Agreement and Public Health", WT/MIN(01)/DEC/2, 41 I.L.M. 755.
46. Adede A.O. (2010), "Origins and History of the TRIPS Negotiations", *Global Media Journal*, Australia edn., Vol. 4:2.
47. Servaas, T. (2003), "Public Health versus Intellectual Property, or How Members of the WTO without Pharmaceutical Production Capacity Could Have Accesse to Affordable Medicines in Public Health Emergencies by using Compulsory Licenses", Geneva, Switzerland.
48. Justin C.W., "TRIPS: Promoter of Innovation or Illusory?",

Intellectual Property Law Server, available at: www.eccb-centralbank.org/Rsch_papers/Rpmr94.pdf.

49. Chon, M., supra.
50. Done at Vienna on May 23, 1969. Entered into force on January 27, 1980, United Nations, *Treaty Series*, Vol. 1155, p. 331.
51. Moniz, P.P. (2005), "The Development Agenda for WIPO: Another Stillbirth? A Battle between Access to Knowledge and Enclosure", unpublished LL.M thesis in intellectual property, Queen Mary and Westfield College, University of London, pp. 29-32, available at: http://ssrn.com/abstract=844366.
52. Ibid.
53. Agreement between the World Intellectual Property Organization and the World Trade Organization, December 22, 1995, 35 I.L.M. 754, 1996, [hereinafter referred to as WIPO-WTO Agreement].
54. Article 66 of TRIPS.
55. Koffi Annan, Secretary General, United Nations UN Press Release SG/2070/AIDS/4, April 5, 2001.
56. The proposal document number WO/GA/31/11, dated August 27, 2004 adopted by the WIPO General Assembly on October 4, 2004.
57. See Annex 1 GATT. Doc. MTN/GNG/NG 11/W71 of May 14, 1990.
58. Khor, M., Third World Network Information Service on WTO and Trade Issues, (October 4/3).
59. Ibid.
60. Khor, M., supra note 64.
61. Proposal document, supra note 62.
62. Khor, M., "Intellectual Property Rights, Technology Transfer and Climate Change", available at: www.un.org/en/development/desa/policy/cdp.../khor.pdf.
63. The Commission Report on Integrating Intellectual Property Rights and Development Policy, Commission on Intellectual Property Rights, 2002, London.
64. Supra.
65. Wayne, S., "GATT and the Uruguay Round", available at: www.eccb-centralbank.org/Rsch_papers/Rpmr94.pdf.
66. The Council for Trade Related Aspects of Intellectual Property Rights, Report on the Implementation of Article 66(2) of the

TRIPS Agreement, New Zealand, IP/C/W/497/Add.3, December 3, 2007, para 3.

67. Ibid.

Part II
Intellectual Property in New Economic Order, Pharmaceutical Industry and Cyberspace

8

Intellectual Property Rights (IPRs) and the New Economy

N.R. Madhava Menon

Evolution of Law and Property Relations:

Historically, with changes in the economy, the legal regime regulating economic transactions and property relations have undergone radical reforms both in substance and in procedure. The concept of "contract" has been basic to the development of trade and creation of wealth. It has been the driving force in capitalist model of economic development even in the agricultural age. During that period, even the concept of property was simple. It included tangible and visible objects neatly divided into movable and immovable properties. Property relations were regulated by the law of transfer of property and the concepts of ownership and possession.

With the onset of Industrial Revolution which India sadly missed, economic laws and the concept of property got changed. Legal system invented the idea of corporation with limited liability. The simple concept of contract got transformed into various forms of specialized contracts to suit industrial and trade relations. Property assumed new forms, neither tangible nor visible, such as stocks, shares, premiums to be managed rather than owned. By and large, the legal regime regulating the economy that we have today is the product of the industrial age.

Slowly but steadily, the role of technology and management in the production and distribution of wealth compelled further changes in the way law regulated the economy. The concept of property assumed yet another dimension which gave importance to innovation and creativity rather than production and management. The advent of information and communication revolution together with globalization of the economy through GATT and WTO changed the way the economy was organized in the post-industrial society.

Inventiveness became the key to economic growth and the law of intellectual property became the supreme instrument to regulate economic and trade relations through the Agreement known as TRIPS (Trade-Related Intellectual Property Rights). In the era of knowledge-based economy of tomorrow, the IPR regime is bound to assume critical importance both for the developed and the developing countries.

Property and the Indian Constitution

In the original Constitution, right to property was a part of the Fundamental Rights. Today, it is no more a guaranteed Constitutional right like right to freedom, equality and liberty. It is worthwhile to remind oneself how this change happened and the risks involved in projecting unlimited rights to property or right to unlimited property.

According to the Constitution, the State could acquire private property only for a public purpose and that too only after paying the requisite compensation. When the Zamindari Abolition Act was challenged in courts on the basis of inadequacy of compensation paid by the State, the Supreme Court came to the rescue of the zamindars and declared compensation to be equivalent of market value. The State could not disturb private property unless it is able to pay market value to the parties. This was not the intention of the Parliament and any way, the State could not have found the money to pay all zamindars who had the bulk of land of the country in their possession at that time. The social justice goals of land reform laws got aborted in the process. The Constitution had to be amended to say that reasonable amount (and not market value) will be paid when property is acquired and the quantum would not be a justiciable issue in a court of law.

Again on the plea of zamindars, the Court struck down the Constitution Amendment itself saying that it is a fraud on the Constitutional right to property. The Western notion of unlimited right to property or right to unlimited property was felt inimical to socialist commitments of the Constitution. The result was the ultimate exclusion of the right to property itself from the list of guaranteed individual rights and reducing it as an ordinary right which the State could amend as found necessary. What followed thereafter by way of abolition of privy purses of erstwhile *maharajas*, nationalization of banks and restrictions in landholdings are demonstrative of the Indian perspective on the nature and scope of individual property rights.

Narrowing of inequalities in income, status and opportunities is a state obligation and this could not have been attempted with a concept of individual's unlimited right to property. In the interest of larger public good, monopolistic rights have to be curbed through law even if it acts as a disincentive to private enterprise and to the so-called capitalist model of economic development. The balancing of private enterprise with social development and individual rights with social justice through what are called "reasonable restrictions" became the focus of a later debate on property rights. It is in this context one has to appreciate the debate on intellectual property rights in the Indian perspective.

With changes in the social and economic content of property, the legal world developed mechanisms which again favoured the monopolistic rights of those who created the new forms of property. The same old issues came back raising the scope of the right to intellectual property, the extent to which a state can interfere with it and what is the right balance between intellectual property rights and the demands of social justice and development. If you allow the technology rich States to dictate terms what will happen to the poor countries seeking development in a highly unequal, competitive world? If you allow the inventor of a new product or service to appropriate monopoly rights to his intellectual property, what will happen to the rest of the society who need his invention but are unable to pay? If society deprives him of his rights on his invention, would it not act as a disincentive to creativity which will stop progress itself causing greater damage? It is this dilemma we need to discuss in analyzing IPR in the new economy.

Today, it is not a dilemma which can be resolved by ourselves because we are inextricably linked to the world economy which protects a property regime not always conducive to our national interests. We have undertaken obligations under WTO and TRIPS which effectively reduced our options and capacity to take decisions on what we perceive as our national interest.

We never treated our knowledge systems in the past as our monopoly, nor did we exploit it on commercial lines. In fact, we have not even documented them to prevent others from copying it. Suddenly, we find many of our traditional knowledges getting patented for commercial interests elsewhere and asking us to pay them the royalty if we want to use our own knowledges! This is an irony which has no parallel in human history. And this makes us think what our national interests are in the existing scheme of things and how we can protect our legitimate rights for our development, given a legal regime which is not friendly to our traditional ways of thinking on property rights.

Intellectual Property Rights and Development

Can intellectual property rights help reduce poverty, hunger, disease and illiteracy—the Millennium Development Goals of the world community? Can IPR enable us to fulfil the preambular promises of the Constitution of India to the deprived sections of Indian humanity? Does IPR act as a stimulus to economic growth, agricultural and industrial production which may, in turn, reduce unemployment and deprivation? Above all, can IPR help improve the quality of life of the poor and lowly and promote sustainable development? If IPR even remotely serves at least a part of the above objectives, one would argue that it is desirable for both developed and developing countries even if it helps to make the rich richer in the process.

On the contrary, if IPR is unlikely to promote research and invention in a country lacking the necessary infrastructure and resources for whatever reasons, IPR may tend to retard its development because of the diversion of available resources in acquiring IPR products and services from developed countries. If the capacity to compete in research and innovation is poor or inadequate, it may result in multinational companies killing domestic competition and compelling imports from developed countries. A strong patent law may lead to increase of the cost of essential supplies including the inputs for improved agricultural and industrial production thereby increasing the cost of living of the poor and the marginalized.

It is between these two policy choices we that have to locate the national interest vis-à-vis IPR protection. India is not a desperately poor country depending on imports for survival. Nor is its research and invention infrastructure too backward that it is unable to compete globally even in areas of modern technology. If we have to import technology in some areas, we are capable of exporting technology in other areas. The human resources that count in an IPR-based development model are immense in India which it exports today because of poor investment in R&D by Government and private enterprises. Otherwise, our capacity is world class and our potential unlimited in a knowledge economy. Whether it is in computing, space, biotechnology, pharmaceutical, software development or health care services, India can be among the leading nations in technology-led development.

As such, national interest demands not a blind opposition to IPR or TRIPS but a fair assessment of our strengths and weaknesses and a well-balanced approach which enables

Indian entrepreneurs to take advantage of opportunities in the global market while protecting the legitimate demands of the domestic market. IPR policies may have to be constantly modified depending upon the impact of the policies of more developed countries. We need to understand the rules of the game and negotiate our destination in the company of other countries similarly placed. Rule of law is our strength in investment and development.

Therefore, what are the issues and concerns we need to consider when we design our IPR law and its administration?

1. Should we be allowing the patenting of living things and materials found in nature, as opposed to man-made products and processes more readily recognizable to the layman as an invention?
2. Should we limit the grant of patents for pharmaceutical substances to new chemical entities or to new medical entities only involving one or more inventive steps?
3. Should we have a *sui generis* IP law for protection of semi-conductors, databases, traditional knowledge systems, folklore, genetic resources etc. and, if so, what principles should govern such a regime?
4. How do we protect the new knowledge and technologies produced in the public sector using the state resources?
5. Given the minimum standards for IP protection under the TRIPS agreement and the legitimate needs of higher standards in certain sectors, should we follow a strategy of regional and bilateral agreements to get a differentiated treatment for trade and investment?

I raised these illustrative questions only to demonstrate the range and complexity of issues that every country has to consider if a national interest-friendly IP regime is to be developed which does not conflict with the TRIPS/WTO minimum standards.

TRIPS, WTO and the National Interest

When India joined the WTO against opposition from

certain groups within the country, it surrendered part of its "sovereignty" to decide disputes involving national interest. The Patent Act was amended amidst opposition in the Parliament and outside and once again the country made its choice where its national interest lies. It is, therefore, of little relevance to argue now, almost 20 years after the agreement that the IP regime is not in national interest unless we are prepared to walk out of the WTO and seek bilateral agreements with countries we deal with.

TRIPS requires all WTO Members to provide minimum standards of protection for a wide range of IPRs including copyright, patents, trademarks, industrial design, geographical indications etc. Apart from existing international conventions administered by the World Intellectual Property Organization (WIPO), TRIPS introduces number of new obligations and measures governing the enforcement of IP rights in Member countries. The interpretation and application of these obligations in the IP systems in Member countries have been a matter of constant concern and the next part of my presentation will address this issue.

Article 8 of TRIPS allows countries to adopt measures necessary to protect public health and to prevent abuses of IP rights provided these measures are compatible with other provisions of the TRIPS agreement. These include the requirements to provide patent protection for pharmaceutical products, limitations on the conditions for issuing compulsory licenses (Article 31) and on the scope of provisions providing exceptions to patent rights (Article 30). Similarly, the extent to which patents should be allowed on inventions relating to living forms, for example micro-organisms and the requirement to provide IP protection for plants, are debatable issues. It is in this context, we also need to question the TRIPS agreement in relation to another important Convention on Biological Diversity.

Disputes over the interpretation and implementation of TRIPS by national laws are raised in the WTO Disputes

Settlement Body which has a multi-level process to adjudicate the issues raised. It is a powerful forum in effect determining the economic prospects of nations in a highly competitive world.

A worldwide IPR system buttressed by TRIPS and WTO may impact development in developed and developing countries differently. Companies, especially in pharmaceutical industry may seek too many patents on matters of negligible importance and patents of low quality may get granted, sometimes blocking fresh research more useful to health. Pharma companies may try to prolong monopolies on valuable therapies. Patents taken at an early stage in the research process may be an obstacle to downstream research and commercialization. Companies may incur considerable costs determining how to organize research without infringing other companies' patent rights, or defending their own patent rights against other companies.

Countries which do not have a robust legal system regulating competition and abuses of monopoly rights may have problems in protecting national interest under a strong patent regime. Similarly, developed countries allowing traditional knowledge or genetic resources originating in developing countries to be patented without prior arrangements for sharing benefits from commercialization can be injurious to the development of developing countries. The continuing harmonization and globalization of IP rights at the instance of the developed countries generally result in advantages for the developed world and development losses for the developing world particularly those developing countries which do not have a scientific tradition, capacity and infrastructure. In short, IPR is related to development directly and indirectly in many ways some of which are not even discernible at present. This is because IPR benefits financially those who have scientific knowledge and inventive capacity while others who do not have these come to pay heavily to access the benefits out of it. The costs and benefits of IPR are not fairly distributed in today's unequal world.

From India's point of view, one of the concerns is the lack of a robust world system of IP rights for the protection of traditional knowledge, folklore and genetic resources. The threat of bio-piracy and patenting of bio-products by developed countries without disclosing the country of origin of bio-materials is indeed real. Another area of concern is the way TRIPS provisions are interpreted, particularly in areas of public health. Very high standards of protection of IPR may not necessarily be in national interest as it was shown in the case of generic manufacturers of life saving drugs. India has to proceed cautiously till such time that its R&D infrastructure and investment is considerably strengthened to meet global competition.

At the same time, the country must seek stronger recognition for IPRs in traditional knowledge, bio-diversity, folklore, geographical indications and software systems in which the country has great potential. India has to take a more active role in the TRIPS Council to ensure that the Agreement provides adequate flexibility to evolve the IP policy in relation to trade and development. The patent infrastructure meanwhile must be made world class with efficiency and standards to ensure that the system is capable of handling the innumerable challenges which may arise in the area of invention and investment.

TRIPS Compatibility of Limiting Patents only to New Chemical/Medical Entity

In 2007, the Government of India appointed a Committee under Dr. R.A. Mashelkar, the then Director General of CSIR to study and report on two questions arising from the amended Indian Patents Act, 2005. The two questions were:

1. Whether it would be TRIPS compatible to limit the grant of patent for pharmaceutical substance to new chemical entity or to new medical entity involving one or more inventive steps; and
2. Whether it would be TRIPS compatible to exclude micro-

organisms from patenting.

The Committee received over a thousand pages of documentation from industry associations, NGOs, patent attorneys and several of them came for personal presentations and interaction with Committee. The Committee felt that in approaching the analysis of the twin issues, the object should be to encourage innovations by Indian industry, ensure access to medicines at affordable cost to the people, dissuade frivolous patents, acknowledge India's research and manufacturing capabilities and, of course, honour India's obligations under TRIPS including the flexibilities provided under it for developing countries.

The Committee answered the questions as follows which deserve close scrutiny and critical appraisal.

On TRIPS Compatibility of Limiting Patents only to New Molecules: "Article 27 of TRIPS, which deals explicitly with the issue of patentability, *inter alia*, states what 'Member States may not exclude from any field of technology from patentability as a whole and they may not discriminate as to the fields of technology, the place of innovation etc. Reading this obligation in the light of the overall purpose of the Agreement, it appears that linking the grant of patents for pharmaceutical substances only to a new chemical entity or to a new medical entity may prima facie amount to 'excluding a field of technology' even when they satisfy the basic requirements of patentability'.

In such a situation, it is possible to hold the provision as being not TRIPS compatible. Furthermore, it is debatable as to whether national interest or the flexibility allowed under the Agreement to Member States would be accommodated by such exclusion (emphasis added)."

On the prospects of proliferating patents on minor changes or fraudulent claims, the Committee was of the considered view that the patent examiner has full authority to decide and exclude such claims. This is what the Committee recommended on the issue of limiting of pharma patents only to new chemical entities.

The Committee was conscious of the ever-greening issue in pharma patents and therefore recommended:

"Every effort must be made to prevent the practice of 'ever greening' often used by some of the pharma companies to unreasonably extend the life of the patent by making claims based sometimes on 'trivial' changes to the original patented product. The Indian patent office has the full authority under law and practice to determine what is patentable and what would constitute only a trivial change with no significant additional improvements or inventive steps involving benefits. Such authority should be used to prevent ever-greening, rather than to introduce an arguable concept in the light of above "statutory exclusion" of incremental innovations from the scope of patentability.

The process of innovation is continuous and progressive leading to an ever extending chain of knowledge. Innovative incremental improvements based on existing knowledge and existing products is a 'norm' rather than an 'exception' in the process of innovation. Entirely new chemical structures with new mechanisms of action are a rarity rather than a rule. Therefore, "incremental innovations" involving new forms, analogs, etc. but which have significantly better safety and efficacy standards, need to be encouraged. What is important, however, is for the patent office to be vigilant about setting high standards of judging such innovations so that efforts on ever-greening are scrupulously prevented".

It is important to point out in this context that the Committee was not asked by the Government to examine the TRIPS compatibility of Section 3(d) of the Indian Patents Act or any other provision of the law. In fact, there is a challenge in Court in this regard. The Committee has expressed no opinion either way on Section 3(d) as some critiques allege.

On TRIPS Compatibility of Excluding Micro-organisms from being Patented: The Committee found that excluding micro-organisms per se from patent protection would be violative of TRIPS in view of the reading of Article

27.3 of TRIPS and the provision contained in Section 3(j) of the Indian Patent Act.

In reaching these conclusions, the Group surveyed patenting practices towards new chemical entities and micro-organisms in countries around the world. In short, the findings were based on evidence and what the Committee considered as promotive of national interests within the flexibility of TRIPS.

On patentability for incremental innovations, the Committee was told by the industry that it will take some more time for it to discover new chemical entities and if they are denied the right to patent incremental innovations, the entire benefit would go to the advantage of foreign multinational companies and national interest would suffer.

Therefore, the Committee concluded that incremental innovations involving new forms, analogs etc. which have significantly better safety and efficacy standards, need to be encouraged in the national interest. In fact, the Committee was told that Indian pharma companies are seeking and getting patents for incremental innovations from other countries at a greater cost because the Indian law is denying them the opportunity [Section 3(d)]. They are objected to in India mainly because they are seen as ever-greening. It need not be so if the Patent Office is careful to exclude such application through a higher standard which it is entitled to do. It is on this interpretation that the Committee concluded that it would not be TRIPS compliant to limit granting of patents for pharmaceutical substance to new chemical entities only. This is because it is a statutory exclusion of a field of technology which TRIPS does not allow.

Conclusion

In conclusion, I would say that the country as a whole needs to give greater attention to the immense potential we are capable of in innovation and creativity. This would mean re-structuring educational policies to promote talents, investing in research and development, encouraging private enterprise in scientific fields, releasing the scientific establishment from avoidable bureaucratic controls and rewarding the innovative spirit at all levels of society. The IPR and trade policies will have to be suitably integrated with development goals and strategies at the Centre and in the States. All these require a robust legal system, which can respond to problems as they arise in tune with India's long-term interests in the knowledge society of the future.

9

Enforcement of TRIPS: Conflicts and Constrains

Syeda Nishat Shadmani

Introduction

One may possibly argue that Agreement on Trade-Related Aspects of Intellectual Property Rights (TRIPS) advocates a set of common international rules and allow nations to adopt higher protection in tandem with their societal, environmental and economic conditions. The standards of protection for IP laws have always occupied a centre-stage in debates and negotiations. Underlying this principle, arises a question of imbalance in the parity of powers viz. the greater powers; developed countries and the lesser powers namely the developing and least developed countries. So outwardly, all nations live in harmony with their own set of Bibles until there are trade and commerce activities among the countries. In economic relations, disputes and conflicts are inevitable. One of the major sources of conflict pertains to the varied interpretation as to the degree of protection accorded by countries to intellectual property rights evidenced during the Uruguay Round of Negotiations.

While strong IP laws are avowed by the developed countries for the protection and realization of their intellectual property pursuits, some of the developing countries on the other hand are still battling economic growth and hence are apprehensive to enforce stringent laws for IP protection. Plausible reasons are for sheltering their domestic industries and markets, avoiding pharmaceutical patents for medicines especially lifesaving drugs for reason of high cost, essentially unavailable to people in those countries that are in urgent need of them.

Arguments are on the rise that maximum protection [1] to IP laws within the framework of TRIPS is the need of the hour for reasons aplenty such as: (a) guaranteeing incentives to the creator/inventor (by tackling the menace of counterfeit goods), (b) protecting the immense amount of effort and investments involved in research and development, (c) facilitating trade between nations etc.

On the other hand, Preamble to TRIPS clearly states that "measures and procedures to enforce intellectual property rights do not themselves become barriers to legitimate trade". In view of the above perspectives and an objective reading of the Preamble to TRIPS it becomes evident that the primary objective of TRIPS is to facilitate and augment trade by reducing impediments to international trade. Clearly evident in the Panel Report *China: Measures Affecting the Protection and Enforcement of Intellectual Property Rights,* [2] a WTO member's TRIPS enforcement obligations entail minimum standards and flexibilities in the TRIPS Agreement. World Trade Organization (WTO) and TRIPS formulated in the Uruguay Round is an attempt to universalize these laws and to bring them under common international rules and settle disputes more systematically both in its substantive and enforcement procedures.

In case of conflict between trade and an intellectual property rights holder, redressal is provided under the WTO Dispute Settlement Mechanism. But what is imperative of dispute resolution is not simply delivery of justice but a swift, amicable and a futuristic one. In order to achieve this, a relook at the enforcement mechanism under the TRIPS Agreement is essential. Articles 41 to 61 of TRIPS provides for the institutional mechanism, procedures and remedies of enforcement. Structurally, the TRIPS enforcement mechanism encompasses remedies both in civil and criminal nature and can authorize the prevention of entry of imported goods (alleged IP infringement materials) into the domestic markets as well as tackling local production of counterfeit goods.

Article 41 encapsulates four cardinal principles of these enforcement provisions:

1. "Specified procedures must be made available under the domestic laws to "permit effective action" against present and future acts of infringement,
2. Pertinent judicial and administrative procedures must be "fair and equitable" and not "unnecessarily complicated" or likely to cause "unwarranted delays",
3. Courts and administrators must base decisions on evidence available to all the parties and should deliver reasoned and written opinions,
4. There must be some form of appellate review for decisions handed down by judicial and administrative agencies of first instance". [3]

After the coming of the WTO, Dispute Settlement Body provided teeth to the hitherto TRIPS enforcement mechanism by conferring compulsory jurisdiction of WTO panels upon nations [4] and binding decision of the Dispute Settlement Body (DSB) with sanctions against member nations as a measure for non-compliance of the rulings of DSB.

In enforcement and interpretations on the limitations and exceptions to TRIPS, history of the negotiations that took place in the formation of WTO cannot be overlooked. In deciding the standard to be adopted, considering the difference between the developed and developing countries, time concession in the nature of transition periods was given. While TRIPS only sets guidelines for domestic implementation of the Agreement, the extent of limitations and exceptions and degree of protection provided by different countries when comes in conflict with the legislations of another trading country or TRIPS per se, is subject to interpretation by the Dispute Settlement Panel and the Appellate Body. It is evidenced by the fact that in all the complaints filed in WTO Dispute Settlement Understanding under TRIPS Agreement, the complainants have been majorly the US and EC against India, Pakistan, and Brazil etc. for alleged violation during the transition period wherein the trade-off between the developed and developing countries came to light. [5]

In another study, facts revealed that despite high success rate (almost 89 percent) in complaints brought before the WTO DSB, there has been considerable decline in cases involving TRIPS; with developed countries being the chief complainants. [6] A plausible understanding may be that: 'the respondent nations saw the benefits in compromising in advance of an adversarial proceeding in which their defeat was practically guaranteed'. [7] It is mandatory to mention here the consultation proceedings [8] and conciliation and mediation measures [9] of the WTO DSU which has laudably minimized the adversarial nature of conflict resolution. For the first time in WTO dispute settlement, TRIPS has been used as a benchmark for constraining additional IP protection [10] which was pronounced in relation to a *Request for Consultations by India, European Union and a Member State Seizure of Generic Drugs in Transit.* [11]

The hypothesis that introducing strong IP rules indiscriminately into the 'legislative and industrial fabric' of a developing economy is unlikely to succeed, whereas it is also fair to assume that a country's technology imports and inward FDI are unlikely to grow without IP rules. [12]

Parallel Trade and Enforcement

Consensus amongst the members of WTO is a prerequisite for the 'balance' sought to be achieved for IP protection in mitigating national differences. From an economic perspective, territorial IP protection weighing differently in various nations ranging from the tenure of patent protection to disputes in parallel trade or the large-scale copyright violations in Asian countries, have hampered international trade and diluted the creator's incentives.

A country engaged in parallel trade involving importation

of goods that enter the markets which also holds intellectual property protected goods, serve as a barrier to the profits/rewards from reaching the rightful owner, leading to a disastrous situation wherein, research oriented firms might step back, consequently affecting the inventions itself. But such an attempt has been justified on the grounds of exhaustion of rights under Article 6 of the TRIPS when the goods have first been sold and secondly safeguarding the interests of the consumers. The incentive for parallel importation is the fact that there are price differences between identical products in different markets. Parallel trade is broadly based on the theory of comparative advantage.

In general, proponents of parallel trade attribute various economic benefits that ensue from parallel trade-consumer benefit. One such benefit prevents the businesses to maintain high prices in certain nations. Therefore, barriers to parallel trade appear incoherent with the principles of free trade suggesting that sometimes free trade does not necessarily benefit the consumer.

Under Article 6 of the TRIPS, [13] 'the exhaustion of rights cannot be challenged as a violation of the TRIPS Agreement under the WTO dispute-settlement mechanism; the TRIPS Agreement allows parallel importation'. The benefits of parallel importation of goods are predominantly important for patents of life saving drugs and public health in particular apart from the advantage of consumer choice.

On the other end, "reductions in tariff barriers have in recent years been accompanied by an increase in the adoption of so-called non-tariff measures (NTMs) (e.g., technical regulations and standards), ostensibly aimed at promoting laudable objectives such as human safety, health and environmental protection, a problem compounded by the difficulty involved in quantifying their impact on trade". [14]

Most IP exporting countries are concerned about the increase in counterfeit and fake goods being traded internationally; essentially creating an imbalance in the free trade market as well as deceiving consumers into buying fake and sometimes even dangerous products. The root cause of lack of adequate IP enforcement in the domestic markets becomes an impediment to international trade. The developing countries, on the other hand believe that imposing non-tariff measures particularly by the developed countries is an attempt to oust their productions from entering foreign markets and majorly affect developing country exporters. [15]

In the recent WTO ruling between *China and the United States*, [16] in an attempt to resolve trade disputes, considering the immense volume of trade between these nations, the clear message that was sent 'signaled to other less developed countries that the TRIPS Agreement does not require the high TRIPS-plus standards of intellectual property protection and enforcement that are now being advanced through bilateral, plurilateral, and regional trade and investment agreements as well as the proposed Anti Counterfeit Trade Agreement'. [17]

Border Measures and Enforcement of IP

"When applied to goods in transit, the IP protection and enforcement standards in the transit country can cause detention and seizures—even if there is no IP infringement in the country of production or destination. Some developing countries consider such enforcement measures as 'protectionist' and their trade restrictive effects as contrary to the main principle of trade liberalization in the World Trade Organization". [18]

Under Article 52 of TRIPS complainants/right holders alleging the trade of counterfeit goods or IPR violated goods who thereby seek the seizure of such goods require to adduce "adequate evidence to satisfy the competent authorities that, under the laws of the country of importation, there is prima facie an infringement of the complainants intellectual property right". Therefore, the seizure of goods in transit although contravening the laws of the country through which the goods are to pass, are not in consonance with Article 52, primarily because both the laws of the country of origin and destination are not transgressed. The case of *Request for Consultations by India, European Union and a Member State for Seizure of Generic Drugs in Transit* [19] amply justifies this position, the facts of the case states that the Dutch authorities suspecting patent infringements seized and returned several shipments of generic drugs transiting via EU ports to destinations in South America and Africa. The drugs at issue were protected in the EU, but not in the countries of origin i.e., India or destination i.e., Brazil, Nigeria etc. Referring to complaints of suspected infringement, customs authorities in the Netherlands detained a substantial amount of generic medicines in transit through the Netherlands.

Such detentions and seizures possibly create barriers to international trade by provisionally stalling the free movement of goods in transit and subsequently destroying them which is not a very comfortable arrangement for the developing countries and particularly in case of generic drugs and goods imported under compulsory licenses. Therefore, the European Union's recent agreement with India to amend its regulation on customs border measures, [20] is considered as a major breakthrough and a positive sign for free movement of goods; crucial for economic development.

Balancing Trade with Non-trade Interests

In promoting the trade interests undertaken by WTO, it has to encounter a number of non-trade interests of various social groups be it the requirements of the least developed countries to import generic and life saving drugs or protecting environment and natural conservation.

In a multilateral system of individual territorial norms and different needs, the art of balancing conflict of interest is an arduous task particularly within the framework of WTO. The flexibilities in the WTO rules lead to discretion on the part of the nations to address these conflicting issues commonly known as 'policy space'. The domestic legislations try to inculcate their own requirements and interests into this policy space while at the same time protecting the interests of the right holders globally. But the primary question that arises is "to what extent is this permeation allowed?" keeping in mind the primary objective of TRIPS i.e., unhindered international trade of intellectual property.

Over the years, there has been a complete shift from reduction of border tariffs (giving an impetus to free movement of goods) to non-tariff barriers such as public health, technical standards, competition policy and a vital concern—environment. Article XX of GATT, 1947 provides for general exceptions in the nature of environmental protections, measures necessary to protect human, animal and plant life or health, more specifically under Article XX (b) to (g). In order to verify the need for such a restriction, the party imposing it will have to prove first that the measures are warranted by either Article XX (b) to (g). Secondly, that it fulfils the conditions mentioned under the Preamble of Article XX. All grounds under Article XX i.e. the general exceptions clause are non-economic and have social considerations.

Article XX relates to the impartiality and neutrality in imposition of restrictions with the aim of conservation. If the national policy is discriminatory in placing all restrictions towards only the foreign product of a like nature in the context of conservation it would be grossly discriminatory, aimed at protecting only the locally produced goods. [21]

It has been applied in two GATT cases involving the United States and Canada. In both disputes, the parties agreed that the fish stocks in question were an "exhaustible" natural resource. In the tuna case, [22] the Panel found that an Article XX exception was not justified because the United States did not have restrictions on domestic consumption of tuna and because its restrictions on production did not extend to every kind of tuna being barred from Canada. In the herring and salmon case, [23] the panel interpreted the proviso to mean that a trade measure had to be "primarily aimed at rendering effective" the domestic restrictions. In the opinion of the panel, the Canadian export prohibition at issue failed to meet this test. [24]

In the US Gasoline case, [25] United States applied stricter rules on the chemical characteristics of imported gasoline than it did for domestically-refined gasoline. Venezuela (and later Brazil) said this was unfair because US gasoline did not have to meet the same standards—it violated the "national treatment" principle and could not be justified under exceptions to normal WTO rules for health and environmental conservation measures. The dispute panel agreed with Venezuela and Brazil.

Moreover, Article XX (b) and (g) should not be applied only to give some colour of protection, occasionally or without intention but must be guided by social and environmental considerations. At the same time, such non-tariff considerations should not themselves become impediments to trade. The Dispute Settlement Panel and Appellate Body have endlessly strived to attain a balance between these diverse objectives, keeping in mind the broad objectives of Article 7 of TRIPS, which reads as "to the mutual advantage of producers and users of technological knowledge and in a manner conducive to social and economic welfare, and to a balance of rights and obligations".

Conclusion

International trade and free movement of goods and enforcement of intellectual property rights within the framework of TRIPS have witnessed a number of bargains in the play of power politics particularly during the period of Uruguay Trade Negotiations.

The Dispute Settlement Mechanism while juggling with the objectives of public interest principles and trade liberalization that guide treaty interpretation in relation to the TRIPS Agreement must bear in mind the extremely important value of "balance" advocated not only by the objectives and principles of TRIPS but adamantly supported by scholars and jurists as well. But 'how?' and 'to what extent?' such a balance is sought to be achieved is still an open question.

'Over a period of time, in intellectual property protection and enforcement, the developing countries have started to avail benefits of flexibilities and 'policy space' in the dispute settlement process than they did in the early days of the TRIPS Agreement. The benefits of the WTO dispute settlement process, indeed, have begun to trickle down to less developed countries'. [26]

It is pertinent to note here that interpretation of TRIPS cannot be an exclusive domain of either the developed countries in pushing for TRIPS-plus standard or the developing countries advocating for minimum standards. Common understanding of the IP laws reveal that until and unless there are strong IP laws between all the member nations, trade facilitation is not possible while at the same time lack of international trade and commerce activities will result in low growth, foreign investment inflow and economic development of a country, consequently hindering the creations and inventions.

While countries have to an extent realized the importance and explored the benefits of IP trade, they are yet to fully comprehend the necessities of proper implementation and enforcement of IP measures in order to protect unhindered and free movement of goods.

Endnotes

1. Henning Grosse Ruse Khan (2009), "Time for a Paradigm Shift? Exploring Maximum Standards in International Intellectual Property Protection", *Trade Law and Development*, 1(1), 56.
2. WT/DS362/R (January 26, 2009).
3. J.H. Reichman (1997), "Enforcing the Enforcement Procedures of the TRIPS Agreement", *Virginia Journal of International Law*, Vol. 37, 340.
4. Articles 6, 7 and 17 of Understanding on Rules and Procedures Governing the Settlement of Disputes.
5. Jayashree Watal (2009), "Intellectual Property Rights in the WTO and Developing Countries", 66-68.

6. Yoshifumi Fukunaga (2008), "Enforcing TRIPS: Challenges of Adjudicating Minimum Standards Agreements", *Berkeley Technology Law Journal*, Vol. 23, 887.
7. *Supra* note 6 at 888.
8. Article 4.3 of Dispute Settlement Understanding: Members shall enter into consultations in good faith within a period of no more than 30 days after the date of receipt of the request, with a view to reaching a mutually satisfactory solution.
9. Article 5 of Dispute Settlement Understanding: Good offices, conciliation and mediation are procedures that are undertaken voluntarily if the parties to the dispute so agree.
10. Henning Grosse Ruse Khan (2011), "A Trade Agreement Creating Barriers to International Trade?: ACTA Border Measures and Goods in Transit", *Am. U. Int'l L.*, 26:3 Rev, 655.
11. WT/DS408/1, May 19, 2010, available at: http://www.wto.org/english/tratop_e/dispu_e/cases_e/ds408_e.ht.
12. Daniel J. Gervais (2005), "Intellectual Property, Trade and Development: The State of Play", *Fordham L. Rev*, 74, 529.
13. Article 6: For the purposes of dispute settlement under this Agreement, subject to the provisions of Articles 3 and 4 nothing in this Agreement shall be used to address the issue of the exhaustion of intellectual property rights.
14. Ubong E. Effeh (2008), "Africa and the Multilateral Trading Regime: Re-examining the Market Access Mantra", *Journal of Politics and Law*, Vol I(I), 84. The author strongly opposes the idea of protectionism of the Western countries by arguing that the observance of the rules of the WTO multilateral trading system, has themselves become an impediment to international trade and thereby negatively affecting the country's (particularly sub-Saharan Africa's) economic prospects.
15. Supra note 10 at 646,647.
16. See, "Request for Consultations by the United States, China: Measures Affecting the Protection and Enforcement of Intellectual Property Rights", WT/DS362/1, April 16, 2007.
17. Peter K. Yu (2011), "The TRIPS Enforcement Dispute", *Nebraska Law Review*, Vol. 89, Issue 4, 1103.
18. *Supra* note 15 at 647.
19. WT/DS408/1, May 19, 2010, available at: http://www.wto.org/english/tratop_e/dispu_e/cases_e/ds408_e.ht.
20. http://www.bbc.co.uk/news/world-europe-11971568.

21. US Gasoline, WT/DS2/AB/R, pp. 20-21.
22. L/5198-29S/91, adopted on February 22, 1982.
23. L/6268-35S/98, adopted on March 22, 1988.
24. Steve Charnovitz, "Exploring the Environmental Exceptions in GATT Article XX", available at: http://www.charnovitz.org/JWT.htm.
25. WTO Appellate Body, US Gasoline, WT/DS2/AB/R, p. 21.
26. Peter K. Yu (2011), "The TRIPS Enforcement Dispute", *Nebraska Law Review*, Vol. 89, Issue 4, p. 1112.

10

Patents in Relation to Biotechnology and Geo-sciences

B.K. Prasad and Rashid A. Faridi

A patent is the right granted by the government of a country to an inventor (applicant) to exclude others from imitating, manufacturing, using or selling the invention in question for commercial use during the specified [1] period of time. [2] When a patent is granted, the inventor becomes the owner of the patent like any other form of property. The patent holder may himself commercialize the invention or he may license one or more parties for the purpose. [3] Protection of biotechnological inventions through patent is concerned with life forms and involves one or more of the following:

1. Methods/processes of generating useful biotechnological products.
2. Biotechnological products such as antibiotics, purified vitamins, hormones etc.
3. Application of the various processes/methods for the product, e.g., application of a bio-control agent to manage a pest.
4. Micro organisms, cell lines, plant/animal lines obtained through biotechnological approaches.
5. Various DNA sequences and proteins encoded by them.
6. Technology for modification of various life forms.

Patenting of Products, Processes and Applications

In developed countries, biotechnological products, processes and application are allowed patents. [4] Indian Patent Act, 1970, allowed process patent but no product patents were allowed for pharmaceuticals, foods and agrochemicals, so that some products could be manufactured by alternative processes. Indian Patent Act, 1970, has undergone three amendments in 1999, 2002 and 2004, which have now allowed product patents in pharmaceuticals, food and agrochemicals whilst making other necessary provisions as required by the WTO. [5] International conventions do not allow patents for processes or product applications concerning alleviation of human diseases. For example, techniques of surgery are not patentable. Similarly, the use of a product for treatment, diagnosis or prevention of a disease cannot be patented. The processes/technologies used for genetic modification of various organisms are patentable virtually in all countries, including India. [6]

Patenting of Genes and DNA Sequences

Genes, i.e. specific DNA sequences are basic to biological functions. Specific DNA sequences, therefore, form the raw material utilized for genetic modifications of various organisms. An artificially synthesized gene is considered patentable in almost all developed countries. Patenting of genes isolated from naturally occurring organisms was first allowed in the US; the gene in question was a bacterial gene conferring herbicide (glyphosate) resistance. It is likely that countries like UK, where natural genes are not considered patentable, will be under considerable pressure to allow patents. [7]

The technology rich countries are gene poor, while gene rich countries are technology poor. Therefore, the desirable genes present in the germplasm developed in the Third World countries will be ultimately patented by developed countries, and the former may be required to pay royalties for their use in crop improvement. [8] A rice bacterial leaf blight resistance gene, *Xa21*, may illustrate the point. A gene for bacterial blight resistance was discovered in *oryza lengiflora* by Dr. R.C. Chaudhary then working at Patna, Bihar. Later, Dr. G.S. Khush, working at International Rice Research Institute,

Philippines, named this gene as *Xa21* and located it on chromosome 11. Ultimately, *Xa21* was isolated and characterized at University of California, Davis, US, and the University holds the patent for gene. [9]

Patenting of Life Forms

After initial reservations, genetically modified life forms are now patentable in US, European Union and Japan. US allows utility patent on plant materials derived through normal breeding procedures; the patent to Rice Tech, Texas for Basmati like rice and gram is a case. [10] The arguments against patenting of life forms are chiefly ethical and moral, while those in favour relate it entirely with financial and material benefits to individuals, societies and nations. It is unlikely that ethical/moral arguments are going to induce business houses and governments to change their priorities/position unless they become convinced that the consumer views are strong and widespread enough to harm their financial interests. One becomes tempted to cite the case of prohibition in various Indian states.

It may be pointed out that the patenting of plants and animals in US is mainly an administrative one. Many non-government organizations have filed legal objections to the issuance of patents in Europe. [11] It is pertinent to note that US judiciary has become increasingly liberal in the interpretation of US patent laws; this becomes obvious from its judgment in the *Diamond vs. Chakraborty* case (1980) in favour of granting patent to a micro organism strain developed by Chakraborty to clean up oil spills. [12]

Terminator Technology

It may be said that developing countries will be under increasing pressure to allow patents on life forms.

Failing this, multinational corporations (MNCs) will resort to develop technologies that will allow them an absolute control on the life forms evolved by them. The popularly dubbed terminator technology or terminator III technology is the most dangerous technology currently available. This technology allows an absolute control by the MNCs on the plant materials developed by them and, if coupled with some other factors, can be used as a very persuasive argument to convince on unwilling nations to accede to the offered terms and conditions in any negotiations. [13]

Broad Patents in Biotechnology

Many patents in biotechnology, especially agricultural biotechnology cover rather broad areas. Some selected examples will clarify this point. W.R. Grace and Co., US, holds separate patents for all transgenic cottons and soybeans. Similarly, Calgene Inc., US, holds patents for all transgenic plants of Brassica family (produced by *agrobacterium* method only), while Mycogen Corp., US, has the patent for any method of modifying the *cry* gene of *B.thuringiensis*. It may be pointed out that *agracetus* (Middketon, US), a subsidiary of W.R. Grace and Co., was granted a patent for all transgenic cottons in India as well. This patent has been revoked in US and India, but it remains effective till all the avenues of appeal are exhausted. [14]

Such broad patents are considered morally unacceptable and fundamentally inequitable. They also demonstrate the vulnerability of the patent granting system. If such broad patents are allowed, MNCs may ultimately acquire the legal right to determine the future of high-technology research for the entire segment of agriculture and biotechnology. Such a situation would be detrimental to scientific and technological progress and would be a threat to global food security.

Geo-science Element in Patent Regime

Geographical indication systems have become very important in patent regimes all over the globe. This adds geographical element to patent regime. A geographical indication is a name or sign used on goods that have a specific geographical origin and possess qualities, reputation or characteristics that are essentially attributable to that place of origin. A geographical indication includes the name of the place of origin of the goods. Agricultural products typically have qualities that are directly derived from their place of production and are influenced by specific local factors, such as climate and soil. Geographical indications may be used for natural, agricultural or manufactured products. Whether a sign is recognized as a geographical indication is a matter of law of that particular country. [15]

GI system is being used in France from the early part of the twentieth century known as appellation d'origine contrôlée (AOC). Products that meet geographical origin and quality standards may be endorsed with a government-backed official certification of the origins and standards. One such product that has such 'appellations of origin' includes Gruyère cheese from Switzerland. Many French wines also are in this category.

Geographical indications have long been associated with the concept of territory. In Europe, where there is a tradition of associating certain food products with particular regions, this concept of territory-based geographical indications is more important.

Geographical indications are protected with international treaties and national laws under a range of concepts, such as special laws for the protection of geographical indications or appellations of origin; trademark laws; laws against unfair competition: consumer protection laws, or some specific laws that recognize individual geographical indications.

Geographical indications are useful mainly because they could protect and reward traditions while allowing innovation; they emphasize the relationships between human cultures and their immediate environment; they are not freely transferable from one owner to another and they can be maintained as long as the collection tradition is maintained.

In a nutshell, it is ensured that unauthorized parties may not use a geographical indication in respect of products that do not originate in the place mentioned by that indication.

Patent Imbroglio

The development of genetic engineering products requires several technologies/materials. For example, production of a transgenic plant would require the following:

1. An otherwise outstanding variety of the crop.
2. A suitable promoter (along with appropriate enhancer sequence).
3. An appropriate reporter gene along with a suitable promoter.
4. The gene specifying the trait to be modified.
5. A suitable transformation method.
6. A specific technology, e.g., antisense technology if needed.

Many of the above would have been patented, while the ownership of the others may be uncertain. Patent/license holders generally do not object so long as the transgenic material is being developed. But once the product is ready for commercialization, legal proceedings are initiated for patent infringements. [16]

This has delayed the release of 'Endless Summer' tomato, (ready for release since 1996) developed by DNA Plant Technology, US. In any case, resolution of such situations requires skilful and capable financial and legal management. [17]

Options for India

Although much has been said for and against intellectual property rights regimes, there is little serious and in-depth analysis of the impacts of the various positions advocated. India seems to have the following two options.

1. To maintain status quo. But this is untenable in view of economic, commercial and political compulsions.
2. To make appropriate changes in the patent and other laws so that our traditional skills, knowledge, innovation, and biological materials are suitably protected. This would

require a complete overhauling of virtually every segment of our activity, beginning with research institutions, academics to civil judicial systems to bureaucracy and governance. The task is phenomenal; let us pray that our will power matches the task. [18]

Endnotes

1. WIPO (1990), "Duration of Patents", Memorandum of the International Bureau, WIPO/HL/CM/INF/1, April.
2. Singh B.D. (2010), "Plant Breeding: Principles and Methods", Kalyani Publishers, Ludhiana.
3. Narayan P. (1985), "Patent Law", Eastern Law House Pvt. Ltd., Calcutta.
4. Holman, C.M. (2007), "Patent Border Wars: Defining the Boundary between Scientific Discoveries and Patentable Inventions", *Trends in Biotechnology,* 25, 539-543.
5. Ganguli, P. (1998), "Gearing up for Patents: The Indian Scenerio", University Press, Hyderabad.
6. Gill, K.S. (1991), "Implication of Intellectual Property Right for Agriculture Sector in India", *Crop Improvement,* 18, 81-97.
7. Kelly P.D. (1992), "Are Isolated Genes "Useful" to Biotechnology", 10, 52-55.
8. Gopal Krishnan R. (1998), "Patent Cooperation Treaty: India Wakes Up to Advantages", *Business Review: The Hindu,* October 21.
9. Singh B. D. (2010), "Plant Breeding: Principles and Methods", Kalyani Publishers, Ludhiana.
10. Singh, S. Singh, A.K. and Singh R. (1998), "Enforced Patenting of Indian Plants and Agricultural Commodities: A Challenging Issue for Future", Proceedings of the National Seminar on Intellectual Property Rights, Organized by Mahamana Malaviaya Mission and BHU Varanasi, December 12-13, pp. 52-56.
11. Birley, R.E. (1991), "Patenting Animals in Europe", *Biotechnology*, 9, 619-622.
12. Sahai, S. (1994), "GATT and Patenting of Micro Organisms", *Economic and Political Weekly*, April 9, 841.
13. Gupta, P.K. (1996), "Transgenic Plants: Some Current Issues", *Current Science*, 70, 654-660.
14. Holman, C.M. (2007), "Patent Border Wars: Defining the

Boundary between Scientific Discoveries and Patentable Inventions", *Trends in Biotechnology,* 25, 539-543.

15. Holman, C.M. (2007), "Patent Border Wars: Defining the Boundary between Scientific Discoveries and Patentable Inventions", *Trends in Biotechnology,* 25, 539-543.
16. Van Wizk J., Lohen, J.I. and Komen J. (1995), "Intellectual Property Rights for Agricultural Biotechnology: Options and Implications for Developing Countries", ISNAR Research Report No. 3, The Hague: International Service for National Agricultural Research.
17. Gupta, P.K. (1996), "Transgenic Plants: Some Current Issues", *Current Science*, 70, 654-660.
18. Singh, S. Singh, A.K. and Singh R. (1998), "Enforced Patenting of Indian Plants and Agricultural Commodities: A Challenging Issue for Future", Proceedings of the National Seminar on Intellectual Property Rights, Organized by Mahamana Malaviaya Mission and BHU Varanasi, December 12-13, 52-56.

11

Indian Bolar Provision and Patent Issues

S.Z. Amani

Introduction

The Patents (Amendment) Act, 2002 (38 of 2002) has incorporated in the principal Act, namely, the Indian Patents Act,1970, what may be referred to as the Indian Bolar provision [1] of the kind of sub-section (a) of Section 107A in comparison to the Bolar provisions of the other common law as well as the continental law of countries each based on the Bolar concept in general that means 'certain acts performed before the expiry date of the patent that would normally infringe it, were allowed as long as they were related to seeking regulatory authority's market approval and did not constitute commercial use'. [2] Section 107A, dealing with "certain acts not to be considered as infringement", was brought in force w.e.f. May 20, 2003. Section 107A with respect to its sub-section (a) that was subsequently amended by Patents (Amendment) Act, 2005, reads as under:

"For the purpose of this Act:

(a) any act of making, constructing, using, selling, or importing a patented invention solely for use reasonably related to the development and submission of information required under any law for the time being in force, in India, or in a country other than India, that regulates the manufacture, construction, use, sale or import of any product;

(b) shall not be considered as an infringement of patent rights".

The provision of sub-section (a) though operates as a defence to an allegation of patent infringement, constitutes in every sense an exception to patent right. The Bolar provision is, therefore, also referred to as Bolar exception. The permitted act of *making, constructing, using, selling or importing* of a patented invention, i.e. the active ingredient(s) to which patent extends, as not amounting to patent infringement, naturally, refers those acts to be of someone a third person or persons other than the patentee, i.e. non-patentee, who may be an 'expert producer' or a 'generic-producer' or both contributing to the production of a generic product. [3]

Again, the above said acts of the third person(s) have been resorted to, obviously, before the expiry of the patent term, because a patent after its expiry is no more a patent. Further, the above said acts of the third person(s) must be resorted to solely for the development of information, i.e. for generating data as respect to generic product/version, and submission of that information, obviously, to some regulatory authorities, under any relevant regulatory law that regulates the manufacture, construction, use, sale or import etc. of any product (including thereby the patented, non-patented as well as generic product) before it is put on commercial market. [4] The Bolar provision is, therefore, accordingly also referred to as early-working exception, regulatory exception or regulatory-review exception.

In fact, a product which is a subject of a market regulatory law is required to get market regulatory approval under that law to be put in commercial market. Before getting such approval, the product necessarily has to undergo two processes. The 'development process' of the product in commercial form resulting in the generation of information/data about that product, and the 'regulatory process' of testing that product requiring the submission of said information to the regulatory authority to assess the product's safety, stability, and effectiveness etc. by appropriate tests. However, the production of generic product (like generic pharmaceuticals) equivalent to a patented brand name product often involves, at the development process, a two-tier production arrangement.

First, to produce or make or construct from the patented

brand name product the patented invention, that is, to manufacture the so-called 'active-ingredient(s)' or, say, 'essential feature(s)' to which patent extends, and sell or import them to another if demanded, and, *secondly*, to assemble the active ingredient with other agents to create the final product—the generic product, in the form that can be used by the ultimate consumers.

A firm may or may not have both the capacities of an "expert producer of active ingredient" and of a "generic producer of generic product". Where the firm is having the capacity as "generic producer" and not as an "expert producer" the latter can sell or import the 'active ingredient' to the firm on demand. In such cases, therefore, either the producer gets engaged in one or more of the prohibited activities of the patentee even if for the purpose of development and submission of information for seeking market approval, but because of Bolar provision they have safe harbour of defence to any successful allegation of patent infringement. "The regulatory review exception applies to these activities of both producers". [5] It "would allow generic producers to complete both development and regulatory approvals during the term of the patent, thus allowing them to enter the market as soon as the patent expires". [6]

The Bolar Provision is said to have both positive and negative bearings on the substantive patent rights as well as patent term or period, and, therefore, requires a thread break task of its interpretation to make the issues clearer for the law making agency to frame a clear policy. In order to better understand the issues of legal importance and judicial construction, it becomes all important to refurbish the concept of patent rights and patent-term in brief before dwelling upon the genesis and general notion of Bolar provision and its peculiar incorporation in the Indian patent system in the context of market regulatory provision, the patent rights and the patent term and other connected issues.

Patent Rights and Patent-Term

Legally speaking, patent right is a kind of intellectual property right always of exclusionary nature. Because, in legal sense, a 'patent' is a term that is used to signify an 'exclusive right' or bundle of exclusive rights or, say, 'monopoly rights' over a specific kind of intellectual creation. Every legal aspect remaining satisfied, it is granted under a given legal system to an intellectual creation as a mundane embodiment [7] of intellectual ideas devoid of any form, appearance, expression or impression etc. such as technical instruction(s)/feature(s), better referred to as invention in a broader sense.

Such invention for the purpose of patent regime, however, ought to satisfy in itself the jurisprudentially professed maximum patentability requirements of novelty (newness), inventiveness (non-obviousness) and industrial applicability (utility). Inventiveness is symbolised with the essential feature(s) or, say, with the active ingredient(s) that solves some technical problem(s) in the production of goods or services. In other words, the particular creation, i.e. the invention, is nothing but inventiveness—the essential feature(s) or, say, the active ingredient(s), and if it is new and capable of industrial applicability in the production of goods or services, then, the particular creation, i.e. the invention, is referred to as a technical invention.

It is said, "it is the cumulative effect of novelty, inventiveness and industrial applicability of an invention that renders that invention a technical invention—a technology". [8] Such creation or invention—the essential feature(s), the active ingredient(s), is generally referred to as 'invention for patent'. When invention is in the nature of being embodied in some product—goods or services, it is customary to call it a 'product-invention' or simply a 'product'.

On the other hand, when invention is in the nature of some process, method or use, thereby, producing or not some product—goods or services—it is customary to call it a 'process-invention' or simply as 'process'. An invention that *could* be granted a patent under a given system of patent law is known as a 'patentable invention'. As such, the patentable product and process inventions in respect of a given system of patent law, on being granted a patent thereunder is known respectively as a patented product and a patented process, and the grantee or proprietor of such patent is known as patentee. [9]

The patent system of a country, like India, after granting patent to a patentable product invention or process invention, thereby, rendering them as patented product and process, confers on the patentee, the exclusive rights of certain defined activities as regards to the patented product and process as well as product obtained directly by patented process. These legally conferred exclusive rights or, say, monopoly rights, thus constitute what one may call the patent monopoly of the patentee. The Indian Patents Act confers this patent monopoly under Section 48 dealing with "Rights of Patentees". This section, as substituted by the Patents (Amendment) Act, 2002, [10] reads as under:

"Subject to the other provisions contained in this Act and the conditions specified in Section 47, a patent granted under this Act shall confer upon the patentee:

- where the subject-matter of the patent is a product, the exclusive right to prevent third parties, who do not have his consent, from the act of making, using, offering for sale, selling or importing for those purposes that product in India;
- where the subject-matter of the patent is a process, the exclusive right to prevent third parties, who do not have his consent, from the act of using that process, and from the act of using, offering for sale, selling or importing for those purposes the product obtained directly by that process in India".

The patent monopoly defined, under Section 48 of the Act, 1970, as exclusive right of the patentee is restricted to a patented product, a patented process, a product-direct-by-patented process as well as to a territorial limit—India. This right further gets restricted, to a reasonable period of time under Section 53 of the Act. [11] The said section dealing with the "Term of Patent" reads as under:

(1) Subject to the provisions of this Act, the term of every patent granted, after the commencement of the Patents (Amendment) Act, 2002, and the term of every patent which has not expired and has not ceased to have effect, on the date of such commencement, under this Act, shall be twenty years from the date of filing of the application for the patent.

Explanation: For the purpose of this sub-section, the term of patent in case of international applications filed under the Patent Cooperation Treaty designating India, shall be twenty years from the international filing date accorded under the Patent Cooperation Treaty.

(2) A patent shall cease to have effect notwithstanding anything therein in this Act on the expiration of the period prescribed for the payment of any renewal fee, if that fee is not paid within the prescribed period or within such extended period as may be prescribed.

(3) [omitted].

(4) Notwithstanding anything contained in any other law for the time being in force, on cessation of the patent right due to non-payment of renewal fee or on expiry of the term of the patent, the subject matter covered by the said patent shall not be entitled to any protection".

Section 53 of the Act, as is obvious, has been made *subject to the provisions of this Act*, that is, the term or, say, the period of patent is to be observed subject to the provisions of the Act of 1970, [12] and the conclusion drawn from Section 53 read with all the subjecting provisions of this Act is that the term/period of the patent granted will be at the most 20 years from the date of the filing of the application for the patent unless ceased earlier as per the provisions of the Act of 1970 and on the cessation of the patent right or on the expiry of that right, as the case may be, the subject matter, that is, the patented invention protected by a patent shall no more be protected.

The commercial exploitation of the patent rights shall, therefore, be consequently determined. In other words, where the subjecting provisions of the Act are not being applied, the maximum period of the commercial exploitation of a patent right is a twenty years term of that patent for every technological invention. Section 53 of the Act of 1970 thus prescribes, like the legal system of every other jurisdiction, the time limit for the due exercise of the patent monopoly by a patentee. In other words, it renders a patent monopoly, a time bound patent monopoly on the expiry of which its subject matter, the patented invention, fall into public domain to be exploited by any member of the public as the very patent over the subject matter ceases to exist in law.

In India, the patent rights of the kind ensured to a patentee under Section 48 of the Patents Act, 1970 and consequently the commercial exploitation thereof through patent agreements [13] say, for example, patent licensing contract or for that matter patent distribution agreement, ensured by Section 70 of the Act are so ensured and protected as long as the term or, say, period of the patent operation has not expired in terms of Section 53. Any activity of the kinds of specified exclusive right as regards the patented invention—patented product, patented process as well as product-direct-by patented process—resorted to by any third person without the consent of the patentee, shall obviously amount to the infringement of patent right unless the same falls within one or more of the defences available under the Patents Act, so as not to be considered as infringement of patent right.

The provision of the kind of sub-section (a) of Section 107A, generally referred to as Indian Bolar Provision, constitutes one such defence to an allegation of patent infringement. The subsequent study is growingly confined to the genesis and concept of the Bolar provision, its peculiar incorporation in the Indian patent system in the context of market regulatory provision, the patent rights and the patent term and other connected issues.

Bolar Provision: Genesis and Concept

The Indian Bolar provision incorporated in sub-section (a) of Section 107A, quoted above, is the result, though of late, of the so-called Bolar exception, that is, the 'exception' what a generic producer Bolar argued, though unsuccessfully, in a case involving Hoffman La Roche and Bolar itself, namely, *Roche Product Inc. vs. Bolar Pharmaceutical Co. Inc.,* [14] to be made to the prohibited use of the patented product. [15] In that case, the US Court of Appeals for the Federal Circuit declared that "taking, during the life a patent, the statutory and regulatory steps necessary to market, after the patent expired, a drug equivalent to a patented brand named drug" [16] is "a violation of the patent laws in the guise of 'scientific inquiry', when that inquiry has definite, cognizable, and not insubstantial commercial purposes". [17]

Bolar argued on the ground of public policy that the policy requires the creation of a new exception to the prohibited use of the patented product during patent term where such use is for the United States Food and Drug Administration (USFDA), a market regulatory approval law requiring pre-market regulatory approval requirements as to development and submission of information as respect generic product for market approval, so that it could be marketed as soon as the patent term expires. But the court declined "to engage in legislative activity proper only for the Congress". [18]

The Court's ruling in Roche case, it is observed, delayed the generic producer of the generic product from entering the market for a significant period of time, even after patent expiry, because it took three to four years for him to conduct all the tests required for market administration approval [19] and, consequently, "the patent holder was thus able to enjoy gratuitous extended patent protection". [20] "In other words, the combined effect of the patent law and the pre-market regulatory approval requirement was to create an effective extension of the patent term", [21] or what one may call 'patentee's de facto monopoly' [22] or 'spilled-over-period of patent protection', so-called because of the spilling-over of the patent term due to the pre-market regulatory approval requirement for generic drugs. [23]

Bolar's public policy-based argument for new exception to the prohibited use of the patented product during patent term, where such use is for the pre-market regulatory approval requirements of development and submission of information thereof for market approval, was considered by the policy makers an important and significant contribution to address the competing policy interests of patent holders and the generic producers with over all benefit to the vast consumers. His public policy-based 'exception' received world wide acceptance through most of the countries' legal frameworks which got fashioned as Bolar provisions or exceptions of the respective countries.

US Congress was the first to seize the opportunity to address, *inter alia,* the Bolar's exception by adopting what is officially called 'the 1984 Drug Price Competition and Patent-Term Restoration Act' and informally known as the "Hatch-Waxman Act". [24] Section 202 falling under the 'Patent-Term Restoration' part of the Act of 1984 deals with the so-called US Bolar provision that got formally introduced as Section 27(e)(1) of the Patents Act, 1994 under 35 United States Code (35 U.S.C.). [25] Like US and Indian enactments, the Bolar exemption is also found to be in vogue in the patent legislations of countries like Canada, Australia, Israel, Argentina and Myanmar (Burma), People Republic of China, Japan and the European Union (EU).

The concept of the Bolar provision is, therefore, said to be the result of the 'generic producers' and competitors' inability to build, before patent expiration, the inventory needed to enter the market immediately upon the expiration of the patent as it requires a lot of research and preparation and marketing approval in satisfaction of relevant market regulatory approval laws and regulations that, obviously, need time.

In fact, there may be some laws in force that regulate the

manufacture, construction, use, sale or import etc. of any product for the purpose, amongst others, of development uses, say for clinical trial, and submission of information (knowledge etc.) received from such development, obviously, to some regulatory authorities of a given system of law, like Drug Controller General of India (DCGI) under the (Indian) Drug and Cosmetic Act, 1940, [26] to get its marketing approval for the products. These laws and regulations equally apply to everyone wishing to market his/her commercial products. In the context of the patented products, the marketing approval requirements is a necessary concomitant to put the product in commercial market, while for a generic producer to put his generic products in the market these requirements become a complex issue much more in the case of his preparing such product equivalent to patented product for market approval well before the expiry of the patent term than after the expiry.

The complexity arises out of the fact that the production of generic product (like pharmaceuticals) often involves a two-tier production arrangement—active ingredient production and generic product production [27]—wherein the producer of either production gets engaged in committing one or more of the prohibited activities of the patentee even if those activities were solely for the purpose of development and submission of information for seeking market approval. To address to such a complexity, the Bolar provision becomes a safe harbour for them to defend any successful allegation of patent infringement.

So far as Indian Bolar provision of the kinds of Section 107A (a) is concerned, it can be said that in order to constitute an act, in question, as an exception to patent rights and, hence, a defence against patent infringement, it is incumbent that each and every terms of the very sub-section must be shown to be satisfied, that is, the act in question is:

- any act of making, constructing, using, selling, or importing a patented invention;

- solely for use reasonably related to the development and submission of information required under any law for the time being in force, in India, or in a country other than India, that regulates the manufacture, construction, use, sale or import of any product".

Now, it is interesting to see the peculiar incorporation of the Bolar provision as such in the Indian patent system as well as in the context of market regulatory provision, the patent rights and the patent term and other connected issues.

Indian Bolar Provision

The Indian Patents Act, it may be pointed out, makes the Bolar provision or exception of the kind of Section 107A(a) to extend only to 'any act of making, constructing, using, selling, or importing of a 'patented invention'. That means Section 107A(a) does not discriminate between various generic products containing the patented invention so as to cover only few, like pharma products and not the rest. It covers all the generic products of any technology uniformly. The only condition is that each one of them could have been covered by one or other kinds of regulatory laws. If any generic product is not so covered that could also be not covered by Section 107A(a) regulatory review exception. Patented invention, be in product or process form, here necessarily means the 'active ingredient(s) or, say, essential feature(s) to which patent extends. This, authoritatively speaking, includes the so-called 'active-ingredient' produced by an expert producer that is equivalent to the patented 'active/essential ingredient(s)'. [28]

Undoubtedly, the most cherished aim of the Bolar exemption is to provide an exception to the prohibited activities of exclusionary rights of the patentee in order to enable the generic producers to carry on the Bolar permitted activities during patent term without the patentee's consent, to ensure that the generic products are ready with necessary marketing approval to be put on commercial market in sufficient quantity generally with consumer affordable prices soon after the patent ceases to exist. But added to this cherished aim is the lurking danger of misuse and abuse of the very Bolar protection mainly arising out of construction of its phrase "*solely for uses reasonably related to the development and submission of information required under any law for the time being in force*". The language "uses reasonably related to" is all that is taken advantage of for committing this mischief and the abuse because of its subjectivity nature [29] and vague meaning [30] not defined by any statute though it is found from various courts' decisions in most continental countries that it has been interpreted broadly.

For example, Cheng Zhang ETH Zueich in his article illustrates one such approach in his own words as: "In *Amgen, Inc. vs. Hoechst Marion Roussel, Inc.*, the court found that "the *use* in question would contribute (relatively directly) to the generation of kinds of information that was likely to be relevant in the processes by which the FDA would decide whether to approve the product" and, therefore, is not patent infringement. Such activities may include carrying out experiments using the patented products to test the production processes, manufacturing extra amount of patented products than that required by the FDA for approval, and making tests to fulfil the foreign standards. [31]

This gives the answer to the many posed questions like "how much quantity of drug may be required for 'uses reasonably related to development and submission of information?", "can manufacture or import of excessive quantity of drugs be allowed under the pretext of 'uses reasonably related to development' in the Indian scenario?" [32] In other words, it is submitted that the questions of quantity of drugs required and the excessive manufacturing or importing of drugs are immaterial if there is a reasonable basis to conclude that the findings of the clinical trial/experiment with them will support any submission of those findings to the marketing approval authority.

Similarly, it could be said that Bolar exception could extend to pre-clinical research despite the fact that "basic drug research at the pre-clinical phase is usually years behind any submission to the drug approval authorities". [33] Nay, it is just a submission and the posed questions in practical India is yet to go under judicial scrutiny at the anvil of "*solely for uses reasonably related to the development and submission of information required under any law for the time being in force*", so as to meet a fair protection to the patentee with a reasonable amount of certainty to the third parties—the generic producers.

Bolar Provision and the Patent-Regulatory Linkage

The Indian Bolar provision of the kind of Section 107A(a) has an important bearing with the regulatory authority, like the Drug Controller General of India (DCGI), under the (Indian) Drug and Cosmetic Act, 1940 as one example. As observed above, Bolar provision constitutes an exception to the patent rights and hence operates as a defence to patent infringement. However, it is equally important to note that "unlike the US, India does not have the concept of tentative approval—it is always a final approval after which generic company is free to enter market without any further go-ahead from the DCGI". [34] This raises the questions whether the Indian Bolar provision gives a statutory go-ahead for the wilful patent infringement with the very getting of the regulatory authority's marketing approval, [35] or it attempts to provide a linkage between the patent office and the regulatory authority so that marketing approval is not actually granted during the term of a valid patent? [36]

It could be seen that an affirmative answer to either question will operate as negative answer to the other in the sense that if marketing approval could be granted during the patent term then there is no scope of patent-linkage, and if, on the other hand, it is insisted that Bolar provision provides such linkage, then, there is no scope of allowing a go-ahead for the wilful patent infringement. The scope of allowing a go-ahead for the wilful patent infringement seems to be hallmarked in the wake of the Delhi High Court's judgment in *Bayer Corporation and Another (Appellant) vs. Union of India and Others (Respondents)* [37] to the effect that "any attempt at bringing in patent-linkage on the basis of the existing provisions (including Bolar provision) of the Patents Act and the DCA (Drug and Cosmetic Act, 1940) cannot be countenanced". [38]

In other words, it can be said now that Indian Bolar provision not only provides exemption for conducting studies for bioequivalence before patent-term expiry but also gives a statutory go-ahead for wilful patent infringement". The decision, thus, becomes subject of much academic debate much more in the light of the TRIPS Agreement, 1994 and TRIPS Harmonized Patents Act, 1970 both harping too much for the protection of patent with necessary leverage for the protection of public interest and welfare. This academic debate is being left to the intellectual minds of the jurists and scholars not to be dwelt upon in this paper.

Indian Bolar Provision in Respect to Patent Rights

It may be pointed out here that the Bolar exemption of the kind of Section 107A(a) to Section 48 patent rights covers the 'patented invention', while Section 48 conferred patent right covers the identified 'patented product', 'patented process' or 'product obtained directly from the patented process' as its subject-matters. Question may be asked whether the Bolar provision's subject matter, namely, the 'patented invention' includes all the Section 48 identified subject matters. The answer may be squarely a 'no'. It is only 'patented product' and 'product-direct-by patented process', and not patented process, that could be said to be addressed by the Bolar provision. Because the Bolar provision identified activities as regards the patented invention shall be considered as exceptions to Section 48 patent rights only when the patented invention made, constructed, used, sold or imported is *used* only for getting marketing approval under any law that regulates "the manufacture, construction, use, sale or import of any *product*".

Taken as such that Indian Bolar's patented invention covers in general only the patented product and product-direct-by patented process, it could be said that it thus tries to do away with the requirement, unlike the US Bolar provision and many of the European Union (EU), of subjecting one or other kinds or species of the genera patented product to itself. For example, it is clear from the above quoted Section 27(e)(1) of the U.S. Patent Act, that the Bolar provision there is applicable only to patented drugs, *other than a new animal drug or veterinary biological product,* instead of covering every patented product in general, though the courts there have given a rather broad interpretation to this statutory exemption to include 'all of the products, except new animal drugs and veterinary biological products, eligible for a patent term extension under Section 201 [of the 1984 Hatch-Waxman Act incorporated as Section 156(f) of 35 U.S.C.] that are also subject to Section 202 [of the said Act incorporated as Section 27(e)(1) of 35 U.S.C.]'. [39]

Thus, it seems that the US "Bolar exemption" covers every generic invention equivalent to patented product including both medicines and medical devices, and with that, the range of activities are also very broad, but restricts the activities of getting FDA approval for generic inventions instead of testing for new animal drug or veterinary biological product. But whether a broad interpretation of the American Bolar provision to cover all patented products including patented drugs except new animal drugs and veterinary biological products, is a reasonable approach in the context of Indian as well as US Bolar provisions is an issue to be reckoned with. Whether, at least in practical India, the term 'patented product' will be applied broadly or narrowly, one has to wait for its courts' interpretations.

It could further be seen that the Bolar exception protects only the making, constructing, using, selling, or importing of the patented invention i.e. patented 'active ingredients' but not its 'offering for sale' which under Section 48(a) constitutes the exclusive right of the patentee, as well as its 'stock-piling/warehousing' which in the opinion of the Panel report, in *Canada-Patent Protection of Pharmaceutical Product,* very much constitutes the exclusive rights of the patentee. [40] It means an expert producer would end up in committing patent infringement, if he resorts to an 'offer for sale' of the active ingredient(s) alike that of the patented active ingredient(s) or for that matter to 'stockpile' such ingredient(s). Question may be asked why this concession has been given to the patentee vis-à-vis Bolar exception unlike Section 55.2(2) of the Canada Patent Act that extends Bolar exception to the stock-piling also. [41]

Obviously, there must be some logic for which one has to wait for the judicial scrutiny by Indian courts in future patent litigation. However, just as a matter of observation, it could be said that so far as 'offering for sale' of the patented invention is concerned despite it having an inbuilt commercial instinct it has nothing to do with the "*solely for uses reasonably related to the development and submission of information required under any law for the time being in force*". So, it is but logical to keep it outside the purview of the Bolar protection. Unlike the patent pre-expiration testing, the 'offering for sale' of the patented invention before patent expiry does not address the time-delay caused by pre-market regulatory approval requirements.

In fact, the act of 'offering for sale' of the patented 'active ingredient(s)' provides only an opportunity to an expert-producer of it first to enter into a standing contract with generic producers, get insured of his manufactured active ingredient to be purchased and with such assurance embark upon to carry on the patent pre-expiry testing activities than what may desist him from resorting to these activities in the absence of any such contract. In other words, the role of 'offering for sale' of the patented ingredient is not to address the time delay caused by the pre-market regulatory approval requirements. It's exclusion from the purview of the Indian Bolar provision is, therefore, justified on this count.

So far as 'stockpiling' of the patented invention is concerned, it can be said that stockpiling, though also has nothing to do with the patent pre-expiry testing requirements, has in a sense a complementary effect to address the time-delay caused by pre-market regulatory approval requirements. In so much so that the expert-producer's pre patent-expiry permitted acts for obtaining the 'active ingredient(s)'is alike that of the patented active ingredient(s), and similarly the generic producer's act of assembling those ingredient(s) with other agents to obtain a final generic product under the pre-market regulatory approval requirements necessarily need the stockpiling of the manufactured 'active ingredients' as well as of the generic products containing those ingredients so that a large bulk of the generic products could be available at hand to be put on commercial market soon after the patent expires than to do the same activities after such expiry thereby leading to the time-delay in such marketing.

It can, therefore, be suggested that the stockpiling activities of the expert-producer with respect to 'active ingredient' and of the generic producer with respect to generic product, though could not be made to fall within the Bolar exception of the kind of sub-section (a) of Section 107A because of it having nothing to do with the patent pre-expiry testing requirements for market approval, however, could be allowed as an additional exception to patent right of stockpiling the patented invention because of their having a complementary effect to the said Bolar exception. In fact, "without the additional permission to stockpile during the term of the patent, competitors who obtain regulatory permission to sell on the day the patent expires would still not be able to enter the market on that day, because they would first have to manufacture a sufficient stock of goods". [42] The Indian Patents Act, thus, needs further amendment to incorporate this additional permission like that of Section 55.2(2) of the Canada Patents Act.

Indian Bolar Provision and the Patent Term

It may be asked whether Bolar provision is a boon or a bane for a patent holder exercising his monopoly power for a limited term of, say, twenty years as provided under the Indian Patents Act, 1970. Without going into minute details as to questions like: why there must be a specified or, say, pre-defined duration for a patent right as a kind of intellectual property rights unlike other non-intellectual properties where no such term or period is ever specified? [43]; why the pre-defined patent duration must be a reasonable one? [44]; can the twenty years limit of patent term for every patented invention defined by Section 53 of the Indian Patents Act be said to be a reasonable one when TRIPS mandate provides laxity in the patent duration even beyond twenty years as the minimum patent term? The main concern/issue of present discussion is the virtual realizing of the statutorily pre-defined patent duration. In the context of Indian patents with a term of twenty years, the question asked may be: is twenty years of patent term virtually realised or, say, enjoyed by the patent holder, and whether the Bolar provision is of any concern to such realization.

Before the TRIPS' 20 years harmonization period for patent protection from the date of *filing of the application* for the patent, [45] the term of patent protection, in some countries, used to be calculated from the date of the *filing of patent application*, in some others from the *date of the publication* of the patent application and in some other countries from the *date of the grant* of the patent. [46] As such, there were found different dates of starting the calculation of the period of patent protection.

The TRIPS Agreement, however, has done away with the different dates of starting calculation of period of patent protection, if not the starting date of patent protection, which protection a country-member to WTO is, however, at liberty to provide either from the date of filing of the patent application, or from the date of the publication of the said application, or from the date of the grant of the patent on such application.

In fact, "The provision (of TRIPS) states the earliest date when the protection may end. This means that protection need not start from the filing date. *But what is important is that the 20 years period of patent must necessarily be calculated from the date of filing of the patent application.* In several countries, protection (in terms of being able to obtain full damages) actually starts only from publication or even grant, which the Agreement allows, subject to Article 62(2)". [47] The idea of starting the 20 years of patent protection from the date of filing of the patent is obviously, as said above, to get the earliest date when the protection may end. So far so is good for it being falling in the public domain as early as possible. Section 53 of the 1970 Act (amended 2002) [48] catering to this idea thus stands for good reason. Section 53 read with the provisions relating to the procedure for acquisition and maintenance of a patent and matters connected therewith, compendiously known as 'patent prosecution', leads to the conviction that to a greater extent the time taken for patent prosecution do not necessarily and significantly mitigate the period of the patent protection of twenty years term and thus does not allow unnecessary delay in the commencement of effective protection.

This, in fact, is a positive approach enabling the patent owner to commercially exploit his patent for a longer period within the Act's maximum twenty years in the absence of otherwise unnecessary and significant delay in patent prosecution. "Time limits are prescribed", says Narayanan, within which parties in the proceedings before the controller have to comply with certain requirements at various stages through which an application for patent has to pass. These time limits are designed to facilitate quick disposal of the applications well within the monopoly period of the patent when ultimately granted". [49] Any artificial measures such as abandonment, reinstatement, non-payment of fees and non-response to a patent examiner's report will not oblige the patent-applicants, tainted with such vitiating measures, to extend the life of their patents up to the maximum twenty years term. [50]

In other words, such patent applicants shall be restricted to enjoy the patent protection for commercial exploitation for a term *equal to twenty years minus time consumed for artificial measures.* The same effect ensues when a country provides patent protection from the date of the publication of the patent application or, for that matter, from the date of the grant of the patent. For example, if the patent prosecution takes 2 years, then the actual realization of patent protection shall be 20 minus 2 equal to 18 years. Similarly, if the patent protection is to start from the date of the publication of the patent application and it takes, say, 3 years to publish after its filing date, then the actual realization of patent protection shall come to 17 years, and if the patent protection is to start from the date of the grant of the patent and it takes, say, 4 years for such grant after filing date of the patent application, then the actual realization of patent protection shall come to 16 years. In a sense, it could be said that 20 years patent term is not virtually realized in true sense.

The period between the date of filing of the patent application and the date from which patent protection actually starts may conveniently be termed as 'time-lag of patent protection'. The question may be asked: is there any means to compensate the patentee for this 'time-lag of patent protection'. Added to this problem is the fact of the time consumed in taking the statutory and regulatory steps to get the administration's marketing approval necessary to put the patented product in commercial market.

In fact, 'two unintended distortions of a patent term are produced by the requirement that certain products must receive pre-market regulatory approval. The *first* distortion occurs at one end of the patent term in the sense that for the holder of the patent relating to such products, the clock on his patent term will be running even though he is not yet able to derive any profit from the patented product. Taken as such, it could be said that at the part of the patent-holder there are two lag-times—one is the lag-time of patent protection and another is the lag-time of market exploitation due to the time taken for regulatory approval. It is “the combined effect of the patent law and the pre-market regulatory approval requirement”. [51]

The combined effect of these two lag-times results in the prolonging of the patent holder’s inability to reap any economic benefit from his patented product until market-regulatory approval gets over. This tension of the patent-holder requires serious consideration. The *second* distortion occurs at the other end of the patent term in the sense that for a non-patentee who plans to compete with the patentee no activity by him as falling within the prohibited use of the patent, even for the sole purpose of applying for market regulatory approval, could be commenced, in the absence of otherwise law, without infringement but only after expiration of the entire patent term thereby creating, because of the time-taking market-regulatory approval for his generic product, an effective extension or spilling over of the patent term’ [52] in favour of the patent-holder which (favour) in the presence of a Bolar Provision becomes bleak to a greater extent leading to further anxiety and worry for the patent-holder in not reaping his patent under the umbrella of the so-called spill-over period.

Before any Bolar provision was known, the pre-market regulatory approval requirement at the end of the generic producer producing the generic product after the patent term gets expired, was a boon in disguise for the patentee to make good for the financial loss he occasioned during the early years of the patent-term due to the combined effect of the time taken for the patent prosecution and pre-market regulatory approval requirements. As a consequence “the patent holder is thus able to enjoy gratuitous extended patent protection” [53] or what one may call ‘de facto patent monopoly’ or spill-over period of patent monopoly generally of five to ten years resulting from the said pre-market regulatory approval requirements. Such an effect is well recognised at the hand of the adjudicating authorities. [54]

This, in a sense, operates to compensate the patentee to a greater extent for the period he lost in obtaining marketing approval for putting his patented product in the commercial market after the grant of the patent.

However, with the introduction of Bolar provision, like that of India and US, the extent or, say, period of spill over of patent term got restricted or curtailed to a considerable extent than what was available to a patentee in the absence of such provision with the result that short period of spilling over of the market exclusivity of the patent holder is considered not sufficient enough to compensate for the long period lost to him for financial gain due to the combined effect of the times taken for the patent prosecution and pre-market regulatory approval requirements. It seems that the Hatch-Waxman Act of 1984 while enacting the US Bolar provision had realised this situation, and, therefore, "allowed patent term extensions of up to five years to compensate for the restriction on the effective protection term because of the time needed to acquire the FDA's marketing approval". [55] But the question is whether such patent-term extension is justified in the presence of Bolar provision/exception.

Indian Patents Act, 1970 does not have, unlike the US patent system, any patent-term extension provision and that too for good reason in one sense that the "patent-term-extension and Bolar exemption are self cancelling provisions, which taken together, have no effect on the length of the exclusive marketing period of most drugs (of the genera patented product)". [56] If it does provide there would have been no need for Bolar exemption provision like the sub-section (a) of Section107A.

Keeping the two provisions in the Indian legal system would mean cancelling of one by another. While the Bolar exemption permits non-commercial use of the patented invention during the patent term only to be exploited commercially just after the expiration of the patent-term, but for the patent-term extension provision the same could not be done. Any ‘patent-term extension’ provision will prohibit the competitors from making, constructing, using, selling or importing the patented invention even after the patent term expiry even if those rights (of prohibition) were exercised legitimately during the pre-defined patent-term under the Bolar exemption. Hence, for good political reason, not to be dwelt at length here, our Patents Act adopted Bolar exemption to patent rights in its right perspective.

That leaves the question of any US like ‘patent-term extension’ provision application in Indian patent system to be debated among the academic circles. As observed above, according to TRIPS Agreement, the period of counting 20 years of patent protection is to be taken from the date of the filing of the patent application. But equally, it is important to note that this 20 year protection is the minimum protection that a State-member to the WTO is bound to provide in its domestic legislation concerning patent regime.

Taken as such, such a country is, therefore, at liberty to provide patent term extension beyond the TRIPS’ ordained protection, and, therefore, there is no hitch or harm to provide for any US like ‘patent-term extension’ provision application in Indian patent system. This extended period could have been equated with the spill over patent term identified with the time taken by the generic producers in getting marketing approval of their generic product after patent term expiry, that is, in the absence of any Bolar provision. Indian patent regime, however, is having its own Bolar provision.

Any suggestion that India must also follow the US policy of patent-term extension to compensate the patent holder for the loss due to the combined effect of the time taken for the patent prosecution and pre-market regulatory approval requirements could, therefore, be made only with this observation that generic producer could be allowed to resort to the Bolar provision not only just well before the expiry of the patent term but also during the period of extended patent-term. In this way, the patent holder shall have the maximum of patent protection for commercial exploitation of his patented product, i.e. the TRIPS' mandated 20 years minus the time lost due to the combined effect of the time taken for the patent prosecution and pre-market regulatory approval requirements plus the Act's extra specified period, on the one hand, and the generic producer shall have the protection against any allegation of patent infringement done not only within but also beyond the patent term, but well before the end of the patent-term extension.

Conclusions

Since the political recognition of the Bolar exemption to patent infringement, most of the countries of the world have incorporated in their legislative embodiments their own so-called Bolar exemptions more or less based on the US Bolar provision of the kind of Section 27(e)(1) of its Patents Act, 1994. India in its considerate policy of remaining abreast with the patent systems of the major countries and harmonization process of the world legislations, enacted Bolar provision of the kind of Section 107A(a) in its Patent Act, 1970 after more than 15 years of the Roche court's ruling. The provision, apart from its own merits, has a bearing with the regulatory approval provision like Drugs and Cosmetic Act, 1940, patent rights and patent term. Though issues like 'patent linkage with market regulatory provisions' arising out of the drafting of the Bolar provision has been settled by the Indian courts in Bayer Corporation's case, yet it is still a matter of academic debate.

Again, Bolar provision provides exception to patentee's exclusive rights except 'offer for sale' and 'stockpiling' of the patented invention. Putting 'offer for sale' out of the purview of the Bolar provision is logical but similar treatment to 'stockpiling' needs serious consideration on the part of the law making agency. It is found that Bolar provision, patent prosecution, market regulatory approval, patent term and patent-term spill over period are inter-connected issues. They need to be synchronized, it is submitted, by resort to US like patent term extension but with this observation that the generic producer could be allowed to resort to the Bolar provision not only just well before the expiry of the patent term but also during the period of extended patent-term.

Endnotes

1. See Chaudhary Sudeep (2002), "TRIPS Agreement and Amendment of Patents Act in India", *Economic and Political Weekly*, August 10, 3355.
2. Cf. the quotation in Graham Dutfield (2003), "Intellectual Property Rights and the Life Science Industries", *Twentieth Century History,* 121, (foot note 31 thereof).
3. A generic product is a product that necessarily contains the same 'active ingredient(s)' as the original brand name product, but its dosage formulation (including the filler, binding agent and coating) usually differs.cf. WTO Panel Report in *Canada: Patent Protection of Pharmaceutical Product*, WTO document WT/DS 114/R, March 17, 2000, (originally: English), para 2.4, 4. Where a patent extends to that active ingredient(s), the brand name product is termed as patented brand name product. The quality of the generic product is as effective as the patented product.
4. The manufacture, sale and import of the products, particularly the drugs and cosmetic products, in India, are regulated by Drugs and Cosmetics Act, 1940 [last amended 1995]. Such regulations in general apply to the manufacture, construction, use, sale or import of any such product regardless of whether it is patented, non-patented or generic product. It may, however, be pointed out that for a vast majority of patented products, there is no marketing regulation law.
5. WTO Panel Report in Canada: Patent Protection of Pharmaceutical Product, WTO document WT/DS 114/R, March 17, 2000, (originally: English), para 7.4, 147.
6. Id. para 7.3.
7. Cf. Hillary Pearson and Clifford Miller (1997), "Commercial Exploitation of Intellectual Property", 3.
8. Cf. NunoPires de Carvalho (2002), "The TRIPS Regime of Patent Rights", 153.
9. Section 2(1)(p) of Indian Patents Act, 1970 reads as under: "patentee means the person for the time being entered on the

register as the grantee or proprietor of the patent".

10. (38 of 2002), w.e.f. 20.5.2003.
11. The requirement of fixing a reasonable period was, in fact, to meet India's obligation under the TRIPS Agreement, 1994. The TRIPS Agreement was adopted at Marrakesh on April 15, 1994 as Annex IC of the Final Act Embodying the Result of the Uruguay Round of Multilateral Trade Negotiations starting 1986 to 1994. The Agreement came into force on January 1, 1995 subject to enjoinment made under its relevant Articles. Its Article 33 reads as under: "The term of patent protection available shall not end before the expiration of a period of twenty years counted from the filing date". It is understood that those Members which do not have a system of original grant may provide that the term of protection shall be computed from the filing date in the system of original grant.
12. These provisions are, for example, Section 53(2), dealing with the payment of the prescribed renewal fee from time to time and effect of such non-payment, Section 55 dealing with the term of 'patent of addition', Section 64 dealing with patent to cease to have any effect on revocation by the High Court/Appellate Board's order, as the case may be, Section 65 dealing with the patent to cease to have any effect on revocation by the Controller (under direction from the Central Government in cases relating to atomic energy), Section 66 dealing with the patent to cease to have any effect on revocation by the Central Government (in case the patent or mode of its exercise is mischievous to the State or generally prejudicial to the public) and Section 85 dealing with the patent to cease to have any effect on the revocation by the Controller (for non-working of the patent).
13. "Patent agreement", as terminology, is usual to be used as a genera covering species like 'patent licensing agreement', 'patent distribution contract' and similar species. For example, one meets with such observation: "Microsoft has nailed a second Android device maker to a patent licensing agreement. The Redmond software giant announced on Monday that General Dynamics Itronix has signed a patent agreement that will provide 'broad coverage under Microsoft's patent portfolio'. In other words, General Dynamics Itronix has agreed to license certain, unnamed Microsoft patents for use with Android-

powered portables.

14. 733 F.2d 858 (CA Fed. Cir. 1984).
15. The patented product in question was the 'flurazepam hydrochloride' (flurazepamhcl), the 'active ingredient' or, say, 'essential feature' to which patent was extended in Roche's successful brand name prescription sleeping pill "Dalmane".
16. Supra f.n. 14 at 860.
17. Id. at 863.
18. Ibid.
19. Id. at 860.
20. Narinder S. Banait (2005), "Authorised Generics: Antitrust Issue and the Hatch-Waxman Act", Fenwick and West I.I.P., November 3at 2. See also supra f.n. 14, at 863.
21. Eli Lilly and Co. vs. Medtronic, Inc., 496 US 661 (1990) at 670-671
22. Ibid.
23. Supra f.n. 8 at 258.
24. The informal name comes from the Act's two sponsors, representative Orrin Hatch of Utah and Henry Waxman of California.
25. The said section runs as under: "It shall not be an act of infringement to make, use, offer to sell, or sell within the United States or import into the United States a patented invention (other than a new animal drug or veterinary biological product as those terms are used in the Federal Food, Drug, and Cosmetic Act and the Act of March 4, 1913) which is primarily manufactured using recombinant DNA, recombinant RNA, hybridoma technology, or other processes involving site specific genetic manipulation techniques solely for uses reasonably related to the development and submission of information under a Federal law which regulates the manufacture, use, or sale of drugs or veterinary biological products".
26. Supra f.n. 4.
27. Supra at 3.
28. Supra f.n. 3.
29. Cf. Aliasgar Dholkawala, "Indian Patent Linkage with Regulatory Approval", available at: http://patentsnmore.wordpress.com/2010/01/18/india-patent-linkage-with-regulatory-approval.
30. See Cheng Zhang ETH Zueich, "The Third Amendment to the

PRC Patent Law and its Potential Influence on the Pharmaceutical Industry", available at: http://www.bepress.com/ndsip/reports/art20.

31. Ibid.
32. See Asghar Ali Dholkawala, op. cit.
33. Gladys Mirandah, "Bolar Provisions in India's Patent Law", available at: http://www.managingip.com/Article/1254871/Bolar-provisions-in-Indi.
34. See Varun C., "Does Section 107A of the Patents Act, 1970 (Bolar-Provision) Gives Statutory Go-ahead for Wilful Infringement?",available at: http://www.linkedin.com/answers/law-legal/corporate-law/intellectual property/LAW_COR_IPP/405442-8368425.
35. Cf. Ibid.
36. Aliasgar Dholakwala op. cit.
37. http://www.cbgnetwork.org/downloads/Bayer vs. Union of India.pdf.
38. Ibid. LPA 443/2009 at 27.
39. Cf. Eli Lilly at 672-673, available at: http://www.cornell.edu/supct/html/89-243.ZOhtm.
40. See WTO document WT/DS 114/R, March 17, 2000 (originally: English), para 7.7, 148.
41. Though on record such provision has been declared violative of the patentee's right to stockpiling. Id. at 156, para 7.34.
42. Supra f.n. 40 at 149, para 7.10.
43. The answer to this question is said to be the difference between non-destructive nature of the intellectual property and the destructive nature of the other property other than intellectual property. Intellectual property, like patent, being of non-destructive nature could, therefore, be considered of infinite duration, and, hence, it becomes logical to subject it to some predefined duration. Cf. NunoPires de Carvalho, op. cit.
44. The answer to this question is said to give, as one of the means of a balancing effect to two extremely equally prejudicial rights —the personal rights of the a patentee to have and enjoy his property—the patented invention, on the one hand, and public rights of the individual public to participate and enjoy that property, on the other. The consequential effect of such balancing leads to neither a permanent monopoly forever in

favour of the patentee to the total exclusion of the individual public interest nor a total extinction of that monopoly to the virtual detriment of the patentee. For detail on the balancing of two equally prejudicial rights, reference could be made to the judgment of 1785 of Lord Mansfield as cited by Jagdish Sagar in his address to the *WIPO Asian Regional Colloquium on the Judiciary and Intellectual Property System*, WIPO Pub. 726 (E), 1994, at 5-6. See also Article 27 of the U.N. Declaration of Human Rights, 1948; Mr. Justice M.H. Kania in his inaugural address to the *WIPO Asian Regional Colloquium on the Judiciary and Intellectual Property System*, WIPO Pub. 726 (E), 1994, at 14; E.S.Venkataramiah (1994): "Intellectual Property Cases in India", WIPO Pub. 726 (E), at 20.

45. See Article 33 of the TRIPS Agreement.
46. See T. Doi (1995), "Japan Legislation: TRIPS Agreement, E.I.P.R., D-42, D-43, and M. Blakenry (1996), "The Impact of the TRIPS Agreement in the Asia-Pacific Region", 10 E.I.P.R. 544. In case of India, before the Patents (Amendment) Act, 2002, the term of the patent protection used to be calculated either from the date of the sealing of the patent or the granting of the patent in circumstances mentioned therein [vide the original Section 53 of the Patents Act, 1970].
47. Daniel Gervaise (1998), "The TRIPS Agreement: Drafting, History and Analysis", at 256. Article 62(2) of the TRIPS reads as: "where the acquisition of the intellectual property rights is subject to the right being granted or registered, Members shall ensure that the procedures for grant or registration, subject to compliance with the substantive conditions for acquisition of the right, permit the granting or registration of the right within a reasonable period of time so as to avoid unwarranted curtailment of the period of protection".
48. For the provision of Section 53, see supra at 6-7.
49. Narayanan (1998), "Patent Law", at 9.
50. Cf. *Canada: Term of Patent Protection,* Panel and Appellate Body Reports adopted on October 12, 2000: WTO document/WT/DS 170/R, May 5, 2000.
51. Supra note 21.
52. Cf. the court observation in *Eli Lilly and Co. vs. Medtronic, Inc.*, 496 U.S. 661(1990), at 670-671.
53. Narinder S. Banait (2005), "Authorised Generics: Antitrust Issue

and the Hatch-Waxman Act", Fenwick and West I.I.P., November 3, at 2.

54. See for example, *Brulotte vs. Thys Co.*, 379 U.S. 29, 33 (1964), *Joy Technologies, Inc. vs. Flakt, Inc.*, No. 89-533-JJF, 1992 WL 188814, at 1 (D. Del, May 29, 1992), *Biogen Inc. vs. Schering AG,* 954 F. Supp. 391 (D. Mass, 1996) at 397, Case C-316/95, *Generics BV vs. Smith Kline and French Labs Ltd.,* 1997, E.C.R. 1-3929, WTO Panel in *Canada: Patent Protection of Pharmaceutical Product*, WTO document WT/DS 114/R, March 17, 2000 (originally: English), para 7.35 thereof where the Panel accepted that "In practical terms, it must be recognized that the enforcement of the right to exclude 'making' and 'using' during the patent term will necessarily give all patent owners, for all products, a short period of extended market exclusivity after the patent expires".
55. Graham Dutfield, op. cit. at 120.
56. Engelberg, A.B. (1999), "Special Patent Provisions for Pharmaceuticals: Have they Outlived their Usefulness? A Political, Legislative and Legal History of US Law and Observations for the Future", IDEA, *The Journal of Law and Technology*, 39(3): 389-425.

12

Pharmaceutical Patents in India

S.K. Verma

Introduction

The decision by Madras High Court in *Novartis AG and Anr. vs. Union of India and Others,* rejecting the patent application covering Novartis' famed anticancer drug Glivec and the other ongoing disputes, such as the one related to Roche's Ertolonib (brand name Tarceva), where the court refused to grant an injunction on the introduction of a generic version of the patented drug, have raised a fair amount of debate worldwide about the veracity of the Indian patent law, which has been brought in line with the Agreement on Trade-Related Intellectual Property Rights (TRIPS) from January 1, 2005. The rejection in the Novartis case stemmed primarily from a unique section in the Indian patent regime [Section 3(d)] that aims to prevent 'ever-greening' of patents. While these cases highlight the efforts in India to interpret the patent regime in the interests of public health, they also raise an important issue of legal certainty that the Indian patent regime needs to establish.

India has demonstrated its potential for innovative IP norms by articulating Section 3(d) in its patent regime, a section that arguably helps to balance pharmaceutical patent protection with the need to preserve access to medicines. But given the importance of India's informal economy, can it be stated with certainty that the new patent regime will provide the space to innovate as well by conceptualizing a set of 'informal' IP norms that will meet the health needs of its vast population? In upgrading its culture of innovation in the pharmaceutical industry, the role of the patent regime is very pivotal.

India became party to the WTO/TRIPS Agreement in April 1994. Around the same time, it acceded to the Paris Convention for the Protection of Industrial Property and the Patent Cooperation Treaty. Together, they have compelled significant strengthening of the nation's patent law. To meet its obligations under the TRIPS Agreement, the Patents Act, 1970, has been amended in 1999, 2002 and then in 2005. The 2005 Amendment Act heralded a new beginning in the protection of pharmaceutical patents in India. It introduced product patents in pharmaceuticals, drugs and chemicals. The amendments, however, have attracted an unprecedented attention, both domestically and globally, because of the presence of certain allegedly controversial provisions therein. While multinational pharmaceutical companies are concerned that the Act may wither away their exclusive rights, the activists and consumer groups are weary about the new product patent regime fearing that it may cause steep hikes in the price of life saving drugs and keeping the health care services out of the reach of common man.

While amending its patent law, India has exploited fully the flexibilities inherent in the TRIPS Agreement in protecting the genuine interests of the inventors and to attain its professed goal of increasing innovative activities. These flexibilities allow India to balance the need to protect its public from the social costs of stronger patent protection and provide the necessary incentives for domestic research and development in medicines and healthcare. In fact, the Indian Patents Act is a test case to use the flexibilities inherent in TRIPS in order to accommodate domestic economic conditions with the international baseline standards on IP rights. The Patents (Amendment) Act of 2005 has introduced some important amendments including the introduction of product patents for chemicals and pharmaceuticals, which were earlier eligible only for process patent that helped India's drug industry to grow by producing generics of well-known patented drugs without indulging into any R&D activity and inventing any patentable molecule. In the face of new changes, the local drug manufacturers may not depend entirely on generics and will be obliged to indulge in innovation for their survival.

The emerging scenario under the amended Patents Act raises a very pertinent question, namely whether it will help to increase innovative R&D activity in pharmaceutical sector. This needs an examination of in-built flexibilities in the Patents Act and other contextual factors. The important factor that may sustain the generic production is that up to 60 percent key pharmaceutical patents are due to expire by 2009 on molecules worth an estimated US$ 44 billion. The new patent regime has enough provisions to ensure that generic drugs are continuously available to the masses and generic manufacturers can continue to copy any pharmaceutical product already available in the Indian market prior to January 1, 2005.

In this context, the reasonable concerns come to mind, *viz*., whether the legislative and administrative measures, which are a part of the new patent regime, will help India in enhancing local innovation and inventiveness in pharmaceutical sector; and whether they will help India to attract foreign investment by providing a conducive IP regime. There are expansive provisions on compulsory licenses, parallel imports and against the ever-greening of patents, which need an analysis to determine that how far they will impact the innovative activities in the pharmaceutical sector. This study reviews the trends in India's TRIPS-compliant regulatory regime to examine whether this will impact positively the innovation in the pharmaceutical sector. The study will first take an account of pharmaceutical patents in the historical context, followed by an analysis of the main features of the new patent law. The structure and R&D capacities of the pharmaceutical industry and its future prospects will be discussed thereafter.

Pharmaceutical Patents: Historical Context

The legislative history of India's patent law starts with the 1856 Act, which was amended and replaced by subsequent

Acts of 1859, 1872, 1883 and 1911, which were adopted prior to India's Independence. All these Acts, including the Patents and Designs Act of 1911, which permitted patenting of pharmaceutical products under Patents Act of 1970, which replaced the 1911 Act, however, excluded pharmaceutical products from patent protection. The new Act, nevertheless, revolutionized the pharmaceutical sector in India. It helped India to develop a world-class generic drug manufacturing industry. The 1970 Act prohibited patents on 'substances intended for use, or capable of being used, as food or as medicine or as drug'. But the processes for the making of such substances remained patentable with a shorter period of five years from the date of sealing or seven years from the date of the patent, while the term of all other types of patents was made to fourteen years from the date of the patent.

The 1970 Act also included provisions on compulsory licensing, including on 'licenses of right' for the above-said substances, that is, the patented processes for manufacturing substances capable of being used as medicine or food were deemed automatically endorsed with the designation 'licenses of right, which could be issued after the expiry of three years from the date of sealing of the patent'. It is however important to note that, although the compulsory licensing provisions remained part of the Patents Act, they were rarely being put to use. The plausible reasons could be absence of local competition and of applications by potential licensees. In the case of pharmaceuticals, the absence of product patents was another reason along with the short span of five to seven years of these patents.

The 1970 Act made India an important player in the generic drugs market of the world. It led to the growth of a strong generic pharmaceutical industry in India, which helped in the sharp decline in prices of medicines. Immediately before the adoption of the Patents Act in 1970, the local pharmaceutical industry in India witnessed a relatively small growth accounting for just 25 percent of the domestic market.

But the restriction on product patent under the new Act and control over prices triggered a rapid development of the industry which now accounts for more than 70 percent of the domestic market meeting nearly all the demands for formulations. Till now, India's generic drug industry was very vibrant and India is a major source of low-priced quality medicines and active pharmaceutical ingredients (APIs) as well as a major supplier of vaccines. Presently, almost one-fourth of the global generics markets is serviced by the Indian pharmaceutical industry.

Patents (Amendment) Act of 1999: The 1970 Patents Act was first amended in 1999, primarily to give effect to TRIPS Article 70.8 (to establish a 'mailbox' system) and 70.9 (to provide 'exclusive marketing rights' [EMRs]), after the Dispute Settlement Body of the WTO found India not in compliance with its obligations under the TRIPS on a complaint filed by the US. The Patents (Amendment) Act of 1999 formally implemented the mailbox procedure and EMRs for patent applications claiming pharmaceutical and agro-chemical products.

A new Chapter IVA was inserted in the Patents Act in 1999, which has been repealed by the 2005 Amendment of the Patents Act. In principle, under this system only those products for which patents were filed after 1995 can claim product patent. For the mailbox applications filed between January 1, 1995 and December 31, 2004, the right of the patentee shall accrue from the date of the patent grant.

Under the 2005 Amendment Act, enterprises, which were producing and marketing the drug prior to January 1, 2005 and which continue to manufacture the product covered by the patent on the date of grant of patent (ongoing generic production), will not be subjected to infringement action and the patent holder will get reasonable royalty only (Section 11A), provided the manufacturers have made significant investment. The Act does not quantify 'significant investment' nor does it specify the parameters of 'reasonable royalty'. The

Act has been criticized for being vague on the issue of royalty. The remedies limitation of Section 11A(7) has also been criticized for effectively conferring on the third parties who marketed the patented drug prior to January 1, 2005 a 'license of right'.

There are 8,926 mailbox applications, filed with the Indian Patent Office during the TRIPS transition period from January 1, 1995 to December 31, 2004, out of which 1,406 were Indian applications claiming product patent for food, drugs and chemicals. However, there have not been many requests for patent examination for these applications and the number of patents granted out of this pool has been very dismal so far. Apart from the first pharmaceutical product patent granted in March 2006 to Hoffman-La Roche for its Hepatitis C therapy sold under the brand name Pegasys, only one more patent has been granted so far in the agro-chemical field.

Patents (Amendment) Act of 2002: The 1970 Act was again amended in 2002 with drastic changes. This was a first step towards India's compliance with TRIPS obligations and it substituted Chapter XVI on compulsory licensing with a new chapter containing provisions on compulsory licensing. The Act extended the term of all patents to twenty years, the compulsory licensing provisions were made TRIPS-compliant while dropping the provisions on 'licenses of right', and made provisions for international filing of patent applications as per its accession to PCT.

It included new definitions of 'invention' and 'inventive step', new exclusions from patentable subject matter, and a new burden of proof provision for cases of process patent infringement. It also enlarged the grounds of revocation and opposition by making non-disclosure and wrongful mention of geographical origin of biological materials, and anticipation based on traditional knowledge as new grounds of revocation and opposition respectively.

Patents (Amendment) Act of 2005: The third amendment to the Patents Act was carried out in 2005, primarily to provide product patents for pharmaceuticals, drugs and chemicals. The Act deletes Section 5 of the erstwhile Act, which excluded product patents in respect of claims intended for use or capable of being used, as food or as medicine or drug; or prepared or produced by chemical processes. It provides for both pre-grant and post-grant opposition of patent application. The grounds of opposition are the same in both the cases. However, pre-grant opposition can be filed by any person and post-grant opposition can be filed by an interested person only. The healing techniques in well established ethnic systems of medicines such as the Ayurveda, Siddha and Unani and formulations are kept outside the purview of the Patents Act and cannot be patented.

The new Act prevents ever-greening of patents and the conditions for obtaining compulsory licenses have been clarified. It incorporates the provisions on parallel imports and a 'Bolar-like' exception (Section 107A). The jurisdiction of the Intellectual Property Appellate Board (IPAB), constituted by the 2002 amendment Act has been enhanced and it now includes the jurisdiction to revoke patents also. A request for examination can be made by any interested person other than the applicant (Section 11B). Most importantly, the Act provides immunity to ongoing generic production by local firms of new drugs, which were in the mailbox (Section 11A).

The resultant consequence of these provisions is that despite switching over to product patent, all products, including those under patent protection elsewhere, which are currently manufactured and marketed in India; and those which are currently not manufactured in India but their patent applications were filed before January 1, 1995, or with priority date before January 1, 2004 will continue to be available in generic form in and from India. Only new drugs, whose applications were filed in India on or after January 1, 1995, would be product patent protected. They cannot be manufactured, sold or exported without the appropriate authorization.

Salient Features of the Amended Act

Scope of Patentability: The amended Act has broadened the eligibility criterion for patenability of an invention. It incorporates a new definition of 'invention' which is in line with Article 27.1 of the TRIPS. It also adds the definition of 'new invention' and 'inventive step', which were not the part of the Act previously. Accordingly, an invention to be patentable should:

- involve an inventive step and be capable of industrial application;
- as a matter of inventive step, it should involve technical advance as compared to the existing knowledge, or having economic significance or both; and
- for being capable of industrial property, it must not be obvious to a person skilled in the art.

But engrafting the 'technical advance' and 'economic significance' criteria on the non-obviousness requirement may make the definition 'vague and arbitrary' that may fail to 'reflect the distilled stock of knowledge' on what non-obviousness means.

'Pharmaceutical substance' has been defined as 'any entity involving one or more inventive steps'.

Exclusions from Patentability: The new patent law includes an extensive list of exclusions from patentability, enumerated in Section 3 of the Patents Act. The Section, relating to the 'inventions not patentable under the Act', has brought in new changes, including those based on TRIPS Agreement Articles 27.2 and 27.3.

The Act excludes the indigenous forms of medicines from patent protection, inventions based on traditional knowledge, topography of integrated circuits, and plants and animals in whole or in any part thereof except micro-organisms [Section 3(j)]. Plant varieties are protected under the Protection of Plant Varieties and Farmers' Rights Act of 2001. The Patent Act does not allow patents on business methods and computer programs *per se* [Section 3(k)]. However, the guidelines on Section 3(k) in the latest Draft Indian Manual of Patent

Practice and Procedure have become controversial. They broadly follow the combination of European and United States practice in this regard. The guidelines permit patents on the embedded program in the hardware. The software *per se* has been differentiated from the software having technical application, which will be patentable. Several recently granted Indian patents appear to be directed to software implemented devices or systems. Rule 4.11.6 of the Draft Manual on Patent Practice and Procedure seeks to draw a distinction between 'software per se' and 'software having its technical application in the industry'.

The newly amended Section 3(d) is of particular relevance to pharmaceutical inventions. It reads: "the mere discovery of a new form of a known substance which does not result *in the enhancement of the known efficacy* of that substance or the mere discovery of any new property or new use for a known substance or of the mere use of a known process, machine or apparatus unless such known process results in a new product or employs at least one new reactant".

Explanation: For the purposes of this clause, salts, esters, ethers, polymorphs, metabolites, pure form, particle size, isomers, mixtures of isomers, complexes, combinations and other derivatives of known substance shall be considered to be the same substance, unless they differ significantly in properties with regard to efficacy.

Although Section 3(d) is applicable to all types of inventions, the *explanation* makes particular reference to pharmaceutical inventions (aimed at pharmacology inventions). The underlying assumption behind Section 3(d) is that derivatives, such as salt forms, polymorphs, isomers, etc. that are structurally similar to known pharmaceutical substances are likely to be functionally equivalent as well, and if this is not the case and the new form of an existing substance works better than the old form, it is up to the patent applicant to demonstrate this and justify the claim. To this extent, Section 3(d) draws a distinction between 'ever-greening' and incremental innovation. By making derivatives with enhanced efficacy patentable, Section 3(d) encourages the sequential development of existing products or technologies to help bring in improved products that address unmet public health needs.

The provision, such as Section 3(d) is unique to the Indian Patents Act, which has been added to rein in 'ever-greening' of pharmaceutical patents by prohibiting the patenting of new forms of existing pharmaceutical substances that do not demonstrate significantly enhanced 'efficacy'. The words 'in the enhancement of the known efficacy' in the provision have generated a lot of debate. For the purposes of this clause, a 'known substance', against which the efficacy of a 'new form' ought to be compared, shall be taken to be a substance which is not 'new', in that it does not satisfy the 'novelty' criterion for patentability. A determination as to whether a difference in property with regard to 'efficacy' is 'significant', shall be assessed with reference to the views of a person skilled in the relevant article. Section 3(d) thus raises both qualitative and quantitative questions, *i.e.*, what kind of data will be required to establish 'efficacy' and how great an improvement over the efficacy of the prior art invention will be required to obtain a patent.

To establish that a 'new form' differs significantly in properties with regard to efficacy, an applicant must provide data comparing the efficacy of the new form with that of a 'known' substance. Such data need not prove this 'difference' in property with a statistical certainty, nor has the applicant to provide actual evidence of trials in humans. The applicant has to demonstrate a reasonable correlation between the efficacy claimed and the data provided in support of this. Such a correlation can be established by relying on, *inter alia*, statistically relevant data documenting the activity of the new form and/or known substance, documentary evidence (e.g., articles in scientific journals), data generated using in vitro assays, or from testing in an animal model, other pre-clinical test data or any combination thereof.

The Draft Indian Manual of Patent Practice and Procedure provides certain guidelines for interpreting the enhanced efficacy requirement. The guidelines broadly observe that "criteria for granting product patents in a particular field i.e. chemicals, foods, pharmaceuticals or biotechnology etc. will have to be assessed carefully within the legal framework and relevant court-rulings". To understand 'known substances' against which the improvement in efficacy of the derivative is measured, Para. 4.5.3 of the Draft Manual provides:

The examiner makes comparison with regard to properties or enhancement of efficacy between the known substance and the new form of known substance. In case the new form is further converted into another new form, the comparison is made between the already existing form and another new form but not between the base compound and another new form.

From the Guidelines, it is not clear that whether 'known' would have the same meaning as of 'novel'. Hence, there is a need to clarify that 'known' would have the same meaning as 'novel'. Further, the phrasing in the guidelines does not cover those inventions in which one crystalline form is converted into another crystalline form. Clarification is required on the standard of proof to establish the increase in efficacy for inventions under this provision. Para 4.5.4 states:

The comparison with regard to properties or enhancement of efficacy is required to be made at the time of date of filing of the application or priority date if the application is claiming the priority of any earlier application but not at the stage of subsequent development.

Based on the judgment in the Novartis case, Para 4.5.5 reads: The efficacy need not be quantified in terms of numerical value to determine whether the product is efficacious because it is not possible to have a standard numerical value for efficacy for all products including pharmaceutical products.

Thus, the standard of proof required to establish an increase in efficacy, the patent office should deem sufficient any data which establishes a reasonable co-relation to the claim of increased efficacy and not absolute empirical accuracy. It may however be noted that the Manual does not carry the force of law; therefore this proposition by the Patent Office is not binding on applicants.

***Novartis* Case:** The first challenge to Section 3(d) came in *Novartis AG and Anr. vs. Union of India and Others.* The case was related to the issue of what qualities elevate a novel and useful material to an invention. Novartis filed a patent application in 1993 for its invention 'Imatinib', for the treatment of chronic myelogenous leukemia (CML), and was granted a patent on May 28, 1996 in the US. Imatinib is the free base, which was further researched upon and converted into a particular salt form, namely imatinib mesylate. From this salt, the most stable version namely the beta crystalline, a particular polymorphic form, was found by Novartis, which then formulated the beta crystalline form of imatinib mesylate into a pharmaceutically useful drug, called Glivec that got approval from the FDA in 2001. The present case in India centred around the beta crystalline form of imatinib mesylate. Novartis claimed that around 40 patents covering this polymorph have been granted to it in various countries.

Owing to the unavailability of drug patents in India until January 1, 2005, Novartis claimed this polymorph in a "mailbox" application and was granted the same in November 2003. Novartis also applied for an exclusive marketing right (EMR) pending grant of a product patent, and was granted the same in November 2003. On the strength of its EMR, Novartis sued Indian generic drug makers such as Ranbaxy and Cipla before Madras and Bombay high courts. The Madras High Court upheld the EMR and restrained the generic drug producers on various grounds. The Bombay High Court, however, did not grant injunction and noted that the validity of the recently issued EMR had been seriously challenged by the defendants. Pursuant to the 2005 amendment, the mailbox application by Novartis was opened and examined.

The grant of the patent was opposed by several generic

drug companies and by an NGO, the Cancer Patients Aid Association (CPAA) on several grounds including the: (i) lack of novelty/anticipation; (ii) lack of significantly enhanced 'efficacy' under Section 3(d); (iii) obviousness; and (iv) wrongful priority.

Agreeing with these grounds, the Assistant Controller of Patents rejected the patent application for the absence of 'novelty and inventive step' and lack of 'improved efficacy' in accordance with Section 3(d). Novartis AG, along with its Indian subsidiary, Novartis India, challenged the rejection in the Madras High Court. Petitioners averred that Section 3(d) is unconstitutional and in violation of India's obligations under TRIPS. The section was termed as being vague and arbitrary that confers uncanalized powers on the statutory authority (patent controller). Novartis claimed that the active ingredient in Glivec (beta crystalline form of imatinib mesylate) is more effective than the imatinib free base, since it displays better bioavailability properties, *i.e.* it is absorbed more easily into the blood.

The court, while rejecting the petition of Novartis, observed that the *explanation* to the section deems that if a discovery is made from a known substance, a duty is cast upon the patent applicant to show that the discovery has resulted in the enhancement of the known efficacy of that substance. In order to grant a patent for such a discovery, the *explanation* presumes that all derivatives of a known substance would be deemed to be the same unless it differs significantly in properties with regard to efficacy. According to the Court, the amended section gives importance to 'efficacy'. The court stated that the medical dictionary meaning of 'efficacy' in pharmacology is 'the ability of a drug to produce the desired therapeutic effect' and 'efficacy' is independent of potency of the drug. The word 'therapeutic' means healing of a disease. It is the responsibility of the applicant to place on record what is the therapeutic effect efficacy of a known substance and what is the enhancement in that known efficacy. The Court emphasized that the properties of the derivate of a known substance must differ significantly with regard to efficacy, which can easily be shown in comparative details based on such science.

The court did not find the provision vague as it has in-built measures to guide the statutory authority in exercising its power under the Act and it cannot be invalidated solely on the ground that there is a possibility of misusing the power. The court held that the object of the amending Act is to prevent ever-greening and to provide easy access to the citizens to life-saving drugs. In discharging the Constitutional obligation of providing good health care to its citizens, the provision is not in violation of the Constitution. The court rejected the argument that the said provision is arbitrary, in the absence of any guidelines as the statutory authority will be guided by the material placed before it. However, it held that it does not have jurisdiction to decide the validity of the amended section, being in violation of Article 27 of TRIPS and to find its compatibility with the TRIPS, the Dispute Settlement Mechanism of the TRIPS is the proper forum.

The Draft Manual of Patent Practice and Procedure has provided some guidelines to process application under Section 3(d), as mentioned above. The provision of Rule 4.5.3 of the guidelines may affect the outcome of the Novartis case, which is presently before the IPAB. Comparison in the application for efficacy was between the base compound and Glivec and not Imatinib Mesylate, an intermediary compound, as to calculate efficacy. But now it will be between the intermediary compound and Glivec. The court did not make any pronouncements about the standard of proof required to establish efficacy either. It is also important to note that Section 3(d), being a part of the section that deals with inventions excluded from patentability, is structured as a patent eligibility test and not as a patentability test. In other words, any pharmaceutical invention that does not comply with Section 3(d) represents subject matter that is not patentable. The case is currently before the Supreme Court.

Section 3(d) has been invoked in number of other cases before the Patent Office for the grant of a patent. In Boehringer Ingelheim Pharmaceuticals [BIP] (USA), the invention was related to a pediatric suspension of Nevirapine Hemihydrate used for treating HIV. The prior art in the application was related to the nevirapine, the active ingredient and known agent for the treatment of infection by HIV-1. The application was opposed, among others, on the ground of Section 3(d). The Patent Office rejected the application of the BIP, while deciding in favour of BIP on the 'novelty' issue. On Section 3(d), the Controller decided that applicant needs to place on record two things: (i) data relating to the therapeutic effect of the known substance, and (ii) data relating to the therapeutic effect of the claimed substance.

In *F. Hoffmann-La Roche Ltd. vs. Cipla Limited*, Cipla challenged the validity of Roche's patent on several grounds, including Section 3(d). In particular, Cipla claimed that Erlotinib was not significantly more efficacious than Gefinitib, an earlier known structurally similar substance. As the present litigation was related to the grant of an injunction against the respondent, the judge did not investigate this issue in detail and determine whether or not Erlotinib, which was merely structurally similar to Gefatinib, could also qualify as a "derivative" under Section 3(d). If it is a 'derivative', then under the explanation to Section 3(d), unless it demonstrates 'a significant difference in property with regard to efficacy', it will be construed as the 'same substance' as Gefatinib and the patent will become invalid.

Compulsory Licenses: India's compulsory licensing provisions give effect to the provisions of TRIPS Agreement and permitted exceptions under the Paris Convention, particularly on local working of the patent. The terms and conditions for the issuance of license are similar to the TRIPS Agreement. The grounds for granting compulsory licenses under the Act are: that the reasonable requirements of the public with respect to the patented invention have not been satisfied; or that the patented invention is not available to the public at a reasonable affordable price; or that the patented invention is not worked in the territory of India [Section 84(1)]. Reasonable requirements of the public shall be deemed to have not been met if due to patentee's refusal: (i) establishment of new trade/industry in India has suffered, (ii) the demand of the patented article has not been met, (iii) a market of export of patented article manufactured in India has not been supplied, or (iv) development of commercial activities in India has been prejudiced [Section 84(7)]. The non-availability of the patented invention at a 'reasonably affordable price' is also a ground for the revocation of the patent.

The Act has made the procedure for the grant of compulsory licenses simpler. It provides that where the applicant has made efforts to obtain a license from the patentee on reasonable terms and conditions and such efforts have not been successful within a reasonable period, the controller can now interpret reasonable period to mean a period not ordinarily exceeding 6 months [Section 84(6)]. The amended Act does not remove the existing requirement that only three years after the grant of a patent, unless there is a national emergency, a person can make an application to the controller for the grant of a compulsory license. However, the Act fails to provide a timeline within which the controller must deal with compulsory license application once made. In cases of national emergency or extreme urgency or in case of public non-commercial use, under Section 92, the Central Government can at any time declare by notification in the Patent Office's official journal that it is necessary to make compulsory licenses available under a particular patent. In issuing the compulsory license, the controller is to ensure that the drugs are available to the public at the lowest prices.

Compulsory Licenses for the Export of Drugs: The Act incorporates a provision (Section 92A) for export of generic drugs to meet public health emergency in a developing/least developed country in accordance with the Doha Declaration on 'TRIPS Agreement and Public Health' and the Council of TRIPS Decision of August 30, 2003. India is the first among the developing countries, with proven manufacturing capacity in the pharmaceutical sector, to give effect to the 2003 Decision. India accepted Article 31*bis* of the TRIPS Agreement on March 26, 2007, which will replace the Council Decision. Under Section 92A, a compulsory license can be issued to facilitate export of patented pharmaceutical products by Indian companies to countries that do not have adequate or no manufacturing/production capacities in the pharmaceutical sector to address public health problems, provided that the compulsory license has been granted by such country or such country has, by notification or otherwise, allowed importation of the patented pharmaceutical products from India. Section 92A provides:

1. Compulsory licence shall be available for manufacture and export of patented pharmaceutical products to any country having insufficient or no manufacturing capacity in the pharmaceutical sector for the concerned product to address public health problems, provided compulsory licence has been granted by such country or such country has, by notification or otherwise allowed importation of the patented pharmaceutical products from India.
2. The Controller shall, on receipt of an application in the prescribed manner, grant a compulsory licence solely for manufacture and export of the concerned pharmaceutical product to such country under such terms and conditions as may be specified and published by him.

Explanation: For the purposes of this section, 'pharmaceutical products' means any patented product, or product manufactured through a patented process, of the pharmaceutical sector needed to address public health problems and shall be inclusive of ingredients necessary for the manufacture and diagnostic kits required for their use.

The controller is thus empowered to set terms and conditions for such a license which will be granted solely for manufacture and export of the concerned pharmaceutical product to a country with no or insufficient manufacturing capabilities as per the procedure prescribed in the TRIPS Decision of August 30, 2003. This provision has no relevance for the domestic market. The provision has not been put into use so far, though it was invoked unsuccessfully by NATCO, an Indian generic drug manufacturing firm, to export generic copies of Pfizer's patented anti-cancer drug Sutent (and Roche's patented drug Tarceva) to Nepal. NATCO's application was rejected by the Patent Office (in September 2008) on the grounds that Nepal's government had not issued any TRIPS notification on pressing public health problem in Nepal; the Nepal Government's letter was merely a permission to import fixed quantities of drugs and was not in the nature of a compulsory license; and the failure of the applicant to set out the terms and conditions of the license which he is willing to accept under Rule 96 of the Patents Rules 2006.

However, India's ability to meet the demands of LDCs is limited by the post-2005 product patent regime. It will require the consent of the patent holder to supply the generics. Thus, Section 92A will be useful only if the drug is already being produced in India. A new generic drug would require 36 to 48 months because of the required investment, bio-equivalence tests and regulatory approval.

Parallel Imports: The amended Act allows parallel imports. Section 107A(b) provides 'importation of patented products by any person who is duly authorized under the law to produce and sell or distribute the product, shall not be considered as infringement of patent rights'. The provision, however, is ambiguous in the context of Section 48 (Rights of the Patentees) which guarantees for the patentee the exclusive right to import the patented product. 'Patented article/product' means an article/product in respect of which patent is in force in India'. Section 107A raises pertinent questions: does it mean that a generic version of the drug manufactured abroad can be imported into India without the authorization of the patentee? What law Section 107A(b) is referring to?

Further, it is also in conflict with Section 84(2) which provides that "[n]o license granted by the controller shall authorize the licensee to import the patented article or an article or substance made by a patented process from abroad where such importation would, but for such authorization, constitute an infringement of the rights of the patentee'. It is, thus, amply clear that the law on parallel importation is quite confusing and may need either the intervention of the legislature or be sorted out by the court in an appropriate case.

However, despite these few hitches in the new patent regime, the immediate impact of this fundamental expansion of patentability in India is a huge influx of product patent applications awaiting examination. The number of patent filing has increased dramatically from about 4,416 in 2002-2003 to 28,940 in 2006. The total filing by both foreign and Indian applicants for the fiscal year 2007-2008 has increased by 17.8 percent from the previous year.

But questions repeatedly arise in the context of the balance required between promoting trade and protecting national welfare issues. In *F. Hoffmann-La Roche Ltd. vs. Cipla Limited*, the court had an occasion to decide on the availability of generics, when a valid patent existed. The issue of public interest in the availability became a focal point in the refusal to grant an injunction. The case is related to infringement of patent rights of the plaintiffs (La Roche) in the drug Erlotinib (used in the treatment of non-small lung cancer) by the respondent (Cipla), the generic drug manufacturer. Tablet formulation of Erlotinib is sold by the plaintiffs under the trade name of Tarceva. The plaintiffs applied for a patent in India in March 1996 and got the EMR approval in December 2005. They were granted the patent on February 23, 2007.

When the news reports came in December 2007 and January 2008 about the defendants plan to launch a generic version of Erlotinib in India and also for exporting it to various countries, the plaintiffs sought injunction, damages, rendition of accounts and delivery of infringing goods by filing a case against Cipla alleging its act as illegal for infringing lawful rights of the plaintiffs. Before the court, Cipla averred that it received approval for manufacturing the said tablet from the Government of Goa in October 2007 and since December 2007 has been selling the drug under the brand name 'Erlocip'.

It alleged that the patent is a new one, being only six months old, and as such no presumption of validity can be attached to it and post-grant opposition has been filed. The patent lacks an inventive step as Erlotinib, being a quinazolin derivative, only seeks to improve from the existing prior art, and is obvious to the person skilled in the art. Plaintiffs failed to prove any improved efficacy of the said drug under Section 3(d) as Erlotinib is merely a derivative of Gefitinib, and it lacks novelty. Cipla also invoked the non-working of the patent as a ground for refusal of injunction. More importantly, it relied on the price difference between the patented drug and its generic manufactured by the defendant. Cipla stated that due to high pricing, drug is not easily available on a commercial scale in India. One tablet of Tarceva costs ` 4,800 compared to ` 1,600 for Erlocip. For proper cure, medicine is required for two months, one tablet daily.

The Court enlisted the three tests for the issuance of an injunction, i.e. existence of a *prima facie* case, balance of convenience, and irreparable hardship (and public interest). The US Supreme Court decision in *eBay vs. Merc Exchange* was referred to, where the US Supreme Court held that patent cases are no different from other cases when it comes to applying the four factor test for determining whether or not an injunction ought to be granted: *prima facie* case, balance of convenience, irreparable injury and public interest. Applying these tests, the court refused to issue the injunction. The refusal of the court to grant an injunction has been termed as 'judicial compulsory licensing' and criticized for creating uncertainty over the patent rights.

Drug Price Controls: India's pharmaceutical regime is monitored by the government to keep prices under control in order to make drugs affordable to a common man. Price control is one of the tools in the hands of the government to protect the Indian public from unreasonably high prices of the patented drugs. For this purpose, the National Pharmaceutical Pricing Authority (NPPA), an independent agency, has been created to enforce the provisions of the Drugs (Price Control) Order [DPCO] that monitor and fix/revise prices of selected pharmaceutical products in the country. The DPCO is in existence since 1964, with various versions thereafter. The DPCO 1995 order has brought down the coverage of price control to only 74 drugs. Presently, there is a new price control policy (of 2006) under consideration, upon enactment of which over 300 different drugs could be brought under price control. Currently, the National Pharmaceutical Pricing Authority (NPAA), created in August 1997, determines which drugs will be included in the DPCO and how pricing for those drugs will be formulated.

The consensus view appears to be that at least in the short-term, the introduction of pharmaceutical product patent protection in India will have a relatively minor overall impact on drug prices. The market share of patented drugs is about 40 percent, out of which many are now off-patent. The Indian government takes the position that '[t]he fear that prices of medicines will spiral is unfounded', noting that "97 percent of all drugs manufactured in India are off-patent, and so will remain unaffected' by the new regime. Another estimate is that in the short-term, prices will be impacted on an average up to fifteen percent of medicines sold in the Indian market.

Indian Pharmaceutical Sector

It is a well-established fact that the 1970 Patents Act has been instrumental in making the Indian drug industry very vibrant, but this did not match with any innovative activities.

The generic drug industry did not become an innovator of new molecules. Virtually no research and development into new molecules was undertaken in India in the pre-TRIPS era. Most of the drug manufacturing industries were involved in the reverse engineering and the so-called R&D was used as a ploy to get the tax cuts from the government. The process patent regime also impacted negatively, the professional expertise in new chemical entity development as potential therapeutic agent. In consequence, it provided less exposure to Indian scientists in conducting advanced clinical trials and drafting patents and patent-related litigation in the areas of new chemical entities, genetic engineering, combinatorial chemistry, agro-chemicals and agricultural products.

Sector Growth and Main Drivers: Recent government figures show that despite India's compliance with the TRIPS Agreement in 2005, its pharmaceutical sector is thriving. According to the Department of Chemicals and Petrochemicals, the Indian pharmaceutical sector has been estimated to be worth US$ 12 billion in 2006-07. India has been a major exporter of drugs since 1988-89, with the exporting done mainly by domestic companies. According to the Department of Commerce and Industry figures for 2006-2007, India exported pharmaceutical products worth US$ 3.1 billion. Of the 20 percent of the APIs produced in the country in 2007, between 55-60 percent were exported and almost two-thirds of its total formulations production was also exported. Drug prices remain lowest in India because of the production cost, which is about 30-50 percent lower in India than in the developed economies due to expertise in reverse engineering processes for APIs, scale economies of production, and lower personnel and capital construction costs.

The Indian pharmaceutical industry comprises of two groups: the multinational corporations (MNCs) and the domestic (entirely Indian-owned) companies. There are around 10,000 registered domestic companies, the organized sector is relatively small and comprises around 300 large and medium-sized firms, which account for over 75 percent of the entire market. Nine out of the top ten companies as of 2007 were local companies and held approximately 30 percent of the entire market. These companies exported mainly generics and active pharmaceutical ingredients (APIs—also called bulk drugs that need to be mixed with excipients to create the final drugs) to over 150 countries worldwide. Dr. Reddy's Laboratories (DRL) is the largest player in the Indian pharmaceutical sector with a market share of 10 percent, followed closely by Ranbaxy, Cipla and Aurobindo.

In addition to the majors, the Indian drug manufacturing sector includes a host of smaller domestic firms, which produce primarily bulk drugs; i.e., the APIs present in medicines. A smaller number of firms produce formulations; i.e., the processing of bulk drugs into finished dosage forms such as tablets and capsules. As is the case for the major firms, exports constitute a major part of the business of these smaller firms, which export mainly to 'unregulated' or small economies, like Vietnam, Syria, Jordan etc.

R&D Capabilities and Spending: In 1992, in a study by Ballance et al., India was identified as one of the countries having innovative capabilities, but it did not produce much patentable molecules. During the past decade, however, the R&D profile of the Indian pharmaceutical industry has undergone major changes. The most obvious of these is the considerable increase in the spending on R&D that was witnessed, particularly since the beginning of the current decade. In 2004, R&D spending of the organized pharmaceutical industry as a whole was nearly US$ 340 million, which was an increase of more than 300 percent from the level existing in 2000.

The ratio of R&D spending to sales undertaken by the pharmaceutical industry for the period 1995-2004 reveals two key features: first, the level of spending in the pharmaceutical industry was significantly higher than that recorded by other industry groups. And second, the pharmaceutical industry was the only one among the leading industries to have consistently improved its R&D spending.

This is also an indication that the pharmaceutical industry in India is allocating increasing amounts of its sales turnover towards R&D spending. The R&D intensity of the industry went up by more than 150 percent since the beginning of the decade.

Industry statistics show that large Indian firms have invested on an average approximately around 10 percent of their total turnover into R&D since early 2000s. In 2005 alone, when India complied with the TRIPS Agreement, the top five companies increased their R&D spending by 47 percent on the whole, which amounted to US$ 192.3 million. A large share of this R&D still goes to developing novel drug delivery systems (NDDS), non-infringing processes, and similar activities that feed into the generics business, thus building upon synergies between the need to be competitive in the present, with the aspiration to build greater innovative capabilities to integrate into the global structure.

R&D Activities of the Generic Industry: Analysis of the R&D activities of generic firms requires examination of two dimensions. These are: (i) the organization of R&D activities, and (ii) specific areas of involvement.

The firms and their strategies regarding R&D remain heterogeneous. Several top firms like Aurobindo and Cipla (predominantly) remain purely generic entities. Other firms like DRL, Glenmark and Sun pursue mixed strategies of generics and drug discovery.

A number of large indigenous companies engage in some original research and development along with generic drug manufacturing, while hundreds of other, smaller firms subsist exclusively on reverse-engineering drugs that are still under patent protection outside India as well as those off-patent.

It is pertinent to note that in recent years, R&D efforts of the industry have received support from the government. This includes exploration of collaboration between the pharmaceutical firms and the large network of public sector research institutions.

Nevertheless, it is expected that the 2005 Amendment Act will stimulate domestic innovation in new medicines and therapies. India has a large trained manpower for this purpose, but it may require a proper mechanism crafted by the government to exploit these pharmaceutical manufacturing skills and capabilities to form a solid base for innovation in the development of new drugs.

The present scenario is unfolding gradually towards this end, which has to match with the IP infrastructure of the country in the form of trained manpower at the patent office, where the examiners until very recently were not trained in doing the search and examination of pharmaceuticals and chemical inventions for product patents. With only a handful of pharmaceutical product patents having been granted in India since 1 January 2005, it is premature to draw any firm conclusions about the impact of enhanced patent protection on the pharmaceutical sector. Nevertheless, Indian pharmaceutical firms are increasing their investments in new chemical entity (NCE) research and development.

Areas of R&D Spending: The R&D structure built by the leading firms in the generic industry has four dimensions. These are: (i) development of generics, (ii) novel drug delivery systems, (iii) development of new processes and (iv) new drug discovery and research. The development of generics is the main field of activity of the Indian pharmaceutical industry, targeting increasingly the US and the European markets. In order to penetrate these markets, the leading Indian firms have deepened their R&D activities to benefit under the laws of the US and Europe. Nevertheless, in general, the Indian generics are considerably behind the global firms having highest R&D intensities. But with leading firms in the generic industry increasing their R&D activities in a consistent manner, the next few years could witness these firms close the existing gap in R&D intensities with the global firms.

In the case of development of innovative drugs, the leading firms in the generic industry are increasing their R&D intensity which is reflected in their drive to obtain patents not only in India, but in several developed countries as well. The top Indian companies filing at Indian patent office are Ranbaxy, DRL, Orchid Chemicals and Pharmaceuticals, Cadila Health Care and Cipla. Further, the top three firms are increasing their international patent filing through the PCT. This is evidenced by the fact that almost 50 percent of the applications made by both Ranbaxy and Cipla have been made through the PCT. Dr. Reddy's (DRL), however, shows a different tendency, with the share of PCT applications in the total patent applications falling during 2004 and 2005.

Although they compete against MNCs in the global generics market, Ranbaxy and DRL also engage in research partnerships and collaborations with the MNCs. These Indian majors are also developing significant independent R&D capabilities. Ranbaxy was the second largest company in the Indian market until the recent sale of a 50 percent stake to the Japanese firm Daiichi Sankyo in June 2008, which has put a question mark on its being a leading player in the Indian pharma market.

The Indian generics are considerably behind the global firms having the highest R&D intensities. The R&D activities remain confined to the generic industry. But there is still low-level of innovation and investment in innovative R&D compared to multinational pharma companies. There is lack of resources to compete with MNCs for new drug discovery research and to commercialize molecules on a worldwide basis.

Concluding Remarks

India's new patents regime while designed to spur domestic innovation is also aimed at maintaining affordable public access to life-saving patented medicines. The new regime is still evolving and a great deal remains to be clarified through implementation. The way the Indian patent regime is being implemented, calls for legal clarity. The cases like *Novartis* and *Roche* have put certain question marks on its veracity, particularly the *Roche* case which leaves one wondering about the sanctity of the patents acquired in India. There is a need for greater clarity on what is patentable in India, on when local companies can apply for compulsory licenses, and on under what conditions patents granted within India can be overridden. There is also a need to establish clearly how patents will be granted and what procedures will be followed for pre- and post-grant oppositions.

It is clear from the new law that the local generic industry will remain the most important sub-sector of the pharmaceutical industry for some time to come and will not vanish soon. Innovation in India's pharmaceutical sector is far from ideal but is slowly on the rise and patent application filings are increasing dramatically, particularly after the coming into effect of the TRIPS Agreement. At the same time, due to the continuing monitoring of the prices of drugs, the price of most medicines has not been severely affected due to the introduction of product patent protection. Longer-term effects of patent protection on drug pricing in India are not yet known, but the government has a number of tools at its disposal to deal with that concern. A number of the new Patents Act's provisions provide the Indian government with legitimate means for balancing innovation incentives against the social costs of pharmaceutical product patents, viz., compulsory licensing and parallel importation.

The Indian pharmaceutical industry has witnessed considerable changes over the past few decades, particularly with the emergence of a strong generic industry. The growth of the industry and its subsequent consolidation was largely contributed by the Patents Act of 1970 which introduced the process patent regime for pharmaceuticals. The new TRIPS-consistent patent regime would limit to a considerable extent, the generic manufacturers' ability to reverse engineer patented products. However, since 1995, the leading generic firms of the industry have been showing considerable dynamism. The consolidation of the Indian firms, which began in the first half of the 1990s, improved considerably since the beginning of the current decade.

Particularly noteworthy has been the increase in the R&D spending of some of the leading firms, in particular, Ranbaxy and Dr. Reddy's. As a result, R&D intensities of the firms have improved significantly. The R&D efforts of the leading generic firms have made them internationally competitive. Both Ranbaxy and Dr. Reddy's have developed improved generics and novel drug delivery systems (NDDS), which have opened the doors for collaboration with pioneer producers in the world.

Although Indian firms are yet to make a mark in the area of new drug discovery, but they seem to be on course for major developments given the sharp increase in their patenting activity of late and improved patent filing internationally. This activity could be strengthened by the increased efforts made by the government to participate in the R&D activities involving the industry. Besides, the R&D priorities are being increasingly set in tune with the global trends, and this focus has increased since the firms have enhanced their level of collaboration with the foreign firms. Ranbaxy's venture with Daiichi Sankyo in June 2008 of Japan is an instance.

The above-mentioned concerns arising from the successes of the Indian pharmaceutical industry is very much embedded in the patent regime of India itself, which has provided sufficient flexibilities in the patent laws so that the domestic pharmaceutical industries can get a chance to develop.

It has provided an enabling environment for the domestic industry by carefully designing provisions that relate to patentable subject matter and compulsory licences, which are, nevertheless, TRIPS-compliant but leave enough scope for the generic drug manufacturers.

It has, however, been argued that the growth of pharmaceutical industry may be affected according to data protection submitted to the regulatory authorities for obtaining marketing approval under Article 39.3 of the TRIPS Agreement. Its ramifications would be felt by most sections of the population not only in India, but also other countries, which have been dependent on the cheap source of generics from India.

13

Copyright and Cyberspace: Issues and Challenges

Shiva Kanaujia Sukula

Information technology is growing faster with the invention of digital technology. The influence of digital technology on information technology is phenomenal. Internet culture is changing lifestyle, way of communication and scholarly publishing. Today, the internet is not only used for educational purposes but also for business. The Government of India by passing the IT (Information Technology) Act, 2000 and further amending it on October 27, 2009 has given fillip to the cyber law. But various issues are not specifically covered by the Act, such as copyright, payment issues, media convergence, domain name, cybersquating and jurisdiction. These do have wide ranging ramifications for the growth of e-commerce in India. [1]

Emergence of Cyberspace and Related Technologies

The term 'cyberspace' was first coined in 1980s by science fiction writer William Gibson. [2] In general, cyberspace represents the new medium of communication—electronic communication—which is fast outmoding, or even replacing, more traditional methods of communication. This includes computers, networks, software, data storage devices (such as hard disks, USB disks etc.), the internet, websites, emails and even electronic devices such as cell phones, ATM machines etc. [3] Further, cyberspace like physical space, can also be categorised in four sub-concepts viz. place, distance, size and route. [4]

Other things which come under this ambit include computer software, sound recordings, novels, pictures, trade secrets, credit card account numbers, maps, and other reference works like encyclopaedias, journals, and the like. In fact, nearly any sort of information, including telephone conversations, television and radio signals, and motion pictures, can be converted to a digital stream of bits and hence can be transmitted through cyberspace. In today's world, a great deal of valuable stuff currently exists in the form of digital information that can be sent through cyberspace. As cyberspace is not a real "place", tangible objects do not exist "there". Computers digitize and process all communication in cyberspace, either during a transmission or at the "end" point of a connection such as a website. In principle, therefore, all transactions in cyberspace could be logged and recorded at low cost.

Copyright and Online Niche

An author is an exclusive owner of its creation. According to Copyright Act, 1957, copyright is a [5] right which enables author of a work to prevent others to exercise that right which has been conferred on him. The precise text to determine whether a person is entitled to copyright is to ascertain whether skill, judgment and experience or labour, and capital has been expended in creating the work. [6] Copyright law protects such works like literary, dramatic and artistic works; cinematography films; sound recording and computer programmes, and databases and compilations. Due to omnipresence of computers and other electronic devices, protection of the intellectual property rights in computer programs has really become an issue since the advent of microcomputers, a much more recent development. [7]

It is seen that it is much cheaper to copy information than to create it. With the advent of information technology, the digital information is often even cheaper to copy than other form of information. [8] If an information producer has a means to restrict copying, but prefers, for whatever reason, not to restrict copying, then the producer can simply not assert or take advantage of that means. In other words, such a means allows those who want and need to restrict copying to do so, and it allows those who do not want to restrict copying to refrain from doing so. [9]

Various digital and information technologies assist the copyright owners in better utilization of their intellectual capital and on the other darker prospect, threatening them loss of control even over their own property. The impact of digital technology, specially the internet, is such a massive one that, even the basic fundamentals of copyright law are under the threat of revisions and modifications. [10] A web page contains text graphics and even audio and videos. The fair use copyright provision exempts certain activities such as: [11]

1. Copying small portions of a work for purposes of criticism.
2. Spontaneous "last minute" copying of a news article for distribution in a school class.
3. Taping a televised movie to watch it at a later time.

The owner's exclusive right to authorize reproduction of the copyrighted works, preparation of derivative works, distribution etc. cannot be strictly applied for copyright on the internet. Very early, Calabresi and Melamed argued: "fair use applies when transaction costs make it impractical for the parties to negotiate ahead of time". [12] In the information age, the economy's greatest assets are ideas and their practical applications and due to the widespread use of computers, the intellectual capital more effectively in large part has been exploited.

It has enabled businesses with greater ease to buy and sell physical products with enhanced efficiency over the internet. The consequences brought about in the content industry as a result of new technologies are already before our eyes. The path breaking scientific and technological advancement has revolutionized the information transaction scenario. [13]

Infringement and Other Issues

New information technologies brought about by

computers, internet and cyberspace widen the scientific horizon posing new challenges and creating problems for the legal world in all aspects of law. The challenges are in almost all major categories of law such as contract law, criminal law, law of torts etc. [14] The system of copyright protects creativity. This has intensified the occurrence of copyright infringements and has led to such violations of the rights of the copyright holder which are protected poorly in various legal systems. [15]

Common issue amongst website owners is to create links to other sites within the design of their own web pages. There is an implied doctrine of public access for linking to other web pages. [16] Infringement over internet and piracy is posing a threat to creative works worldwide and the resultant growth of internet, e-commerce and the digital economy. Copyright owner's exclusive right of distribution applies to e-mail attached or forwarded. This is precisely due to involvement of various factors like the worldwide reach of the internet and millions of websites. [17]

It has been established and an obligation has been created on the part of bulletin board operators to ensure that the system is not being used to display and download copyrighted materials by the customers. There must be at least some minimal degree of creativity and what should be protected by copyright were the fruits of intellectual labour and not just sweat of the brow. Further, it is a violation of copyright owners exclusive statutory right of display by making available videotape over the internet without authorisation and posting unauthorised copies of electronic clipart on web pages.

The temporary copies made into a computer RAM are copies. But in year 1995, in *Religious Technology vs. Netcom*, [18] the US District court held that temporary copying involved in browsing is the functional equivalent of reading and does not implicate the copyright laws. Unauthorised reproduction or "scanning" of a copyrighted printed document into a digital file, and uploading, downloading a copyrighted file to a bulletin board system is a copyright infringement. [19] With these security measures being applied on the internet, it is hoped it will generate greater confidence in customers so that the internet becomes a secure medium. [20]

Digital Environment and Intellectual Property Rights

The internet is characterized as a digital means to disseminate information and promote free expression on a scale that was never possible before. Digital technologies have become principal tools for creating and storing information due to its speed and easy access. An application of copyright law to digital information has become critical. It is difficult to make the intellectual property rights apply on the internet, enforceable due to following factors: [21]

1. Ease of reproducing works in digital format is inexpensive and there is a near-perfect quality of copies.
2. Fundamentally transforming the nature and means of publications and thus making their works extremely vulnerable to internet piracy.
3. The decentralized nature of internet's management allows users to publish for a vast audience, heretofore unavailable because of the restricted character of conventional publishing.
4. A user can easily distribute a work to news groups through e-mail or on personal website.

Due to sophisticated copying methods, it becomes almost impossible for the copyright owner to control further dissemination without adequate protection. [22] Although the copyright originally protected only the written work, it has subsequently been extended to cover artistic and visual works together with rights in respect of the performance of works. [23] In the light of the new electronic environment, the existing exceptions and limitations to the rights would have to be reassessed as: [24]

(a) To what impact, the access controls have on the ability to engage in fair use;

(b) To what extent, circumvention of access controls affect the market for, and value of works protected by copyright.

Cyberspace: Issues at the Forefront

The transmission of information and transacting of business in cyberspace across borders, have cropped up on legal front. Some of the major issues include determination of jurisdiction, cyber crime, intellectual property, cyber forensic, e-commerce, electronic evidence, privacy and contract. The absence of a comprehensive law anywhere in the world and disproportional growth ratio of internet and cyber law have added to the injury. In India, the enactment of The Information Technology Act, 2000 (ITA), amendments made to the Indian Penal Code, Indian Evidence Act etc. and the problems associated with the regulation of cyber crime have further aggravated the situation.

The ITA does enforce and control a level of cyber-related problems. Dealing with information technology itself, the ITA in many ways falls short of international standards. New provisions added through Information Technology (Amendment) Act, 2008, [25] could be a way out from all these challenges. Functional equivalence and technological neutrality warrant few more changes. The cyber laws in India should be redefined as per the international scenario.

Various Challenges

Cyberspace is international in character. The opportunities and threats also emanate internationally. Laws related to cyberspace have two key issues: determining the jurisdiction and the formation of e-contracts. These issues have been taken into consideration worldwide. [26] In cyberspace, there is no geographical boundary. No judicial body exists to deal with legal commercial problems arising between citizens of different countries. In US and UK, there have been various principles and tests laid down by the courts. India is also following an elaborated scope of jurisdiction. [27] There is no uniform international jurisdictional law with universal application, and as such the questions are generally a matter of conflict of law, particularly in private international law. It is also seen that the contents of a website are legal in one country but illegal in another. Such aspects lead to a conflict among law practices. The international character of internet warrants international legal solutions. Therefore, a logical hypothesis could be drawn that effective protection of copyright in cyberspace can only be guaranteed through a strong international copyright legal regime. [28]

For example, in Europe, the Brussels Convention is the controlling document for jurisdictional issue within the European Union. In India, all cyber laws are governed by the IT Act. In India, where more than one court has jurisdiction in a certain matter, an agreement between the parties to confer jurisdiction only on one to the exclusion of the other(s) is valid.

In cyberspace, the problem began when unrelated parties started using intellectual property of others or of famous brands with the intention to use it otherwise. In the area of IPR violations and infringement across borders, a universal law is yet to develop.

While discussing about contractual difficulties, the ITA deals with some contractual [29] aspects in e-commerce. Indian courts, following the traditions of common law, have developed the doctrine of "last-shot rule". [30] The online contracts require attention in this aspect. [31]

Cyber Crime and Electronic Evidence

Cyber crime is a crime committed over the internet, against the government, property and against any person in various forms. Today, cyber crime has emerged as a bigger threat in comparison to physical crime. In India, cyber crime is increasing everyday in various forms. [32] The quality of evidence poses a serious challenge before the investigation agencies to collect and preserve the evidence in context of cyber crime. A contract is formed, only when the acceptance of an offer is absolute and same as the terms of the offer. [33]

The Indian Evidence Act, 1872 (Section 3) and Information Technology Act, 2000 (Section 4) grants legal recognition to electronic records and evidence submitted in the form of electronic records. In the leading case of *State vs. Mohd. Afzal and others* [34], it was held that electronic records are admissible as evidence. The person challenging the accuracy of computer evidence on the ground of misuse of system must prove the same beyond reasonable doubt. The basic principles of equivalence and legal validity of both electronic signatures and hand written signatures has gained acceptance worldwide. [35]. For admissibility of electronic records, specific criteria have been made in the Indian Evidence Act to satisfy the prime condition of authenticity or reliability.

Technological Challenges and Right to Privacy

Globalization and ICT (information and communication technology) revolution has presented mounting security challenges for both the providers and the consumers. It is increasingly difficult to determine the physical and logical boundaries of networks. The right of privacy is a part of Article 21 of the Indian Constitution, but it is not absolute. The right to privacy is to be read within the ambit of Article 21 and construed as a fundamental right. [36] It is suggested that the right of privacy may be infringed by:

- Unauthorized reading of e-mails of others.
- Sending of unsolicited e-mails or spamming.

The following sections reflect the provisions in the Information Technology Act (ITA) relating to privacy:

- Section 43: Protection against unauthorized access to the computer system including unauthorized downloading, extraction and copying of data.
- Section 66: Protection against hacking.
- Section 67: Protection against unauthorised access to data.
- Section 69: Protection against cyber terrorism.

- Section 72: Protection of individual's privacy and confidentiality.

Data Protection in Cyberspace

The relative significance of legal measures is due to the apparent limitation other measures may suffer. Copyright threats emanate globally due to the international character of cyberspace and potential legal measures must be developed to improve copyright protection.

Social or economic measures should be strengthened. Legal measures on the other hand could be an effective set of tools in improving the global protection for digital copyrights. [37]

Data Protection and Room for Improvement

The ITA should look into the following aspects to match with international standards and data protection:

- Data types: definition, classification and categories of data.
- Unambiguous definition of data controllers and data processors.
- Standards and technical measures: for the collection, storage, access to, protection, retention and destruction of data.
- Safeguard and penalties: against the breaches.

WIPO, WTO and TRIPS

The WIPO has been instrumental in the protection of IPRs. It concentrates on:

1. The territorial nature of the IPR systems;
2. The need for introducing minimum IPR standards across jurisdiction; and
3. The reliance of IPR system on registration as a means of enabling protection of certain rights. [38]

As per WIPO, the limitation of conflict of law solutions states the need for a vibrant international legal regime protecting copyrights in cyberspace. The range of challenges pertaining to copyrights in cyberspace and the scope and limitations of related international initiatives prompts an investigation on WTO regime. It is seen that WTO protects IPR under its TRIPS Agreement as the member states adhere to the TRIPS Agreement. Many states have either introduced or modified domestic IPR legislations. The provisions of the TRIPS Agreement provide an effective IPR protection covering all three major forms of protection including copyrights. Various IPR instruments like the Paris Convention, 1883 (as amended in 1967: generally "Paris Convention"), Berne Convention, 1886 (copyright), Rome Convention (neighbouring rights), Washington Treaty, 1989 (integrated circuits), UNESCO Universal Copyright Convention, 1952 etc. can be taken into consideration.

Copyrights and Other Related IPR in Cyberspace

Apart from copyrights, there are other IPR related issues in cyberspace. Few IPR issues that are significant in cyberspace are listed below: [39]

Trademarks and Domain Names: The issue of trademarks in the context of domain names has surfaced at significant levels in cyberspace. The domain name is considered as the main identity in cyberspace. Trademark owners are concerned about the infringement as well as the dilution of their trademark caused by domain name threats. The main area of controversy has been the issue of domain names. Conventional trademark principles have not contemplated domain name rights as part of the trademarks, and this has led to the initial confusion as to whether trademark principles can be expanded to domain names. Cyber trademark issues require attention at the international level. The ranges of trademark issues that may specifically arise in the context of cyberspace are:

- Issues of trademark dilution.
- Abuse of trademark online.
- Unauthorized use of trademarks in meta tags etc.

Patent of Software: The issue of patenting of software is associated with diversity of views. It is pervasive that the patentability of software is not uniform worldwide. Anyone who uses a patented invention without authorization of the patent holder is generally held to violate the rights of the patent holder. In the context of an online operation, the issue of infringement by use is bound to raise a lot of controversies as many of the online operations may make use of different patented software. Use of a network may trigger the running of infringing software at some remote sites without the knowledge of the online user. Commonly, software programs are protected through copyrights. Patent protection for software programs is on the rise due to limitations of other types of protection. Copyright protection is an insufficient form of protection for software since the emphasis is on the literal copying rather than protecting the innovation in software.

Copyright and Indian Scenario

Information Technology Act, 2000, in India was enacted to provide the legal infrastructure for e-commerce in India. The Amendment (2008) came to deal with some major legal issues such as jurisdiction, protection of domain name, infringement of copyright law etc. [40] This led to the formation of various challenges before the Indian legal system. While copyright has shown flexibility in accommodating new forms of creation, it still fails to protect ideas, methods, and functional characteristics. Few aspects such as Copyleft, the Open Source Movement, Fairshare, and Open Street Protocols require consideration in the perspective of copyright. [41]

Endnotes

1. Ahmad, Tabrez (2010), "Copyright Infringement in Cyberspace and Network Security: A Threat to E-commerce", *The IUP Journal of Cyber Law*, Vol. 9, Nos. 1 and 2, pp. 17-24, February and May; available at:
SSRN: http://ssrn.com/abstract=1511187.

2. Cotton, B. and R. Oliver (1994), "The Cyberspace Lexicon: An Illustrated Dictionary of Terms from Multimedia to Virtual Reality", Phaidon Press Inc., p. 54.
3. Rohas Nagpal (2008), "IPR and Cyberspace: An Indian Perspective", Asian School of Cyber Law, p. 4.
4. Rebecca Bryant (2001), *Minerva: An Internet Journal of Philosophy*, 5, pp. 142-143.
5. Deepak Printings vs. Forward Stationary Mart (1981), PTC 186 at p. 189.
6. Mac Milan vs. Cooper (1923), 93 LJPC 113 and 117.
7. Charulata Chaudhary and Ishupal Singh Kang, "Pirates of the Copyright and Cyberspace: Issues Involved", available at: www.igi-global.com/chapter/pirates-copyright-yberspace/50714.
8. Raymond T. Nimmer and Patricia Ann Krauthaus (1994), "Copyright on the Information Superhighway: Requiem for a Middleweight", 6, *Stan L. and Policy Rev.*, 25.
9. All rights can be waived except those that are protected by a rule of inalienability.
10. Charulata Chaudhary and Ishupal Singh Kang, "Pirates of the Copyright and Cyberspace: Issues Involved", available at: www.igi-global.com/chapter/pirates-copyright-yberspace/50714.
11. Ahmad, Tabrez, "Copyright Infringement in Cyberspace and Network Security: A Threat to E-commerce", available at: www.site.technolexindia.com.
12. Wendy J. Gordan (1982), "Fair Use as Market Failure: A Structural and Economic Analysis of the Betamax Case and Its Predecessors", 82, *Colum. L. Rev.*, 1600, 1628.
13. Charulata Chaudhary and Ishupal Singh Kang, "Pirates of the Copyright and Cyberspace: Issues Involved", available at: www.igi-global.com/chapter/pirates-copyright-yberspace/50714.
14. Ahmad, Tabrez, available at: www.site.technolexindia.com.
15. Charulata Chaudhary and Ishupal Singh Kang, "Pirates of the Copyright and Cyberspace: Issues Involved", available at: www.igi-global.com/chapter/pirates-copyright-yberspace/50714.
16. Ahmad, Tabrez, available at: www.site.technolexindia.com.
17. Charulata Chaudhary and Ishupal Singh Kang, "Pirates of the Copyright and Cyberspace: Issues Involved", available at: www.igi-global.com/chapter/pirates-copyright-yberspace/50714.

18. 907 F. Supp. 1361 (N.D. Cal 1995).
19. Ahmad, Tabrez (2003), "Cyberlaw, E-commerce and M-commerce", APH Publishing Corp., New Delhi.
20. Civil Services Chronicle, April 2000, p. 67.
21. "Green Paper on Copyright and Related Rights in the Information Society", available at: http://europa.eu.int/scadplus/leg/en/lvb/l24152.htm.
22. David Bainbridge (1996), "Intellectual Property", 3rd edition, p. 19.
23. "Rhys Bollen Copyright in the Digital Domain", available at: http://www.murdoch.edu.au/elaw/issues/v8n2/bollen82_text.html#t20.
24. Ahmad, Nehaluddin (2009), "Copyright Protection in Cyberspace: A Critical Study with Reference to Electronic Copyright Management Systems (ECMS)", *Communications of the IBIMA*, Vol. 7.
25. The IT (Amendment) Act, 2008.
26. Longarm Statutes enacted in US and Minimum Contacts test.
27. 'Minimum Contacts test' as developed by the U.S. Supreme Court in International Shoe Co. vs. Washington, 326 U.S. 340 (1945); 'Sliding scale test' as laid down in Zippo Manufacturing vs. Zippo Dot Com, 952 F. Supp. 1119 (D.C.W.D. Pa. 19997); 'Purposeful availment test' as laid down in Hanson vs. Deckla, 357 U.S. 235 (1958) .
28. Perumal, R. Muruga (2006), "Copyright Infringements in Cyberspace: The Need to Nurture International Legal Principles", *International Journal of the Computer, the Internet and Management*, Vol. 14, No. 3, September-December, pp. 8-31.
29. Section 10, Indian Contract Act, 1872.
30. The 'last shot rule' is also known as mirror image rule. According to Indian law, a contract comes into existence only when the acceptance is a mirror image of the offeror's exact offer. Indian laws provides for the mirror image.
31. However, the UNCITRAL Model Law has a specific provision regarding validity of contracts.
32. http://ncrb.nic.in/ciiprevious/Data/CD-CII2007/cii-2007/.home.htm.
33. Section 3, Indian Contract Act, 1872.
34. 11 (2003) (71), DRJ, 178.

35. Krishna Kumar, "Cyber Laws: Intellectual Property and E-commerce Security", at 295.
36. 13 AIR 1963 SC 1295.
37. Perumal, R. Muruga (2006), "Copyright Infringements in Cyberspace: The Need to Nurture International Legal Principles", *International Journal of the Computer, the Internet and Management*, Vol. 14, No. 3, September-December, pp. 8-31.
38. WIPO, 2002
39. Perumal, R. Muruga (2006), "Copyright Infringements in Cyberspace: The Need to Nurture International Legal Principles", *International Journal of the Computer, the Internet and Management*, Vol. 14, No. 3, September-December, pp. 8-31.
40. The IT (Amendment) Act, 2008.
41. "Indian Copyright Laws in Tune with Time or Unfairly Opt Out", *PSA*, Issue XIII, March 2010.

Index

Index